saur

Information Handling in Offices and Archives

Edited by
Angelika Menne-Haritz

K · G · Saur
München · London · New York · Paris 1993

Die Deutsche Bibliothek - CIP-Einheitsaufnahme

Information handling in offices and archives / ed. by. Angelika Menne-Haritz. - München ; London ; New York ; Paris : Saur, 1993
ISBN 3-598-11146-0
NE: Menne-Haritz, Angelika [Hrsg.]

∞

Gedruckt auf säurefreiem Papier / Printed on acid-free paper

A Reed Reference Publishing Company
Printed in the Federal Republic of Germany
Druck: WS Druckerei Werner Schaubruch GmbH, Bodenheim
Binden: Buchbinderei Schaumann, Darmstadt
ISBN 3-598-11146-0

TABLE OF CONTENTS

PREFACE

The Symposium on the Impact of Information Technologies on Information Handling in Offices and Archives took place in Gladenbach near Marburg in October 1991. The Archivschule Marburg thus followed a proposal of the ADP-Committee of the International Council on Archives to organize an expert-meeting on the subject. The VW-Foundation gave the financial support without which the meeting could not have taken place.

I would like to thank all those who contributed to the success of the symposium, all the colleagues from different disciplines who prepared papers and took part in the lively discussions and all the staff of the Archivschule who sacrificed a lot of time and worked hard in the organisation of the meeting. Especially I would like to acknowledge the contributions of Ann Thurston, Wolf Buchmann, Michael Cook, Jörgen Martinsen and John Walford, who chaired the sessions and summarized the main topics of the discussions, of Máire Mulloy, who translated the introduction and of Werner Engel who produced the lay-out of the manuscript.

Angelika Menne-Haritz
Archivschule Marburg

SYMPOSIUM ON THE IMPACT OF INFORMATION TECHNOLOGIES ON INFORMATION HANDLING IN OFFICES AND ARCHIVES MARBURG, OCT. 17th - 19th 1991

INTRODUCTION

By Angelika Menne-Haritz

In October 1991, Gladenbach was the venue for a three-day symposium on the consequences of modern information technology for archives and records management. Attended by twenty-five information professionals from nine countries, the symposium was made possible by the financial support of the VW Foundation's symposium program. Besides special guest speakers, invitations were sent to the members of both the ADP committee of the International Council on Archives (ICA) and the German data processing committee of the archive representatives' organization of the Federation and the Federal States. Both bodies have long been engaged in discussions on this field. The organizational form of the symposium facilitated an in-depth exchange of experiences and ideas, and the lively discussions with the appointed experts were continued afterwards by smaller conversation groups. The resulting open atmosphere proved most stimulating, and was commented upon favourably by the participants. Almost all the guest speakers had prepared papers for distribution which have been revised for the present publication. In a final round of discussions on the last day, the most important topics of the symposium were aired again in context and potential solutions to particular problems were given serious consideration.

This meeting took its place as one of a series of similar rounds of talks by international experts in the field. A 150-page paper contributed by one of the participants (now available in German translation: Charles M. Dollar, The impact of information technologies on archival principles and methods, trans. and ed. by Angelika Menne-Haritz, Veröffentlichungen der Archivschule Marburg, Nr. 19, Marburg 1992. The forthcoming English edition will be accompanied by an Italian translation) had already been the subject of a conference held at the University of Macerata, Italy, in May 1991. Several participants at the Marburg symposium had just come from a seminar for archivists which they had organized in Velthoven (NL) with the support of UNESCO from Oct. 13 - 16, and in the following week the ADP committee of the International Council on Archives, which has likewise extended its field of interest to include office automation, met in Vienna. In this way the discussion topics could be dealt with in overlapping blocks with varying emphasis and ingredients. Due mainly to this close incorporation in a series of similar events, the symposium did much to articulate and clarify various conflicting standpoints.

One positive aspect of the Marburg symposium was the fact that this was a meeting of experts from the fields of archive science, public administration, psychology, economics and standards with practising archivists from public administrations and archives. For some of the experts from other subjects, in fact, this meeting was the first, most welcome opportunity they had had to become familiar with archivists' problems. In return, their very varied contributions and queries opened up new perspectives for the on-going archive discussion and also helped formulate new approaches. This interdisciplinary effort, combined with the high thematic standard, resulted in an intensive and profitable discussion of particular innovative approaches. As the subsequent meeting of the ADP committee in Vienna showed, this series of conferences led to the open questions being more precisely pinpointed, which in turn clearly exposed the problems confronting all engaged in the field.

The symposium was conducted in English only, with no concessions to any of the participants in the form of intermittent translations etc. While this encouraged spontaneous discussion, it cannot be denied that it also led to serious misunderstandings, mainly because English archive terminology - and likewise the technical terms used in records management - sprang from a different tradition, with the result that English terms frequently denote something quite different from their "equivalents" in the terminology of the other languages represented. Thus a straight translation is usually no guarantee of mutual understanding; to achieve this, the discussion partners must, at the very least, be familiar with the basic principles of the respective administration and archive structures involved. The more precise a technical discussion is intended to be, the greater the risk that the participants talk about different things. These problems soon became apparent at the symposium, though admittedly they can be cleared up more easily as they occur in a smaller round of specialist discussions than at large conferences. In our case, the semantic confusion prompted the suggestion that an investigation be carried out of the differences between the European and American administrative traditions in their dealings with recorded documents.

Another difficulty was how to integrate the different approaches from different areas of research and national traditions into a common basis of discussion. It is not unlikely that a number of potentially useful and interesting new suggestions did not make the impact they deserved, simply because they were so new and packed in an as yet unfamiliar context. Nevertheless, these new impulses were at least registered, and in this respect too the advantages of the smaller stage became apparent in the ensuing specific queries and explanatory answers.

The chief aim of the symposium was to define basic archival problems by comparing and contrasting European and American experiences regarding the introduction of modern information technologies to public administrations. At the same time, it was intended to provide the European archivists present with an opportunity to hear of the first-hand experiences of their North American colleagues in this field, and thus also of the problems surrounding the technology imported from North America from a point of view other than that of the manufacturers. It was hoped to assess more realistically the risks for archival practice involved in alleged circumstantial constraints impeding acceptance of the new technology, but also the risks involved in this progressive technology itself, so that adequate precautions could be taken on the basis of more exact knowledge of both the technically feasible and necessary as well as of the user's unavoidable professional requirements.

The starting-point of the round of discussions was the established fact that offices and public administrations produce the raw material for the recorded tradition which the archives' task is to assemble. Modern electronic records are revolutionising the way information is handled in public administrations and are jeopardizing the long-term safekeeping of the administration's memory as well as the safe conservation of permanently relevant information. Obviously, computers cannot be regarded merely as new-fanged tools. Their use transforms archival working methods, the nature of the recorded material and hence also the reconstructibility of decision-making processes.

To date, neither the comparative importance of written records nor the functional role placed by administration records in conventional and new decision-making processes has been seriously investigated. The only hesitant initiative in this direction so far is to be found in specialist archive publications, particularly in North America, where occasional attempts are made to identify the underlying, on-going virtues for modern archival working methods of the traditional archive principles adopted in the 19th and early 20th centuries.

Seen against this background, the symposium was intended as a forum for constructive ideas that would lead to the development and scientific substantiation of appropriate methods for dealing with new, electronically recorded data. At the same time, it was meant as an opportunity to determine the limitations of the traditional methods and the extent of their adequacy for dealing with the new tasks. It was hoped that attempts would be made to define promising approaches for the necessary further developments in this area. In sum, the symposium was designed to produce new impulses to enliven the professional archive scene by providing a forum for the direct exchange of experiences, opinions and ideas between archivists and other specialists from related disciplines. In return, it was expected that the archivists would have constructive suggestions to offer other disciplines, such as the administration sciences, as well as their technical cooperation in pushing issues of mutual interest.

1. TOPIC: INFORMATION TECHNOLOGY OVERVIEW

Rick Barry, Information Manager of the World Bank in Washington, described the current state of information technology and the developments issuing from it. He stressed the fact that it was not his intention to paint a futuristic scenario with undefinable practical relevance, instead he outlined the potential latent in the technology available today. Thus the use of telefax, for instance, increased by 400% between the years 1988 and 1991 and that of E-Mail by 4000% in the same period. E-Mail is heavily used for delegating jobs, and this despite the absence of any provision for the storage of incoming data and despite the extremely low level of awareness for records management wherever E-Mail is used. Consequently, new procedures for information management are required, and they should be based on business processes. Revealing in this context is the ever growing number of archivists engaged in electronic records management in large companies. As his own view of things to come, Barry described the changing role of records managers and archivists as shifting away from that of information specialists towards that of process specialists. As such, they will preserve the visible traces of past transactions, they will maintain operational continuity, they will keep circumstantial evidence relating to decisions open for inspection and facilitate access to documents and other records. For the archivists employed in historical archives this development brings with it an additional challenge: how to make history accessible to everyone.

As the next speaker, Charles Dollar, Assistant Director of Archival Research and Evaluation Staff at the National Archives and Records Administration in Washington, outlined the consequences of these developments for archive work, which he summarized in the statement that the electronic transformation of records administration actually reaffirms the durability of the 100-year-old provenance principle, but also that archival working methods will nevertheless have to undergo certain modifications. He went on to suggest presumably necessary and appropriate measures relating to the following points: technical obsolescence, functional demands on information technology systems, how to identify the provenance of electronic records, the definition of the concept "record", archival appraisal, retention and preservation of record stocks.

In the discussion that followed, attention was drawn first to the character of administration information as the result of processes, then to the demands of the public and the resulting conflict with the archivists' striving to preserve transaction contexts, and finally to the predominance of technological imperatives.

1.1 Administration Information as the Result of Processes

Items of administrative information are generated in the course of processes because of their necessity for this course. Therefore information specialists in administrations and offices act as engineers and controllers of actions, as it depends on them how well processes are backed up by the information necessary to make decisions. Experience has shown that information structures work effectively as long as they are tailored to meet the respective business requirements and targets. False decisions, which impair the efficiency of the administrative tools used to take them, can have serious consequences for all the established decision-making processes and courses of action. This is why the ultimate responsibility for the technical form of the information and decision-making structures should be entrusted to those at the most senior decision-making levels. Naturally, this would not prevent organization experts or technicians from taking over the responsibility of working out the concrete, practicable requirements of the adopted structures.

A significant organizational development is currently taking place: the continuing improvement in the lines of cooperation within organizations accompanying the increased use of information technologies is leading to more highly motivated staff. However, this development also distracts attention towards the actual current activity itself and away from the documentation thereby produced, an effect which seems to be stronger here than when pure paperwork alone is involved. In addition, it is becoming more and more difficult to achieve a consensus of opinion regarding records due for longer-term conservation as important documents in cases of precedent or even as historical evidence. A further effect is the appearance of multifarious individual applications wherever operators are able to make use of their technological equipment to devise new applications to meet their own specific needs. This trend alone brings with it the risk of limiting both the transferability of data and even, due to the absence of uniform formats, the extent of communication between individual departments. This is where international standards such as OSI really prove invaluable as guarantees for unhindered lines of communication, not just from one organization to another but within internal organization structures. In general, the scope of clerical jobs is becoming much broader and more varied; as a result, the traditional divisibility of labour into clear-cut areas of limited competence no longer holds, and the control of decision-making processes no longer plays the major role it used to in records management.

1.2 Public Users' Demands versus Contextually oriented Archival Systems - A Conflict of Interests

The demands made on archives and archivists are rising all the time, they are increasingly expected to make their records more and more accessible to the public. This development is linked to the claimed right to popularize historical research, whereby it is the factual information to be gleaned from the records that attracts attention, not the contexts essential to its understanding. Public users are not attuned to the problem of evidence, indeed they hardly understand its implications. But the public needs to understand the circumstances and contexts from which transactions originated to the same extent as conventional research historians need to go back to the original sources. The context forms the framework; it is indispensable for the proper appraisal and understanding of the factual information about persons, places and incidents contained in the records. Hence, it is the archive appraisal and description systems that bear more and more of the responsibility for the comprehensibility of the contextual circumstances in which the records in question originated.

1.3 The Predominance of Technical Considerations

In the electronification of records management technical considerations predominate, whether in specialist discussions, the development of systems or the goods put on the market. Posing as "electronic archives", the usual records management systems are geared towards the storage of single pieces of writing without any connection to preceding or subsequent communications and without any regard for the originating contexts. At least the sales representatives and manufacturers of electronic records management systems show very little awareness or sympathy for administrative procedures and instruments such as co-signatures of approval or procedural instructions. They concentrate almost exclusively on the technically feasible, and neither their training nor their range of previous experience gives them the slightest idea of the instrumental role played by administration records in guiding and controlling the processes involved in getting jobs done. Clearly, it is imperative that the true requirements be precisely identified, formulated and explained to the manufacturers if the joint interests of archivists and administrators are ever to influence the design of applications software.

Because of this technical dominance, archive aspects likewise barely figure in the design of office automation systems. Yet items of information obtained from administration processes are potentially of archival value, because they disclose further information on the environment influenced, shaped and regulated by that administration as well as information on the procedures employed to influencing, shaping and regulating. However, the loss of the context of a case transaction, the originating context which gave rise to the text in question, will make it impossible to identify the archival value of the text which will continue to be the prerequisite for its permanent conservation. The basic criterion for the archival storage of administration records is the evidence they contain about the course of transactions. This appraisal and selection of records of permanently relevant importance - a typical task for the archivist - could not be done by anyone else, not even in the case of electronic records. Possibly none other than the European archive tradition with its characteristic provenance principle and *respect des fonds* could prove a source of inspiration to the profession as a whole. Important open questions would have to be answered, of course, such as whether the traditional working procedures, principles and methods are still applicable or whether they need to be augmented or modified.

2. TOPIC: THE CHANGING NATURE OF WORK

Three contributors examined various aspects of change in the nature of work in public administrations, and all three papers corroborated the observation that information technology does indeed effect changes and cannot be regarded as a mere working tool. Tom Finholt, a psychologist at the University of Ann Arbor, Michigan, spoke about the erosion of time, geography and hierarchy, describing as an example the case of the Tandy company which operates world-wide. He set himself the question how staff members of such an organization procure information about working procedures. The answer, he found out, takes the form of two data bases at the disposal of all the staff via e-mail, the first of which comprises "field archives" with "working expertise", the second "expert archives" with "canonical expertise". It turned out that the first of these data bases was consulted more frequently, despite the fact that its information was not backed up by expert opinion but was simply the result of open communication. But here the user received information set in a transparent context. Therefore he was in a better position to judge the applicability of the information received for his own purposes, especially as the context information was linked to examples of solutions for typical problems. Obviously, context is of vital importance.

This paper was followed by a discussion on the character of administration records. Should the data bases referred to by Tom Finholt be included under the heading record-like documents or not? It was suggested that files or administration records should be defined as communicated transactions, and that therefore the data bases mentioned do not properly belong to this group.

Victor Bekkers, an administration specialist from the Catholic University of Brabant, outlined current developments based on the findings of a project on the consequences of E-Mail. He described how the electronic exchange of documents between Dutch government ministries and the parliament is leading not only to the whole handling of written data becoming more formalized, but also to the increasing decentralization of their distribution. As opposed to pure paperwork, the electronic system requires the operator to make new evaluation decisions at an earlier stage in the work process which determine its further course. The findings of the project show that the implementation of E-Mail improved the transparency of the decision-making process, removed the risk of missing information links and simplified the parliament's execution of its control duties, even though the members may not yet have realized the potential or the risks of this information technology.

Heinrich Reinermann, Rector of the College of Administration Sciences in Speyer and its Professor of Administration and Information Technology, demonstrated that applied technology can never be neutral but always brings about changes in working methods. Administration information technology deals with the influences of information technologies on administration and vice versa. Today, almost every operation in public administration could, in theory, be computerized. Its patterns of behaviour are directly linked to the working techniques available. Thus the administration has to be triggered into action by an outside mechanism, e.g. by a citizen submitting a formal application. But this presupposes that every citizen has a grasp of the techniques for claiming his rights. The reason for the principle of formal application is to be sought in the working technology customary today. However, the implementation of modern information technologies opens the way for new administration procedures, which in turn make it conceivable that filed applications will be granted automatically on fulfilment of the legal requirements. In sum, the consequences of the implementation of electronic processing systems in public administrations can be seen in changes in the structures of the data, the organization, the staff and, finally, the prescribed functions. As an example, the speaker cited the "community centres" set up in rural areas in Germany to establish at least the "telepresence" of a variety of public administration departments, banks and insurance companies which have moved their physical presence to the cities. Such phenomena encourage the tendency towards holistic concepts of work. Through the integration of several different areas of work into one workplace, the outsider finds himself faced with a parallel series of several similar workplaces, and this in itself can lead to the development of a hitherto unknown element of rivalry between the various administration departments. The speaker's central thesis was that information technology functions as a catalyst, and that it is fully capable of exercising a decisive influence on the course of organizational procedures and hence cannot be regarded simply as a new-fanged tool. Without a proper assessment of these consequences, the implementation of information technologies cannot be adequately planned.

The discussion that followed concentrated mainly on questions relating to data privacy and work with computerized files in public administrations.

2.1 The Problem of Data Privacy

In the past, it was an easier matter to obtain information from and about administrative procedures. In the meantime, a number of laws have been passed in reaction to the potential dangers of the new technology, and this legislation has resulted in the cooperation between public administration departments and archives becoming strictly regimented. Thus, for instance, the data privacy regulations forbid the archiving of data wherever this is not expressly permitted by law. The entire field has become more complex, impenetrable, and difficult to deal with. In fact, the data privacy legislation often goes further than intended or even needed, and can actually be a handicap by spoiling the cooperative atmosphere of mutual trust between citizen and administration. As regards practical functionality, the borderline between the desired degree of transparency in the work of public administrations (after the legal privacy term, if prescribed, has expired) and the need to protect the privacy of personal data is not always easy to find. Indeed, one is led to conclude that the laws regulating data privacy were formulated in a hurry and passed too soon. The latest amendments seek to correct this situation by adapting the existing legislation to cater for the real needs of the citizen.

2.2 What Happens to the Traces Left by Administrative Operations?

Today, the body of material upon which administrative operations are based is commonly stored in huge data bases jointly accessible to the various departments. How is the archival concept of provenance to be understood in this situation? Can the term be attributed to the data stored in the data base? Or rather to the transactions based on this data? Is there a way to connect transactions permanently with their informational content and fix them in the data bases? In the old days, the spheres of responsibility were evident and clearly demarcated; they could be retraced by following the chain of clues through the file from the stamped date of receipt to the delegation to a particular clerk, co-signatures, memoranda etc. Where are these traces to be found today? If the origin of an item of information is the jointly used data base, where is its provenance to be sought? If it were to be pre-established during processing, how could it remain identifiable once the task assignment is completed? It should be investigated whether the functions of record registries could not be performed by computer software, as the tasks and procedures of records management, i.e. those involved in the control of administrative processes, remain basically the same, even though they may now be interconnected in broader contexts.

Administrators in senior positions are often particularly hesitant about coming to grasps with modern information technology themselves, as they consider this a matter more appropriate for the lower levels of the hierarchy. In fact, however, the implementation of the new technologies raises a need for many strategically vital decisions which can only be taken at top level, e.g. concerning legal stipulations, spheres of work responsibility, norms, policy matters etc.

Information technology can act as a catalyst, in that it can facilitate the formulation of new ideas for the organization of administration work. It can prompt the will to reform and encourage debate, e.g. on the issue of privatization. Once task assignments and the desired results become clearly definable, because a decision has to be taken whether to stick to the old administrative procedures or to change them, then it is time to consider whether the corresponding software could not be bought on the market. In other words, the concept of outsourcing could be worth considering from the administration's point of view. At any rate, information technology will bring more open market economics into the public administrations and thus bring about changes in organizational structures, job processing and the keeping of records.

3. TOPIC: THE CHANGING NATURE OF DOCUMENTATION

Richard Kesner, an economic scientist from Babson College, described how information management is turning more and more into process management, so changing the professional demands placed on archivists. This means, naturally, that the professional qualifications to which training courses are expected to lead are likewise changing. He sees a particularly challenging task for the archivist in the proper treatment of virtual documents consisting merely of a "shell" of procedures for request and linkage and which are supplied with content as required from the labelled stock of stored data. Although there is not yet much awareness or sympathy for the new problems confronting records managers and archivists, this is no reason not to start thinking hard about the electronic possibilities for saving evidence or about the continuing applicability of archival principles.

Peter Bohl, commissioner for office automation at the State Archives Authority of Baden-Württemberg, then gave an account of the Federal State's automation concept. One of his concerns was to draw attention to the rift forming between archive working methods and the way documents are handled. But he still thought it unlikely that new working procedures which contravene current legal stipulations would be introduced, simply to keep pace with technological progress. In his opinion, it is still and will continue to remain necessary to present records for safekeeping to the archives in analogue form, i.e. on paper. At present, information systems can only archive chronological cross-sections in the form of printed output.

The discussion that followed these two contributions concentrated on the definition of a record in the electronic office scene, and looked at differences between the European and North American public administration traditions in so far as they affect archive work.

3.1 The Record as a Working Instrument

Advancing office automation means that things that used to be considered self-evident are now raising question marks, and indeed require a new theoretical basis and justification if they are to remain valid. Before we can decide whether we can continue to work with records we have to establish what exactly a record is, whether it is inherently linked to the conventional physical form, or whether the term is more a description of a certain indispensable functionality which can be activated even without a material series of written papers. Should a definition be found which both corresponded to the conventional understanding of what a record is and also proved to be a functional basis for documents produced with the aid of modern information technology, then that in itself would confirm the fundamentally identical features already remarked upon in the old and new working methods used to deal with records in public administrations. However, in the same way as an address index in an administration department would hardly count as a record, for instance, a computerized file alone would not count as a record either. The shared features are rather to be found on the functional level than in the outer form, and for this reason the jointly valid definition of a record has to be founded on the functions of this type of document. Records are not merely an instrument of communication, of the transmission of news, but serve to carry out task assignments. To the transmission of information the action carried out with the help of this information has to be added. Both together constitute a record, which thus can be understood as a communicated transaction. An electronic record, therefore, can be defined as a unit consisting of data and procedures for their linkage. Many new developments are to be expected in the outer form or the electronics of such units, however, such as the combination of E-Mail documents with Voice-Mail leading eventually to the development of multi-media documents impossible to reproduce as analogue paper records.

One problem is obvious in this form of documentation and that is the transmission of evidence. The transmission of the actual data or pure information is less of a problem, it is rather the procedures for processing it that are far more liable to interference and loss. But in order to conserve the complete evidence, the procedures for processing the data and their respective status would have to be just as transparent as the data content. Virtual documents consisting of procedures and references to other documents or electronic files are particularly difficult to deal with in this respect. We find ourselves here in the field of object-orientated programming, which is the study of the logic of such virtual documents and their attributes. It is not only in the linkage of data and procedures, but also even on the apparently straightforward level of the representation of these computerized files in print or on the screen that the operational parameters of the software prescribe the procedures used to process and generally deal with the material. Here again contexts are created which can have an effect on the evidence.

3.2 Differences between the European and North American Traditions

Organizational and legal parameters play a less important role in the changeover to and installation of information technologies in North America than in Europe. In the US, public administrations will install anything that works, without stopping to wonder about possible restrictions. In Germany, it is not the archives but the internal administration offices that check and authorize all purchases which could have repercussions on organizational structures. The reluctance on the part of German public administrations to introduce modern information technologies to their departments could be a reflection of the (barely registered) fact that the methods employed in traditional German records management are efficient and functional, and so the need to replace them is less urgent. Besides, the state auditors insist not only that written records be kept, but also on their storage in analogue form so as to ensure the workings of the administration remain verifiable. Electronic files are, of course, in increasing use in public administration. Nevertheless, neither the file itself nor the query addressed to it with the resulting answer constitutes a record. The latter comprises, for instance, the initial query with the draft answer based on the information obtained in answer to the query.

An outstanding illustration of the legal constraints binding administrative transactions is the personal file. The only transactions considered necessary and hence permissible in the case of these personal records are defined by law or are available for consultation in the relevant state administration department. The laws and regulations only prescribe the objective of the procedure, however, the objective as it "ought to be". The factual "is" has to be found out by examining the documentation, as this is the only way to obtain evidence on the way the information was really handled and thus reveals the way the laws and regulations were actually applied in a concrete case. In order to gain this insight it is not so much the personal information on the subject of the file which is required, such as name, date of birth, employers' references etc., but rather the clues and evidence contained in it for the way the data was used and what for, in other words, information on associated transactions. The demand for evidence, then, diverts attention to the transaction associated with the answer. The less legally regulated the procedures, however, the more difficult it becomes to acquire knowledge about them and the greater the need for evidence on cases of precedent. This consideration appears to be a major starting-point for the criticism of information systems expressed by North American contributors. Nevertheless, despite big differences in the European and North American traditions surrounding public records management and archives, the analyses of their current requirements also show that they have plenty in common.

4. TOPIC: LIMITS AND FUTURE DEVELOPMENTS OF TRADITIONAL INSTRUMENTS AND PRINCIPLES

John McDonald, head of a department in the Canadian National Archives in Ottawa, described a records filing system devised jointly by an organization department in his archive and a software company. This new filing system, designed specifically to handle electronic records, classifies the texts systematically and produces document profiles which provide additional contextual information. Here again the pressure imposed by the automation to regiment work processes even further was evident. Not only were task assignments automated, but processing procedures were altered as well. In all probability, the records management systems of the future will be coordinated more closely with the relevant business operations and will even have to be developed on the basis of the latter's requirements. So a registry of files will not be a classified index of documents, but a repository of objects containing both the items of information of common relevance necessary for carrying out assignments as well as, for example, testimonials of transactions required for the statement of accounts or for the corporate memory.

Michael Cook, archivist to the University of Liverpool, spoke about the effects on records management of the introduction of e-mail and electronic office communication. The following are likely components of an electronic registry system: outline lists of the documents, transfer lists, lists of expenses, and archival procedures. The use of E-Mail for these purposes is still relatively rare, although it is fairly widespread in the university scene. This state of affairs appears to be connected with organizational structures and work procedures: managers are not accustomed to operating computers themselves, they still tend to delegate all such tasks to the clerical staff.

The implementation of an electronic system of the kind referred to makes it possible to work more flexibly and efficiently, but a weak point in the system is the purely chronological order it imposes on incoming and outgoing documents. Without doubt, systems of this kind will undergo some of the most significant developments in the field of information technologies in the next couple of years. Although technologically simple and inexpensive, their effects and consequences must be kept under sharp observation. Their potential to influence and change social and hierarchical structures is enormous.

The discussion afterwards concentrated mainly on the possibilities open to administrative staff to come to terms with the demands of electronic records management, on the psychological consequences of the implementation of E-Mail, and once again on the similarities and differences between the North American and European administration traditions.

4.1 File Processing and Registry

In the comments on John McDonald's contribution, the point was made that a precondition of the electronic registry system he described is the operator's awareness of the concept of corporate memory, as it is the staff operating the central filing system who decide which texts should be put through it and which should not. Is it realistic to expect the operators responsible to have the necessary far-sighted awareness of the possible consequences of their selectivity? After all, their main task is to deal with the content of the documents, not with filing technicalities. There have been attempts to install automated procedures for deciding what should be filed and what should not, but the operators using them felt ill at ease; they insist on the right to decide themselves. Further problems are caused by the fact that the mental model the operators have of their system tends to drift further and further away from the reality. This is where object-oriented programming comes to the rescue. Experience has shown that it is not necessary to understand the way the system functions in order to be able to operate it. For instance, if a user linked to a PC network enters the command "send", he assumes he is transmitting an item of information. In fact, however, he is not sending off anything but merely altering a right of access to the advantage of the addressee. Consequently, there are several ways of capturing the action "send" as part of the contextual material of a text (commonly documented today by the verified date of dispatch on the sender's copy and also by the presence of the communication in the addressee's file): on the technical level, the command entered can be protocolled, or the altered right of access, or else, on a more complex level, the fact of the transmission of an item of information can be documented. In other words, the transaction can be saved and conserved in several forms, either as a written text, or as the state of the system at a certain point in time, or as a symbol. This causes hitherto unforeseen problems for the saving of the context of a transaction, particularly from the archivist's point of view.

4.2 E-Mail and Styles of Communication

E-Mail works somewhat like an ongoing virtual seminar and is changing our style of communication. It is very informal. Bulletin boards, because of their inherent difficulties, are less popular. This does not mean that there are no strings attached to E-Mail. One of the disadvantages is that a small number of acknowledged experts in their fields are inundated with queries. Another is that the level of acceptance of this medium varies widely from one scientific discipline to the next.

4.3 North America and Europe - Shared Problems

Again the differences between North America and Europe were discussed. It soon became apparent that the participants represented either of two camps, the first of which aired expert opinions on a high level while the others were eager to broaden their knowledge. The Europeans urged each other to think carefully whether they really wanted to jump on the speeding bandwagon or whether the differences between the two traditions were too great after all. These differences are obviously not merely due to the amount of money made available for information technologies in each case. Archivists in the US, for instance, have always considered themselves responsible for a document from the moment of its coming into existence, whereas their German counterparts accept responsibility for a document only when it is handed over and entrusted to the care of the archive. European archivists could probably gain much by paying more attention to administration matters, while North American archivists show a growing interest in European traditions. American interest is focused mainly on such issues as the nature of a record or file and criteria for defining it and its function.

5. IMPLICATIONS FOR ARCHIVES

Claes Gränström, deputy director of the National Archives of Sweden in Stockholm, went into the question whether current archive theory will continue to provide adequate solutions for the new problems already confronting archivists. In Sweden, archive principles are fixed by law to a very great extent. The guiding principle is that of provenance, legally binding since 1900/1903 and practised in state, community and private records offices. The concept of provenance here covers "respect des fonds" as well as the restoration of the original sequential order of records. File description is a continuous process that starts in the administration as soon as a record comes into existence and must be completed before its appraisal. It is forbidden to rearrange or alter the order of records so as not to destroy the surrounding contexts in which the information was compiled and filed, i.e. the evidence. This concept of provenance is complemented by a comprehensive set of regulations determining public accessibility. The cornerstone of all this legislation is the definition of what constitutes a record, also in the case of electronic processing. In addition, the National Archives support a research program with the aim of defining a record, establishing authenticity, accessibility and the technical preconditions for long-term storage.

Bruno Delmas, professor of archive theory at the Ecole des Chartes in Paris, considered various possible and necessary approaches towards solving the new problems on the basis of his scientific discipline. He described the objectives of this discipline as the definition, consideration and study of the functionality of records as administration tools. Contrary to Claes

Gränström, he refuses to understand the principle of provenance as something materially compulsory, but instead as a functional imperative, as a scientifically substantiated necessity for the proper treatment of this kind of information. Seen in this light, "respect des fonds" is nothing other than the presentation of records in the same functional context as that in which they came into existence, regardless of their actual physical order. The same applies to electronic files, as long as the functional context of their origination and utilization can be reproduced. The corresponding archiving system is based on a two-level model, the first level being the physical system of storage and communication and the second comprising an intellectual system of administration and control as well as the adaptation of archiving instruments and procedures. For archivists engaged in archiving administration records, this functional interpretation of the principle of provenance provides the key to the analysis and conceptual planning of new systems.

David Bearman, a Pittsburgh management consultant and editor of the journal "Archives and Museum Informatics", then spoke about archival principles and the office of the future. This he combined with a summary of the discussion up to that point as well as with a review of the results of similar meetings. His main thesis was the increasing necessity to treat provenance as the central and fundamental archival principle. "Respect des fonds" and the restoration of the original order could be regarded as working methods derived from this principle which are closely associated with the keeping of paper records. In an extended sense, provenance is required as the starting point for any effort to elucidate evidence. Evidence remains accessible if the origination context of the record concerned remains clear. Evidence is understood here to mean the sum of all the items of information on a reconstructable transaction; it links the recorded information to the actions. Information on structure and context is mostly available already in implicit form. In the case of electronic records, however, it has to be made explicit. To suit different administrative needs, different types of records are created. For instance, a chronological series is created wherever the main route of access to certain records is via relevant dates. When clients or applicants are the focal point, personal files (as client, parallel or mass files) are created, and when the chief concern is the execution of assignments or responsibilities, this is documented in object files.

Electronic systems for making and administrating records make it possible to retain larger amounts of evidence information than was usual in the past. At the same time, however, these electronic systems bring with them the very real risk of totally obliterating the evidence, as they do not, unlike clerks, automatically or unconsciously make tracks of their own. But it is just when recorded information is stored in coded form and thus incomprehensible to the user that he requires additional context information in order to understand it. Integrated meta-data systems in the office communication systems could probably be designed to retain structural information on the contexts of actions. A possible task for the archivist could be to determine the measure of evidence necessary both for working on the recorded information and for information regarding the actual procedure itself.

The discussion on these three papers focused on the extent of legislation regulating records management, e.g. records appraisal in the Swedish system, which again raised the question as to the character of administration records. The question of evidence dominated the comments that followed David Bearman's contribution.

5.1 What are Records?

According to the Swedish definition, all written records and even empty folders are to be considered as records because they provide evidence on administrative operations. This definition even applies when empty folders indicate no more than the fact that an activity is planned for which written communications are expected, even if the plan never materializes. In fact, a Swedish court order ruled that even E-Mail communications are to be treated as records. Is the definition of a record as a written communication adequate? Or does this communication also have to have initiated some activity or to represent its result? Traces left by people dealing with written communications belong to the classic terrain of diplomatics, traditional and modern, both of which disciplines will probably have much to offer and should therefore be involved more closely in this definition controversy.

5.2 What is Evidence?

Generally speaking, archive records are read on two levels, that of content and that of form. Structural information is accessible via the form level. The whole archive concept is built around the precondition that the semiotics of the outer, formal features is understood. In the case of large data bases, e.g. statistics, it is especially important to be able to reconstruct the operators' actions. Here again there are two access routes, one leading to the content information and the other to the structures. The difficulties concerning the proper access to the content information have been more or less solved since the 1970's, the problem facing us now is how to preserve the evidence. In fact there are two problems involved here. The first is to find a permanently valid answer to the question as to which recorded items of information were collected by a public authority for what purpose, who had access to them, what request and linkage possibilities were available and what programs were used to process the data. This kind of information can be formalized to a great extent. The second problem is how to preserve the evidence of the actual activities carried out. This problem occurs frequently nowadays with regard to business graphics linked to dynamic data bases in the now commonplace electronic office communication systems. These graphics merely illustrate the current state of the data base at the time the query was addressed to it, and besides, they only manifest the audited results produced by invisible formulae contained in preparatory spread-sheets. Furthermore, as the trading figures or the statistical premises for such an electronic business graphic are not static and so cannot be reproduced a second time, the corresponding graphic looks different each time it is generated. The user's mental models no longer resemble the actual electronic processes involved in software application. Strangely enough, however, this discrepancy is a necessary and even deliberately planned precondition for the effectiveness of electronic office systems. So the saving of the evidence must take place on a level below that of its manipulation within the system, whereby a decision has to be made whether it should be saved and stored in the form of the operator's entered commands, the technical processes or the results of the internal processing. Also, each time a set of data is transferred from one system to another a new appraisal of the records has to be carried out and a new selection of the context information to be transferred too has to be made - as a precaution against the loss of "evidential historicity". And it is just this that makes a record a record - without it we are dealing with nothing but plain data. Yet decisions which in fact affect the preservation of the evidential nature of records are taken for granted in the normal course of everyday business administration. This is where the difficulty lies: on the one hand, controlling the course of work processes is quite a different task to the actual information processing itself and hence difficult to combine with the demands of an effective, truly work-related administration, but on the other hand it seems to be just this combination that will be required in future, since - contrary to the situation up to now - the job of carrying out a task assignment will, at the same time, impose upon the clerk the job of continually making appraisals of the usefulness of the records both for the further completion of his task assignment and for future reference.

6. CONCLUSION

There was general consensus about the symposium having contributed much to the discussion on archive theory. It demonstrated how records management as such was at last coming in for critical but constructive scrutiny. As long as records were kept on paper only, the processes to which they were subjected and the procedures involved were applied more or less automatically. Then came the development of electronic information processing, which brought with it the hitherto unknown phenomenon of the conceptional separation of information for processing from its carrier medium. Parallel to this phenomenon, the processing of the stored records and their administration began to drift further and further apart into independent areas of work. In the administration of paper records in the old days, processes were controlled unconsciously. There is no place for the unconscious in modern electronic records, which demand of the user a clearer, more purposeful attitude towards predetermined aims and procedures and where the mastery of the working processes can only be a conscious act.

In today's office environment, records management is becoming less important for the staff because of the increasing independence of the actual processing from the administration of the records concerned (much as information and carrier media are no longer inseparable). On the other hand it is becoming ever more important to understand the context of information, and this presupposes the preservation of the evidence which used to be a by-product of the administrative processing procedures but now, because of the new technology, is no longer being produced automatically. The role of technology is so dominant that it is actually diminishing the significance of process control in the administration of electronic records even further, thus endangering both its instrumentality and the evidence.

Administrative working methods change with automation. Data privacy is just one of the new problems raised. Work on modern dynamic data bases leaves no trace. Processing procedures that used to materialize in the records now end up as sets of data. Nevertheless and independent of their form, records can remain useful if they are functionally defined. Electronic records then become units comprising data and regulations as well as the established procedures for linking them. The dividing line separating the data from the regulations and procedures is very definite, however, and the latter run a greater risk of getting lost than the data. The risk of losing evidence does not appear to be so great in the European administration traditions as it is in North America. The traditional instrument for controlling processes in records management, viz. the registry or central filing system, is approaching its limits, even though the basic task for which it was invented still remains. But both the records and the procedures are changing. While he is actually processing recorded information, the operator is now expected to take more decisions relating to the functionality of the records administration system, e.g. to make appraisals of usefulness and relevance. E-Mail has made communication much easier and so it is heavily used, but as a result traditional forms of communication are being reduced to mere information carriers. As this development is particularly pronounced in

North America, records managers there are beginning to show interest in European administration and office management traditions. North American archivists hope to gain new insights and borrow useful ideas on how to retain and preserve the instrumentality and evidence of administration records by tapping the experience not only of the various European professional archive disciplines and theories but also of classical and modern diplomatics, which developed in the archives of those European states with long-established administration traditions in the 19th and early 20th centuries. Archivists are now expected to formulate the preconditions necessary to enable evidence to be manifested as the intended aim or purpose for which the respective information was collected by an administration office, and as the use to which this information is put. Before this can happen, criteria have to be agreed upon for the continuous appraisal of electronic records for two purposes, for carrying out the task assignment and for preserving the institutional memory.

6.1 What Are the proper Tasks of Archives as Institutions?

Is their task limited to the production of evidence? Surely state archives especially have a more far-reaching contract, namely to retain and preserve the nation's entire social memory? In order to fulfil this contract they require vast amounts of information from non-state sources. But this information also needs the context of the circumstances in which it originated. The US National Archives in Washington, for instance, are currently taking over large data bases that used to be in the care of data libraries and universities. This takeover causes two major problems, first, how to provide evidence and secondly, how to make it clear to the user how the stored data was originally used.

Thesis 1: It is the archives' job to make information and evidence available, and especially to make evidence accessible in those cases where information is incomplete without a knowledge of the contexts which formed and filtered it.

6.2 Do We still Need Theoretical Archive Science?

The methods practised up to now in applying the principle of provenance are methodical procedures rather than applications of a real theory. But now we need to forge ahead and work up the theoretical foundations, as it is here that the key to many of the phenomena and problems raised by electronic record-keeping lies. A specifically archival function is to open access to evidence. Yet is it just the producers of large quantities of data, including even many state authorities, who have an eye for nothing but their current requirements and show little understanding or sympathy for the necessity of evidence. This is so even though the acts of looking up cases of precedent or rendering accounts are utilizations of evidence, on a par with research historians' utilization of preserved sources.

Thesis 2: In extreme cases, information values could be kept by other institutions. But the only access route to evidence is via archival methods, and it is these that mark the special character of archive science. Here lies a solution formula for the main problems besetting office automation.

6.3 Making Evidence available Places special Demands on Archives

Providing evidence is a very complicated task. Electronic records offer the archivist more ways of capturing evidence than paper-based records, but also subject it to a far greater risk of loss.

In the case of E-Mail communications, for instance, it is not sufficient simply to add standard formal marks to clarify the context. Even the act of distinguishing between business and personal communications constitutes an appraisal which is made on the basis of the intended purpose of the communication. A complicated but necessary task is to select which elements of the evidence are indispensable. This entails further appraisal. It also presupposes a preparatory analysis of what items of evidence can arise at all within the range of certain transactions and which of them are needed for maintaining the continuity of the administration, for rendering accounts and for qualifying a record as a historical source. Archivists will be expected to analyse information from administrations and systems devised to process it according to the operations conducted with their aid, and according to their purposes and aims. In future, therefore, it will be the task assignments, executed operations and systems which will form the basis on which appraisals for securing evidence will be carried out, less so the individual documents.

Thesis 3: Appraisal is a major problem in the extraction of evidence from electronic records. The appraisal of a document may not focus upon its content, it has to be based on task assignments and operations.

It has become apparent that there is a real need for some fundamental inter-disciplinary research in new fields. The somewhat nebulous theoretical questions raised occasionally in recent years are now becoming much more precise, although nothing like answers can be formulated as yet. Questions relating to the former and future functionality of administration records independently of their physical carriers were hardly touched on up to now. How can the instrumentality of records for a smoothly running, transparently efficient and conscientious administration be transferred to new carrier media? At the same time, how can historical tradition be secured and preserved as a preventative measure against social amnesia? Up to the present, both the instrumentality of records and their historical evidence were inseparable. Will it still be possible to guarantee this in future, or will the transmission of historical sources have to be incorporated in the design of the electronic system?

English translation: Máire Mulloy

GETTING IT RIGHT: MANAGING ORGANIZATIONS IN A RUNAWAY ELECTRONIC AGE

By Richard E. Barry

[N.B. This paper covers, in an abbreviated fashion, materials used in a workshop which the author has conducted on this subject. References to specific information technology products are for purposes of illustrating particular technologies only. They do not constitute any endorsement of those products.]

INTRODUCTION

This discussion is about the growing impact of the use of electronic media in modern organizations on how information is managed. One of its important underlying messages is: information managers of all stripes must join together in managing organizational electronic files right now, in order to minimize the rapidly increasing costs of unnecessary paperwork and paper storage in the short and medium term, and to avoid chaos in the long term. "Information managers", includes archivists and records managers along with information technology specialists, communications specialists and others dealing with the physical or electronic organization, transport, storage, retrieval, and disposition of organizational files.

The following sections outline: some comparative results of two surveys taken of some 30 United Nations Organizations in 1988 and 1991 in the use of electronic media (not every organization answered every question); outline some of the major symptoms, problems and opportunities surrounding the use of such media by organizations today; and suggested strategies for approaching the associated challenges.

SCOPE OF DISCUSSION

The focus here is on the **management of organizations with organizational electronic files**, with concentration on two major forms of electronic documents. First are those which are created, communicated, received and used in electronic form (e.g., electronic mail or "e-mail"). In principle, these documents should never need to be converted to, or be kept, in paper form. In reality, this type of document, more often than not, is simply not stored in any form outside the creator's or recipient's personal computer (PC). They are thus not accessible to appropriate officials across the organization and, therefore, become lost to the institutional memory; or they are printed to hard copy form (perhaps in several places by creators and recipients) for the purpose of storage and future access. In the broader sense, it may also include products of computer-based transaction systems (e.g., payroll) or management information systems. Certain products of these organizational systems may be of mid-term, long-term or permanent value in terms of official records or archives interests. Even if these products are converted to microform or paper and traditional ground rules for handling the 'copy of record' are followed, this is done at increasingly high and unnecessary human and facilities resources costs to the organization.

The second type comprises documents which have been converted from paper to electronic form. This includes incoming mail and other documents *external* to the organization which are not presently accessible to the receiving organization in electronic form. Regrettably, and with considerable cost implications for many modern organizations, it also includes the bulk of documents which have been *internally* generated in recent years. These documents were originally created in electronic form (e.g., word processing documents), but were subsequently converted to and communicated, received and maintained in paper form. The original diskettes for most of these documents either have been erased or lost, or reside in the desk of the originator's secretary. At best, they exist on some outdated type of diskette or require the use of a machine which may or may not be available in a nearby museum. In short, for all intents and purposes, these documents no longer exist in useful electronic form.

This pattern continues, even today, including in many organizations using state-of-the-art technology. Thus, we have the extraordinary situation in which documents are being created in electronic form, are then printed to paper and subsequently must be electronically scanned in order to convert them back to their original electronic state, if we are to take advantage of electronic file technologies. Even if an original diskette copy is extant, it will more likely than not have to be converted to some 'altered state' (e.g., ASCII) - or if an ODA/ODIF-like document transfer standard is used - some other state which is not exactly what it was originally. This, in turn, becomes a source of misunderstandings and disputes between information technology (IT) specialists and archivists - i.e., the requirement for copies of record to be in original form.

This discussion does **not** focus on the important and more widely understood area of using computers to manage paper files, although it will touch on some transitional considerations. Employing a small play on words, the focus here is not on the **automation of records management**, but rather on the *management of automated records.*

ACCIS REPORT

Portions of this material draw heavily from work which was done by a multi-organizational, inter-disciplinary, Technical Panel on Electronic Records Management (TP/REM), which was sponsored by the United Nations Advisory Committee for the Co-ordination of Information Systems (ACCIS) in Geneva, Switzerland. This work is documented in a book entitled ***Managing Electronic Records: Issues and Guidelines,*** 1990, and is available for sale by the United Nations Sales Office, N.Y., N.Y., or through ACCIS headquarters in Geneva. In the near future, other related reports which have been developed by a follow-up group to TP/REM will also be available through the same sources.

THE PLACE OF THE ARCHIVIST

There is no need to justify the place of archivists or the importance of what they do in the unfolding human drama. Their position is long and well established, as are their many contributions to organizational and societal well-being. Although it might not have been written about what archivists do, the Old Testament certainly testifies to the importance and timelessness of much of the human endeavor which archivists seek to preserve. It is written in this familiar chapter of the Old Testament:

> **To every thing there is a season, and a time to every purpose**
> **under the heaven:...**
> **A time to get and a time to lose, a time to keep, and a time to**
> **case away....**
> **That which hath been is now; and that which is to be hath already**
> **been; and God requireth that which is past...for there is a**
> **time...for every purpose and for every work....**
> **Wherefore I perceive that there is nothing better, than that a man**
> **should rejoice in his own works; for that *is* his portion:**
> **for who shall bring him to see what shall be after him?**
>
> **- Ecclesiastes (The Preacher), Chapter 3**

The ever emerging art and science of archival work (Archiv-Wissenschaft), and the willingness and ability of modern archivists to meet the challenges and opportunities of today's information age, may make the difference in future years - whether men and women will truly be able to rejoice in the works of this and earlier times and ages, and whether they will be able to see what shall be after them.

WHAT TRENDS DO WE SEE IN RECENT EXPERIENCE?

To set the stage for the future, it may help to consider what has happened over the past few years in the use of electronic forms of information. To do this, let us briefly discuss the results of two surveys of UN Organizations - one which was done in 1988 and the other in 1991. The next table shows figures for average daily usage of telex, facsimile and electronic mail, and shows what has happened over the three year period ending in 1991. It does not include word processing, which is assumed to be ubiquitous in most organizations.

Comparison of 1988 and 1991 Results of surveys of UN Organizations

Avg. Daily Usage:		1988	1991	% Difference
TELEX:	(Sent)	552	212	- 62
	(Rec'd)	447	135	- 70
FAX:	(Sent)	85	464	+ 446
	(Rec'd)	83	425	+ 412
E-MAIL:	(Sent)	149	1668	+ 1019
	(Rec'd)	148	1995	+ 1250

TRENDS IN FORMS OF ELECTRONIC COMMUNICATIONS

What the experience clearly shows is that there has been a dramatic shift away from the use of telex and toward alternative forms of communication: specifically facsimile and 'e-mail'. It is worthy of note that this change in mode of communication does not herald a reduction in communications, but rather a major shift in media. Indeed, the newer media, if anything, have increased - not lessened - the volume of communications.

As interesting as the trend-line information from the UN survey is, what is also very interesting is that survey respondents felt sufficiently strongly about the subject that many were compelled to add write-in comments of their own. And what is very important to the archives profession is what they said. Below is a sampling of those comments:

- "The delegation of authority always used to be done by memo. Now it sometimes just goes as an electronic message."
- "We will authorize offers of jobs, for example, in e-mail. This is an official action. But it's usually printed and put in a file."
- "E-mail rests too much responsibility with end-users.. there is no proof of decisions taken..."
- "Appraisal and control [of electronic] documents is a problem we have no systematic approach to yet."
- "'Retention policies do not presently exist."
- "The move to a decentralized computing environment makes it difficult to implement corporate-wide records management applications."

- "Important policy decisions will need to be taken in the next few years....Perhaps the most important issue we will face is being in a position to see what decisions need to be taken."

These are sobering comments from people in the trenches. They suggest that the time for debate has been overtaken by a time for action jointly by all information managers, including information technologists, telecommunications specialists, records managers and archivists.

WHAT HAS CHANGED SINCE 1988?

The ACCIS report on the survey results concluded that between 1988 and 1991 there was clearly a growing awareness of records management problems related to proliferation of electronic media. This may have been brought about in no small part by the emphasis placed on this whole subject matter in the past several years, including the conduct of the first ACCIS survey. With the significant and continuing growth in volume of electronic communications, the report also noted the rising tensions between centralized/decentralized approaches to electronic communications. It observed greater knowledge about and attention to information technology standards in general, and the Open Systems Interconnection approach to standards in particular. Finally, ACCIS observed that many more exploratory and transitional activities were beginning to be put in place to begin to address at least some near-term electronic records issues.

WHAT HAS *NOT* CHANGED?

Although the second survey showed an increasing awareness of risks and issues surrounding electronic records, it did not detect the development of any specific examples of new over-arching policies that define the nature, role and importance of electronic records in relation to basic organizational missions. Nor did it reveal much by way of implementation of systematic procedures for the life-cycle management of electronic records - aimed, in any integrated fashion, at their identification, capture, control, appraisal and disposition management.

WHY DID THE SHIFT COME ABOUT?

I would like to add some comments on my own observations and interpretation of the results of the UN survey, because there may be some lessons for the future in these events. The shift from telex to fax and e-mail is no doubt due, in part, to the lower telecommunications costs of the alternative forms. This much was predictable. In the case of facsimile, it is also because of the simplicity afforded by that technology, especially for people who find e-mail still technically formidable. Furthermore, - as became the case with copy machines some years ago - fax machines are beginning to become ubiquitous in the workplace - in offices, retail stores and restaurants. There are early signs of this phenomenon extending to the home, a movement being led by small businessmen and independent home-based consultants who find it an essential way in which to do business and overcome the lengthy delivery times of the postal service. It is also seen as the most universally accessible way in which to communicate the written word electronically and is a growing expectation of clients and associates. This is due mainly to the fact that - unlike most e-mail systems even today - facsimile has already established the standards necessary to ensure inter-connectivity. In an increasingly mobile world society, other pressures will act to make fax literally a household word. It may become a prescription for families with grown children who are too busy to write home or for avoiding the trip after the long day to the local carry-out restaurant. Rapidly dropping prices for fax machines will ultimately make them as much within the reach of the average family as answering machines are today.

What about the dramatic change in the use of e-mail ? Instead of the one-way nature of telex, which typically requires someone's authorization and can be initiated only in the physical workplace where the person works, in the case of e-mail (despite the fact that it is not everyone's cup of tea) the user interface and, more importantly, individual control over the communications exchange are vastly changed and improved. With e-mail, we may have one or more electronic *conversations* in real or near-real time, and cumbersome authorizations are not normally required unless, perhaps, there is some violation of normal chain-of-command communications. Moreover, people did not typically have direct and ready access to telex machines from their office desks, homes or everywhere away from their home or office where they might have traveled. They need only a PC and modem in their home, or a portable computer when they travel, to have full and immediate access to e-mail across geographic and time zones. As an added bonus, along with their access to e-mail comes immediate access to whatever electronic files they may have.

In both the fax and e-mail cases, we see something similar to what we observed earlier with the advent of the PC: the decentralization of technological resources followed by decentralization of information resources, or access to information resources. It is apparent that users prefer this mode of operation. Whether we agree or disagree, the challenge to provide for institutional interests in the management of organizational records in electronic form is there, and it is formidable.

Unlike the cost advantage, some of these advantages to e-mail and fax over telex would have been predictable only to those paying close attention to the rapidly maturing 'groupware' technologies as well as to the associated results of the growing body of research in the field of computer supported collaborative work, or CSCW as it has come to be known. It would appear that most people in the initial UN survey population, who completed the telex portion of the survey, were not. When asked in 1988 what they felt the trend would be over the next 2-3 years, the staff who completed the telex portion of the survey of UN Organizations generally stated that they expected the use of telex to continue to rise marginally, fax to rise at about the same rate and e-mail to rise somewhat more than in the preceding 2-3 year period. They did not anticipate anything near the fourfold growth in the use of facsimile, or the tenfold increase in the use of e-mail; nor did the people who completed the e-mail portion of the survey (typically those in charge of e-mail systems).

While the survey did not ask which part of the organization was responsible for which information services, it is probably safe to surmise that telex and facsimile services were typically under the responsibility of the communications function. Most e-mail systems pre-dated PCs. For this and other reasons, early systems which quickly gained primary market share (e.g., the IBM PROFS system and the DEC All-in-One system) were host-based on centrally operated computers. E-mail services, were thus typically established under the domain of the mainframe computer manager.

Tradition has continued the dichotomy in the management of telex and e-mail services with the exception of organizations which, mainly in the past five years or so, have consolidated both functions under the same information resources manager. This has been done in order to make the most favorable economic gains for the organization as a whole. In many such cases, telex services have been made available at the individual workstation level. Without reference to organizational arrangements, the UN survey showed both a convergence of telex, fax and e-mail services at the workstation level in more than half of the responding organizations, and corresponding decreases in the central control of these services. This trend exacerbates electronic records problems, but it simplifies messaging options within and outside the organization, and facilitates the system selection of least-cost-routing, invisibly to the user. This is similar to what has been practised by many large organizations for several years for long distance phone calls.

Thus, there may also be another lesson in the UN survey results, i.e., that the internal 'purveyors' of particular information services are not necessarily the best ones to judge future trends - especially where growing user market shares in competing technologies may be involved. Stated another way, organizations in general, and information services managers in particular, who fail to keep abreast of trends in alternative technologies do so at their own peril. What is the next surprise? Will it be voicemail? Voice recognition e-mail ? Some intelligent medium which integrates all of the above? Stay tuned. And stay tuned *in*.

WHAT IS THE ORGANIZATIONAL RESPONSE?

Telex

While telexes were originally prepared in paper form and thus were easy to capture in traditional records systems, they are increasingly being prepared in electronic form on PCs and communicated wholly in electronic form. As these communications go through central offices, there is no reason why they cannot be captured electronically. However, as with backup tapes for data processing systems, the manner in which telexes are captured and stored in many organizations is simply in serial form on magnetic tape. As with most other computer back-up systems, this form may be satisfactory for disaster recovery purposes, but it is not for the kinds of access and information retrieval needs that the archivist (or records manager, or typical user) faces from day to day. We lack electronic records or document management systems with these kinds of requirements designed into them. Because of this, the more usual approach to telex management today is to convert the electronic form to paper for official records purposes - again, at considerable unnecessary additional costs to the organization in terms of paperwork, facilities storage costs and the human costs of processing and finding paper document.

Facsimile

In principle, the same thing happens with facsimile. The problem may be exacerbated in the case of facsimile, however, because we find that facsimile facilities are being decentralized to end-user offices at a faster rate than telex facilities. In fact, in the extremely competitive PC industry, high speed fax-modems are being bundled into new PC models as standard features. However, ways for centrally capturing decentralized facsimile communications have not normally been developed as decentralization happens. We can only legislate and hope that originators sending facsimile from hard copy will, where appropriate, ensure that another hard copy gets into the traditional paper records system. Once again, however, in the absence of systems designed to meet these requirements, we lose the advantages of digital storage of, and access to, such documents.

Electronic Mail

The most elusive case is that of e-mail. Although e-mail systems provide a capability for individual storage and filing of electronic messages, they do not typically have the ready made capability for corporate or institutional electronic files. Even where the capability exists from a technical standpoint, it is not normally developed by the systems people, because they have not been made aware that there is an organizational requirement to do so. Moreover, even if the IT people were to agree to such a requirement, nothing could happen until management has allocated the substantial resources implied in doing such a thing, and that is not likely to happen until managers are made more aware of the problem. The largest bottleneck, however, toward realization of such a capability is that the records management and archives specialists have not done the massive job which needs to be done on the logical or intellectual side of the problem, which dwarfs the technical problems of implementing such a system. Issues of information management and file organization, indexing vs. full-text retrieval strategies, flat vs. multi-level security access, revisable vs. non-revisable storage forms, character vs. image approaches to document storage, distributed vs. centralized archives architectures, etc., and combinations of these choices are simply not being addressed in most organizations.

WHAT DO THE RESULTS OF THE UN SURVEY MEAN?

The main message from these surveys for the UN Organizations, in my opinion, is a simple one. It is that most of the UN organizations are in the same boat - at least for the 24-28 of the 32 organizations which responded to the survey. To be sure, some are further ahead than others, and some are further ahead in some aspects while others are further ahead in others. This is a disarming, and in many ways comforting, message. It has helped these organizations avoid a great deal of posturing and other non-productive responses which might occur if individual organizations (in the absence of broad and convincing survey data) felt embarrassed about the possibility that they might be far behind their sister organizations. Although we do not have the benefit of comparable information in national public sectors, or in the private sector, there is little evidence to suggest that what has been observed in the UN Organizations is not also representative of these other sectors. In the private sub-sector defined by the manufacturers and producers of information technology products, with few exceptions, e.g., Thinking Machines Inc. of Cambridge, Massachusetts, the absence of electronic records solutions is as prevalent as it is anywhere, if not more so. This being the case, it is not surprising that even the enlightened among their customers find it difficult to jury-rig such products to begin addressing electronic records issues with any kind of user-friendly results, with the exception of the most innovative companies, e.g., the Sverdrup Corporation's office in Company of Arlington, Virginia.[1]

ASSESSING WHERE AN ORGANIZATION STANDS

Most organizations are unaware of where they stand in all of this, or remain unaware or unconvinced that they have a problem. One simple way of gauging where an organization stands is to examine the symptoms which are characteristic of many organizations which recognize that they already have, or are in danger of having, runaway electronic records. If most of the same symptoms reflect the way things are today within another organization, then one might fairly assume that that organization is also at risk. Alternatively, if this is not yet the case, that organization has a jump on the problems and has a small window of time in which to address them. In the following discussion, symptoms are addressed before problems, because we need to recognize them when we see them; however, we need to treat the problems, not the symptoms.

What are Some of the Main Symptoms?

Some of the most common symptoms, which organizations experience before recognizing the underlying problems, are most obvious by observing the manner in which records are currently created and managed in the organization.

- Different organizations responsible for paper and electronic files
- Lack of coordination in managing paper and electronic files
- Inability to maintain a single internal word processing standard and infeasibility of doing so
- Rapid diffusion of document control to users
- Dramatic shifts in information mix

[1] Initially, because it could not find a suitable electronic records product on the market, Sverdrup developed its own Document Control System, especially designed to meet its needs as a construction management firm and the needs of its clients. As it became clear that this need was shared by many other organizations, Sverdrup made its product available for others in the construction industry and has embarked on generalizing the system for broader application beyond the construction industry.

- Increasing use of new communication vehicles
- Growing presence of mixed-media
- Loss of *access* to official records
- Loss of the official records themselves

Other symptoms are more readily apparent by observing the manner in which staff skills are exhibited and in the way in which staff function. Some of the major human telltale signs of impending problems with electronic records are the following:

- Records (in Europe, the Registrar function) & Archives staff often unskilled in modern information technology and information engineering
- Information Technology (IT) staff unskilled in: text-based information systems, archives and records management
- IT staff insensitive to institutional archives/records needs
- Diminishing secretarial control over paper files & file systems
- Users often unaware of their changing role in maintaining the integrity of organizational records, files and information

What are the Problems?

If many of these above symptoms in the human behavior or document arenas sound familiar to an organization, then it is probably facing the same kinds of problems prevalent in most organizations today. Time does not permit a detailed discussion of problems stemming from the increasing use of electronic media for official purposes. For now, let us just observe that they appear at many levels of the organization and mention a few, with primary focus on the top management level.

Top Management's Problem

At the highest levels of the organization - the top management level - there are two main problems manifesting themselves by the symptoms outlined above. One is substantive in nature. It is the creeping loss of managerial accountability throughout the organization, due to lack of documentation - not so much of decisions taken but of the behind-the-scenes debates leading up to decision making, and of the *reasons* for decisions which have been made. In many organizations, this kind of documentation is growingly recorded only in the form of electronic mail.

Executives have long understood the necessity for maintaining and managing organizational records and archives for purposes of managerial accountability and evidence thereof, operational continuity and institutional history. It is not clear that they appreciate how the infusion of modern information technology into today's organizations threatens continued accommodation of these top management objectives. This is true even when they appreciate that technology is essential to the achievement of other mission-critical organizational objectives; and even though the technology can be as much a part of the solutions as it is the problems. One needs only to observe recent events in U.S. industries producing building products (e.g., asbestos insulation) and pharmaceuticals (e.g., breast implants) to see this phenomenon. Similarly, the auto industry has been quick to see the tremendous competitive advantage which can be realized through requiring suppliers to do business through electronic data interchange (EDI); but has the industry been as perceptive in managing the rapidly increasing share of its information base represented by electronic documents?

The other top management problem is economic in nature. The cost of physically processing and storing paper is becoming prohibitive. With stricter government regulations for record-keeping (for environmental reasons, limitations on the export of strategic arms, etc.), and as rates of records accumulation continue to rise, they are beginning to outstrip the capacity of records and archives organizations even to properly schedule and appraise them, if this isn't already the case. Even if these problems could be solved by putting more money into the management of paper records assets, we have or soon will reach natural limits in our ability to process and quickly access specific documents or document groups needed to satisfy a particular information requirement.

Similarly, the direct and indirect costs of paper*work* are becoming prohibitive. Simply moving paper from one end of the organization to another and using it as the token for conducting business, is getting to be very costly. It is also unsatisfactory from a service-needed point of view and unsatisfying from a service-delivery point of view. Lack of recognition of this fact of modern life in a private sector operation is already a recipe for extinction. However, because of shrinking revenues and the growing budgetary squeeze, academic and public sector organizations cannot escape these considerations either. More and more, even these latter institutions are looking to more appropriate technology to help solve these problems, or face the serious threat of their functions being outsourced to the private sector.

The IT Manager's Problem

The information technology manager's problem is one of facing up to the corporate records issues and the jurisdictional problems to which that gives rise. Their traditional lack of interest in paper-based systems illustrates this point. In the past, and still so today, the management of copier services in most organizations has resided in the print shop. Now, with the advent of such products as the Xerox DOCUTECH digital copier,[2] and its forthcoming local area net-

---

[2] This technology represents a major change in information services, because it is a shift from xerographic platform to a digital-image platform, bringing it out of the analog world and into the middle of the digital-based information management environment which is common in most modern organizations today.

work version, remote copying services will be introduced into the family of services which will be available to all workstations which are members of a local area or enterprise network system. Similarly, the opportunities for solving the growing need for document management systems which are afforded by document-based technologies (image, full-text) tend to be foreign to most IT organizations. Faced with their own political and budgetary problems, IT organizations are often unskilled and poorly equipped to take on these blossoming technologies. In the face of these changes, and the changing expectations of their client communities, IT managers can ill afford to overlook what in most organizations now represents the lion's share of information assets - text. This means taking on deeply entrenched traditions in print shops and mail rooms, not to mention records offices and archives.

The Archivist's Problem

The symptoms described above present mounting problems for the archivist in preserving the historical perspective of the organization when, growingly, the history of the organization is becoming digitized and resident in remote PCs. The human resources allocated to the archives function is woefully inadequate to face the problems at hand; not only in terms of numbers of staff but in terms of needed skills. Even if the archivist is 'invited to the table' by the IT manager to address these issues, many predict that no one will show up. Lack of time, resources, computer literacy and prestige in the organizational structure on the part of many archivists makes this prediction credible. Archivists must be agents of change if this scenario is to change.

This is not a matter purely of interest to the public sector. Similar arguments can be made with respect to records managers in the private sector. Moreover, there appears to be a growing interest in the private sector in the establishment of an archives function. Although information is episodic, and statistics are not readily available, at least some of the largest and most successful private enterprises see the need for some kind of archives function, if only as a way for ensuring their place in the history of the industrial and information ages.

The Records Manager's Problem

The challenges to the records function are great. As with the archives function, lack of resources and organizational priority, which have plagued this function for many years in most organizations, are factors which are greatly exacerbated with the advent of electronic records. As with the archivist, records managers need to overcome enormous skill gaps in the use of modern information engineering methods and tools. This has begun in some organizations, where records managers are taking stronger leadership in the use of IT in their own operations and coordination with the IT function on global IT issues.

Even assuming that top management appreciates the need to overcome electronic records issues, they tend to view such matters in the same mold as most other technology/labor tradeoffs. If human and capital resources are to be injected into the records or archives functions, there generally comes with it an expectation of a return for reasons of productivity elsewhere in the same functional areas. However, the records function will continue to have to deal with historical paper records for many years to come - and some believe forever. This is true because it is either economically prohibitive to covert all existing records to digital form or because the organization considers it infeasible to do so for other operational reasons. Thus, in most cases, it will be necessary to operate parallel paper and electronic records systems for the foreseeable future. This does not reduce the resource requirements for the records or archives functions. On the contrary, it increases those requirement. There are, no doubt, significant productivity or quality gains to be made by making needed and relevant information from these systems more readily and easily available to staff throughout the organization. However, these gains accrue to the users of the official records, not to the staff maintaining them. Records managers need to articulate this issue and the steps which can be taken to move ahead.

Everybody's Problem

The people who suffer the most from inattention to the electronic records issues are the people across the organization who require access to the 'institutional memory' to carry out their daily programs of work. Denying staff at large the rich assets which the organization now has - at least potentially - at its disposal, is a penalty devoutly to be avoided. Firstly, it represents a waste of scarce resources, just as if it were financial resources or real estate being squandered. Few organizations can afford that luxury today; and in most organizations, similar ineffective use of financial or real resources could constitute cause for disciplinary action.

Secondly, the generation of new blood coming into modern organizations, fresh from public and private schools, and institutions of higher learning, has high expectations for discovering the responsible use of information technology and information resources in the workplace. The best of these products of modern education will want to be associated with the organizations which exhibit at least a commitment to, and plan for, tackling these questions if not some already implemented smart solutions.

Up until very recently, the penalties for lack of appropriate information sharing within and external to the organization were high but perhaps not fatal. Now, with the advent of inter-organizational electronic information exchange systems (e-mail, EDI), the penalties for failing to capitalize on such capabilities, and for not adapting present business processes to take advantage of them, are becoming potentially fatal. This is true not only in the private sector but also in the academic and public sectors where open exchange of information has been a long-standing tradition. In short, the overall problem for all members of the organization is one of how to bring about sufficient gains on IT investments to make them worthwhile in ways which are economically justifiable, and in terms which bear on the core aims and processes of the organization.

WHAT INFORMATION TECHNOLOGIES ARE RECEIVING THE GREATEST ATTENTION?

It is reasonable to ask the question: what technologies which are relevant to the problems associated with the management of electronic documents, are readily available today? Although individuals might argue on their ranking or completeness, most would agree that the technologies most needed to address the electronic records issues include: full text and imaging technologies to capture and organize massive textual data bases; optical storage systems and large-scale, very fast, massively parallel processing technologies to house and efficiently manage massive text bases; local and wide area networks to provide needed client services and to communicate textual information; smart and artificial intelligence systems to address the infeasibility of individually indexing each document; advanced information retrieval systems with 'fuzzy logic' to facilitate navigation through very large text bases and retrieval of relevant documents; and high-speed communications vehicles over which large documents can be quickly transmitted.

As surprising as it may seem, there are substantial developments in all of these areas, although the imaging technology is advancing much more visibly than is the full-text area. The IBM Image Plus system has been piloted in the United Services Automobile Association (USAA) in San Antonio, Texas - one of the largest and most competitive insurance companies in the United States. It illustrates the enormous potential of this technology for document management purposes in a 'bottom-line' profit-and-loss environment. Incoming correspondence received from USAA clients is indexed and digitized in image form, the versions of which are destroyed. This technology has reduced mail and other paper handling, delivery and paper storage enough to convince this private sector company that this is the most efficient and effective manner in which to conduct business.

Apparently this has not created any significant legal problems for USAA, since the courts accept the 'best' available form of a document as evidence. If originals are kept by the organization, then only that form will be acceptable to the courts as evidence. If the company files only paper copies of the original documents, then only that form may be used as evidence. If, however, the company does not have the original, or a paper copy of the original, then the courts will accept an electronic image as evidence, or a demand paper copy thereof.

Substantial gains are being made in the development of local area and wide area networks, worldwide. The notion of the enterprise network has come of age and many organizations have installed, or are in the process of installing, such systems across their entire structures. Increasing use of this technology has also helped to bring about **de facto** standards which, in turn, will assist in intra- and inter-organizational information sharing.

One of the most promising new developments in information technology is the recent use of the massively parallel processing capabilities of supercomputers in business applications. Up until very recently, such computers were dedicated primarily to scientific computation and space applications. Yet, this technology is a natural one for handling very large text bases and for making them more accessible than is feasible in other more traditional technologies. To illustrate, the Thinking Machines Inc. supercomputer - called the Connection Machine - comes in several models offering storage and processing capabilities which would stagger the imagination of many managers of traditional mainframe systems. These vary from 5000 to 100,000 parallel processors - thousands of times greater in processing capacity and effective access time than most business mainframes. They make it possible to search hundreds of documents simultaneously to see if they meet the needed search criteria. Such a system, the Wide Area Information Servers (WAIS) System has been installed on a Connection Machine and has been operating on a test basis internationally for approximately two years. The system was developed by a consortium of large information users and purveyors and computer manufacturers - Thinking Machines, Apple Computers, Dow Jones and Peat Marwick. It includes a large network of distributed data bases on geographically diverse PC platforms. Although it was designed principally as an electronic library, it is used within Thinking Machines for certain aspects of the management of electronic records.

What we observe is significant advances in most of the relevant technologies individually. What we have yet to see is real strides being made in the integration of these technologies, principally because the vendor world has not become sensitized to the electronic records problem, nor has it been told that there is a real market for products aimed at these issues.

WHAT ARE THE IMPLICATIONS?

We have looked at what is happening in UN Organizations today and postulated what we see as likely to be typical in public and private sector organizations more generally. We had discussed some of the symptoms and problems facing organizations in the management of information resources in general and electronic records in particular; and we have touched on some of the technological developments most relevant to solution of electronic records problems.

What can we sensibly draw from this information?

- Solutions are not mainly technology bound
- The issues are mainly ones of policy, organization, and management commitment
- The principal technological hurdle is in the integration of existing technologies
- Vendors have not heard the demand

The leadership is not coming from the usual sources - neither the internal information technology groups nor the system producers. IT managers thus need the prodding and assistance of archivists and records managers in better understanding and articulating systems requirements for electronic records management, and they should be able to expect that assistance. Archivists and records managers should not wait to be asked but should exercise that leadership themselves. They must enter into a 'strategic alliance' with their IT colleagues and begin to address strategies for the management of important organizational electronic records assets.

MANAGEMENT STRATEGIES FOR GETTING IT RIGHT

What should organizations do once they have recognized some of the symptoms discussed above - or even before most of these symptoms have manifested themselves? It is difficult to find models to replicate. If there are no fully working models, then there can be no experts either. Thus the best we can do here, until some better models are available, is to make known what we know about those aspects of the problem set which have been, or are being, addressed - and there are several partials solutions which can be 'seen and touched'. We can also share our different visions of nirvana, and our perspectives, strategies and tactics for solving existing problems in the management of organizations with electronic records, or for avoiding such problems before they arise.

Not only are we lacking in good, replaceable models of success, but - as noted earlier archivists and records managers have not been very successful, to date, in closing the gap with their information technology colleagues. They have not typically become sufficiently conversant and experienced themselves in the use of modern information management techniques and associated information technology to be able to convincingly articulate functional requirements for electronic records and electronic records management.

Why is this? In some cases, archivists and records managers are not convinced themselves that there is a problem, or that the solution rests anywhere other than in converting electronic documents to paper for traditional treatment - i.e., that, the term "electronic record" is in itself an oxymoron. In other cases, archivists or records managers see no need to question or change their ways of doing things when it comes to electronic records, because they believe that electronic records and archives can be managed in the same way that their paper forms are and have been for many years. For most, however, it remains a failure in coordination among some of the key stakeholders of the electronic records issue - IT managers, telecommunications managers, archivists, records managers and managers of the organization's primary operating arms. This comes from a need for a greater awareness of both the problem set and the interdependency of these groups in solving it, as well as from the traditional (and powerful) barriers of organizational 'turf'. As a result, there has been a failure, in most organizations, in getting top management insights into the risks attendant with *not* doing anything new or different, and in getting the necessary commitment to coordination and cooperation in planning, staffing and budgeting terms.

What follows is a discussion of three strategies which archivists and others interested in addressing organizational electronic issues may find helpful in promoting a common understanding among themselves and their IT colleagues. It may also be of assistance in showing executives that there is a way out, once senior management has become aware of the breadth and potential seriousness of a 'do-nothing' approach to electronic records.

The three strategies proposed are ones which are not at such a level of detail that they would fit into only a very limited number of organizational settings - although some specific ideas for implementation are suggested. On the other hand, they are not so general as to be of little use to anyone. They may be used as a way of setting directions or as a check-list for assessing how far a particular organization has come in addressing these issues. They are: (1) linking information and technology to core organizational processes; (2) reassessing roles and rules for managing organizational information assets and services; and (3) basing procurement of IT on emerging Open Systems Interconnection standards.

1. LINKING INFORMATION AND TECHNOLOGY OF CORE BUSINESS PROCESSES

What is Meant by "Business Process"?

Every organization has a central purpose. Most are organized both to directly carry out that purpose and to provide various indirect support services to ensure the efficient and effective implementation of their primary purposes. A 'business process' is something which any public or private organization does to carry out its principal aims and support functions. The term 'business process' is used here because it is the one most commonly used in the literature; however, it should not be misinterpreted as applying only to commercial or private organizations. The term 'organizational process' could equally well be used in its place.

Core Business Processes

The important thing to recognize is that there are *core* processes which get to the heart of the organization's existence because they most closely represent its purpose. Expressions of these processes normally begin with verbs, because they represent what the organization **does**. Examples might be to:

- perform social services
- collect taxes
- provide technical assistance
- carry out disaster relief operations
- educate students to meet specific national needs
- lend money
- construct office buildings (to sell to others)

Support Business Processes

Just as there are core processes, there are also support processes which are more representative of the inputs necessary to carry out the stated aims of the organization. Examples of these might be to:

- hire staff
- purchase supplies
- maintain records and archives
- provide automated information technology services
- construct office buildings (for an organization's own purposes)

Why are They Important to Archivists and Other Information Managers?

Business processes tend to remain relatively stable, even when organizational structure does not. It is seldom that an organization changes its basic purposes; and even though the personnel department may be reorganized every few years, the associated business processes remain relatively the same. Staff must be recruited, hired, trained, promoted, etc. And although the manner in which the process is carried out may be streamlined and the physical or electronic tokens or documentation of these processes may change over time, the process nonetheless remains an excellent anchor for tracking what an organization does. Clearly, the closer that support processes can be brought into line and integrated with core processes (without contradicting institutional or extra-institutional (e.g., legal) interests), the more relevant they will be to the organization's principal aims and the more important they will be seen by managers responsible for core processes and by the organization's executive management.

This is important to the archivist and records managers for both political and substantive reasons. Politically, it is important because the business processes for which the archivist and records managers are responsible are themselves important support processes. The closer these processes can be integrated with the organization's core business processes, the greater support there is likely to be for what archivists and records managers do, and this will facilitate obtaining advantageous organizational placement and resource allocations. It is important for substantive reasons, because the business process offers a very stable platform against which to associate paper and electronic records. Information systems tend to be closely tied to business processes, or should be for the reasons outlined above. If they are, it means that the associated electronic records will be also.

Competitive pressures among and within private enterprises are causing increasing attention to be paid to how key business processes are carried out in those organizations, especially those which cut across internal organizational boundaries where jurisdictional considerations often create unnecessary process transactions and paperwork - and associated records. In the past, managers and staff in public sector organizations have often taken the position that they are not subject to the same pressures, since they are not for-profit, not market-driven, organizations. Very often, in fact, they constitute monopolies. In recent years, however, public sector organizations *have* experienced competitive demands as old forms of governing have given way to newer forms, largely because they were not sufficiently responsive to public (market) needs. This phenomenon has not been limited to the widely heralded events of eastern Europe. Some large cities in the United States and other highly developed countries, including in western Europe, are facing enormous economic problems and must weigh public demands for improved services against the needs for increasing taxes, just to continue performing at current service levels. At a more micro-level, many public and private sector organizations are reexamining 'make vs. buy' alternatives in rethinking (or 're-engineering' as it is commonly referred to in the business literature) how business processes are carried out. 'Out-sourcing' work, in which organizations turn to private sector organizations to more efficiently or effectively carry out specific support processes, has become a more common approach to service delivery in public and private sector organizations as they both face increasing demands and shrinking revenues and budgets. Thus, it may be said that public sector organizations are no less under pressure to re-engineer core and support business processes in order to survive than are their counterparts in the private sector. It simply takes them longer to go broke.

Information resources, including both paper and electronic records, are a major factor in both articulating existing business processes and in re-engineering those processes. Archivists must play a strong role in both cases to ensure that institutional interests are protected and to most efficiently and effectively carry out their own support processes. This requires an alliance between archivists, IT managers and those responsible for the major business processes being served.

2. REASSESSING ROLES (AND RULES) FOR MANAGING ORGANIZATIONAL INFORMATION ASSETS AND SERVICES

As we look deeper into the issues related to electronic records, as noted above, it becomes apparent that an essential part of any attack on electronic records problem involves a rethinking of formal and informal organizational relationships and models for information management. This requires first determining who the stakeholder or participants are in the management of the life cycle of electronic information and records, followed by some definition and agreement on the roles and relationships among those 'key actors'. The answers will not be the same for every organization, nor even within the same organization depending on its stage of development in the use of electronic forms of information.

Who are the Players?

There are several factions within any organization which may be needed to contribute to the development of a sound program for the management of electronic records. As electronic information is created on, or normally resides in, some automated system (both hardware and software), the organizational entities responsible for those systems are both a part of the problem and a part of the solution. This may include one or more of the following: central IT functions, responsible for computer operations; functional managers responsible for systems development of specific applications (depending on the degree of centralization or decentralization of information resources management this may be the central IT organization or a functional manager (e.g., Personnel, Accounting, etc.); department-level users, where local area network are in place and information is controlled at that level; or individual end users, in cases where certain information resides only in end-user personal computers.

Archivists and records managers are also key players now, because they have long-standing institutional responsibilities for: the appraisal and preservation of organizational records (in whatever form); making such information easily accessible over time to staff and others with a legitimate need; and for managing the ultimate disposition of such records. In the paper world, the creators of information have also played a key role in the life cycle of documents. In many organizations, it is the originator's responsibility to ensure that something is copied to files. With electronic records, this may or may not be the case, depending on how much the system is relied upon to capture electronic information and get it into appropriate records and archives channels (which may also be automated to varying degrees).

Information technologists and archivists have different points of reference and view about information and information processing - and about the life cycle of information. As most managers responsible for the IT function today are people whose early professional careers developed before the advent of personal computers, IT specialist tends to hold the well-established model of information processing:

- Input
- Processing
- Output

This model places emphasis on the capturing and preparation of data as input to a computer, to the input and software which will be used to process the data, and to the presentational form in which data output will be organized. In the past, the output presentation has more often than not been in the form of paper reports. This is giving way to more modern practices of organizing data in such a manner as to make it accessible to users on demand in whatever form they wish - both in terms of report format and in physical terms, whether in paper form or electronically on a video display terminal at the user's workstation.

The archivist and the records manager see information in a different way in terms of the life cycle of a typical document. While there are variations on what constitutes that cycle, it is generally patterned chronologically according to the manner in which paper documents have been processed for many years: creation, use, preservation, appraisal and disposition. At the risk of oversimplifying in order to make the point, the emphasis of the IT specialists has focused mainly on the creation and use of electronic documents or information, whereas the emphasis of archivists and records managers has been principally on their preservation and disposition.

Changing Roles and Rules

IT Managers

If organizations are to meet their institutional needs for electronic files, IT specialists will have to embrace a broader life-cycle concept to information management. It will not be enough for IT managers, or functional managers responsible for specific applications, to simply provide for disaster recovery copies of electronic files and purge on-line files as quickly as possible due to storage constraints and system performance considerations. As noted earlier, backup files which are maintained on magnetic tape in off-site storage facilities (often where no computer is available to immediately recover and make use of the files) may be adequate for purposes of re-establishing vital business operations after a disaster of some sort (although this is also questionable). They do not, however, normally serve the purposes of on-going and easy access to historical information. Nor, for all practical purposes, have the appraisal needs of the archivist been addressed in the disaster recovery back-up process. In short, historically, IT managers and applications managers have not provided for information scheduling and disposition management as, and along with other, legitimate system specifications; nor, in most cases, have they been asked to. If archivists tend to lack computer literacy, IT managers tend to be seriously lacking in their literacy of records management and archives. In some ways, this is a strange state because, in principle, they share many common interests, even though they use different words to talk about them. Until there is some closer understanding among these groups, there can be little by way of resolution of electronic records issues.

Archivists and Records Managers

Archivists and records managers will have to re-think the life cycle which has served their purposes for many years. In particular, they will wish to reexamine the location and timing of the appraisal function in the life cycle, the level at which it is (at least initially) performed (document, file, series, system), and the extent to which this function should be automated. This is so for a number of reasons. Principal among them is that, for most organizational environments, it will not be economically feasible for archivists and records managers to physically inspect all electronic documents. Thus, they will have to rely heavily on the systems where the electronic records are maintained to also automatically schedule and perform associated disposition management functions. Needless to say, that must be done according to scheduling and disposition management rules designed by archivists and records specialists.

Life-Cycle Information Management

The life-cycle model which was embraced by the ACCIS Technical Panel on Electronic Records, and which is spelled out in more detail in the UN ACCIS publication *Management of Electronic Records: Issues and Guidelines* (1990) offers a model which can serve the needs of line managers, IT managers, records managers and archivists alike. It can also be used to evaluate the business processes of those groups and the formal and informal organizational arrangements for the maintenance of organizational records. Finally, the life-cycle model below can play an important role in opening the needed dialogue among IT and records specialists and managers, and in sorting out sensitive role issues.

- *Creation and Identification:* To create a new document, record, or file and provide unique identifying information.

- *Appraisal:* To determine the ultimate disposition of documentary material and schedule it for future destruction or archival retention, typically in terms of years after creation.

- *Control and Use:* To store and retrieve information for use by its creator and others with authorized access rights or to convey information to others as part of administrative or secondary use.

- *Disposition:* To destroy information according to the schedule determined at the appraisal stage, or to transfer it to an archival repository. The latter also may include reappraisal and the imposition of restrictions on access in order to protect personal privacy or confidentiality.

Preservation vs. Public Access

Information technology, while constituting a major part of the new problem environment, also offers a major part of the solution. If properly employed, it offers a great opportunity to open up possibilities for future analysis of today's and tomorrow's history - facilitating scholars to locate, work with and analyze source material which previously was simply impossible to physically handle in the paper world - even assuming one could get access to such source material. Not only does this open great possibilities for scholars and researchers, but it also offers heretofore impossible means to open up representations of historical source information to the general public. The opportunity is, literally, to place current and selective ancient history at the fingertips of primary and secondary school students and 'the man on the street' in the form of living images of documents as they appeared when they were created, while at the same time protecting the actual originals from unnecessary handling and exposure, e.g., from Dead Sea scrolls to genealogical research files such as those of the Mormon Church.

The American Memory Project of the US Library of Congress has as its objective placing the Library's information stores at the disposal of anyone with a personal computer. This is estimated to involve in the order of 20-30 terabytes of information, and ways and means of effectively managing and accessing target information. Manufacturers of supercomputers, such as the Thinking Machine Inc., are now developing this class of computer. Application of such engines to electronic records management will greatly facilitate public access to historical information. This possibility offers new roles for librarians, archivists and historians in promoting and making such systems work.

Physical vs. Intellectual Control

A shift in emphasis is needed in the archivist's thinking and work - from one in which (in many places) their is a predominance of concern about the physical preservation aspects of records, and relatively little emphasis on the intellectual control aspects. What is needed in the case of electronic records is much greater emphasis on the intellectual control or organization of information. This is so because of the magnitude of the inventory that will be available and in order to make it all easily accessible in future years. Similarly, a shift in emphasis is needed in the thinking and work of some information technologists, in which there is as much consideration for the message as there is the medium of information storage and processing.

In addition to the fact that an enormous amount of effort is required to organize large text and data bases, there is also the question of whether electronic files are more effectively housed in many disparate applications systems or in a central electronic repository as often has been taken for granted with respect to paper archives. In the case of electronic records, the physical control of electronic records is more easily managed in computers. Thus, archivists and records managers may not enjoy the same advantages in exercising physical control over electronic records as they do over paper records.

The ACCIS report argues, as do many consultants in the field, that the physical control of electronic records should rest with the same organizational units which are responsible for the applications systems which produce the records - whether that is the corporate IT manager or the applications functional manager (e.g., Human Resources Department), depending on the extent of decentralization of systems development in the organization. There are some strong arguments in favor of this approach. By tying the records to the applications systems, the IT or applications manager must carry the responsibility for successfully migrating historical records, as the systems are upgraded to new software and hardware platforms. If the role falls to the IT manager, that person will have to take account of the significant costs of conversion in considering any new platform.

Similarly, if it is the applications manager, the issue cannot be escaped when upgrading software. Moreover, the ACCIS report also puts forward the suggestion that applications programs include scheduling and document disposition management algorithms (albeit designed by archivists and records specialists). This point can be advanced as an argument for the placing physical control of electronic records with the IT or system application manager, rather than in a separate records or archives system. This is especially the case as archivists and records managers have not normally developed skills and experience in the management of electronic systems.

There is also a case for the development of a corporate level integrated records and archives management system. This approach may be the most practical one for some years to come. Apart from some non-trivial technical problems associated with maintaining and integrating numerous independent applications level electronic archives, there are advantages to the development of a single corporate system approach. Applications and IT managers, as well as end-users, have a strong interest in using and re-using information. They do not normally require the information in its original form, e.g., with signatures, logos, etc., but place a heavy weight on easy access and retrieval. In technology terms, their interests, therefore, tend to be more character oriented and better served by character-based, full-text systems.

Records managers and archivists, on the other hand (and especially archivists) place heavy weight on the representation of the document which most closely mirrors the original paper form (if there was one). That means that things such as signatures, logos, marginalia, etc., are very important to the archivist. This, in turn, suggests a different (or additional) kind of technology which is image based rather than character based. The archivist will probably require both character- and image-based technologies - one for the purposes of automatic indexing, the other for preservation of the original electronic form. This consideration will have to be factored into any discussion of the organization's need for a separate electronic archives system under both the physical and intellectual control of the archivist.

As a separate issue, but one which must also be factored into the debate on physical and intellectual control, is the issue of security and access. It is one of the most difficult corporate electronic file issues which must be tackled. It is not enough to have corporate files. They must contain multi-level access rules which ensure that there is not unauthorized access to records. For some time to come, this may more easily be managed through a centralized electronic records and archives system than through numerous independent applications systems. For the archivist and records manager, there is also a time line associated with electronic records - the former with a declassification schedule, the latter with a disposition schedule.

Moreover, not all systems fit the mold of the classical applications system which is embodied in the typical payroll or personnel system. A corporate electronic mail system is a case in point. Such a system may yield many organizational electronic records. As archivists and historians know so well, what happened in an organization, and who was accountable for it, is often less obvious from reading the final documents on a subject, with all the agreed decisions, than it is from the debates which led up to the decisions and the alternative which were discarded. This is the kind of information less likely to be found in formal memoranda than it is in e-mail files, most of which - today - are either not accessible at the corporate records level or are routinely destroyed. Yet, like the telephone, the facsimile, telex and electronic mail facilities constitute communications media, rather than being applications systems. They do not, therefore, lend themselves easily to the same kinds of electronic records treatment as do most applications systems.

The applications system usually contains highly structured data, tends to be highly transaction oriented, contains information about a single application, and is amenable to mass retention scheduling. They normally reside on centrally operated mainframe computers which have limited physical and logical access. By contrast, e-mail contains highly *un*structured text, is not ordinarily transaction oriented, contains information potentially about all applications as well as other information, requires document level application retention scheduling, and is typically widely accessible throughout the organization.

There is another argument in favor of a corporate records and archives system. It is that such an approach provides for better security and for checks and balances. Official organizational records must be maintained in a fashion which least subjects them to accidental or intentional alteration or destruction. It may be argued that the keepers of official records are less likely to have a self-serving interest in altering or destroying those records than are those who are responsible for the applications which produce the records. E.g., would the records of an organization's procurement activities be served better by locating the physical control of those records in a system in the office carrying out those organizational functions where the records are produced, or in a separate system and office which has no special interest in those records, except their appropriate retention without alteration.

Like so many other things which involve the use of advanced information technology, there is not likely one answer to the physical control question which will be right for all organizations at all periods of their organizational development. It may well be that a hybrid approach in which a combination of approaches is most appropriate. The important message here is that this question is one which each organization should address and, for many organizations, very soon.

Training for Archivists and Records Managers

If archivists and records managers are to assume responsibility for the operation of electronic records systems, they will have to possess the necessary skills and other human, technological and financial resources necessary to fulfill that role. The lack of these resources will surely cause the role to fall to others by default, whether that is the best thing for the organization or not. Either way, and even if the large majority of this electronic information is not of long-term or permanent value, it will be impossible to appraise electronic records without incorporating information engineering and meta-data design into systems containing them. Archivists must be in a position to meet information systems designers and business process engineers on their own playing field. To achieve that status to address these problems - means that archivists must be aware of, learn and use the tools of modern and rapidly evolving business process engineering and information engineering and management. Archives schools would serve their educational aims well to include such tools in their curricula, at least for those students who wish to avail themselves of such training.

Early vs. Late Appraisal of Information

Decentralization of the creation, and much of the control, of information requires centralized approaches to information organization and management (including appraisal and disposition management). The magnitude of the information to be managed requires structured, system-level, archival assessment rules (algorithms). The technology makes it possible to do it. The advantage, therefore, swings from appraisal late in the document life cycle to appraisal at the time electronic information is created and identified as a 'information of record' or 'information of permanent value'.

The Archivists' Contribution to Systems Design

As has been advanced by many spokespersons on the subject in recent years, the challenge is thus for archivists to step into the breech and join with their information technologist colleagues and other functional specialists to provide for computer-based management of electronic records at the design stage of automated systems. This includes definition and structure of meta data, 'rules of engagement' for retention scheduling, appraisal and document disposition management. In the process, new alliances will be (*must* be) forged - either through the informal organization or through structural organizational changes. Ultimately, it is likely that this alliance will be forced as and when management more fully appreciates the increasing risk to which the organization is exposed. Archivists have the opportunity to exercise leadership in bringing that alliance about, or to wait for it to happen. This is not a new role for archivists and records managers, who have always carried out this kind of coordination with functional managers in establishing retention schedules, for instance. What is new is bringing the IT partner into the picture, closing the technical loop and dealing with the changes in their traditional way of doing things which may be inherent in managing the processing of electronic records.

3. MAKING THE CASE FOR OPEN SYSTEMS INTERCONNECTION (OSI) STANDARDS

This subject is covered extensively in the literature in its more general applications and in technical terms. It is covered in the ACCIS publications as it pertains especially to the management of electronic records. What follows is a brief description of what OSI is and why it is important to the archivist.

What is OSI?

The Open Systems Interconnection model is a seven-level model of information systems standards. Because it is *non-proprietary* in nature, it offers a means for facilitating the exchange of information and applications among *proprietary* or vendor-specific systems. The model includes standards at various levels of system interface. This includes standards at the very low (physical connectivity) end of the spectrum to the very high (logical) end of the spectrum. Thus, the aim of OSI is to provide full spectrum services from *inter-connectivity* (system 'handshake') to *inter-operability* (inter-systems operations).

Why do You Need It?

Information managers of all kinds, including archivists and records managers, need something like OSI because it enables information sharing among organizations and among disparate systems within organizations. It also affords one of the best solutions to the question of technological obsolescence of information which is created or maintained on proprietary systems. In the absence of such standards, it would be necessary to associate with each electronic document the particular version of software in which it was created, and possibly maintain the associated hardware. As this would constitute a totally infeasible approach, most organizations simply turn away from addressing electronic records and convert to paper whatever they can capture, even though this does not afford an economically feasible long-term solution to the growing records problem. Use of standards therefore makes sense for both operational reasons and because it makes good business sense.

Operational Reasons for OSI

In operational terms, such an approach can significantly increase the exchange and usability of electronic information, thus increasing the rate of return of an organization on its information assets. It can also be used to reduce user 'unfriendliness' common in so many electronic systems, by minimizing the need for multiple interfaces. Because it would overcome most of the problems associated with proprietary systems, it could reduce the need for single hardware and software standards, which have not worked well in most organizations anyway, and thus avoids the necessity of individuals or organizations to forego the benefits of new technology. As noted above, it can also facilitate operational continuity by 'future-proofing' technology and data.

How soon it will be possible to fully implement OSI is, as yet, uncertain. This is because most products are still not OSI-compliant. Most vendors state that they are committed to the OSI model, but few have developed the products. OSI standards are also not yet fully defined in such a way as to ensure that they will be implemented in the same manner by all developers. Thus, there may be different interpretations of the model, even where there is commitment to the idea. Until OSI is better defined so that this can happen, or until someone's version of OSI becomes a **de facto** standard, the alternative is for organizations to establish their own specifications for OSI or adopt someone else's - e.g., the U.S. Government's GOSIP standard or similar models of other national governments. Similarly, organizations can ride existing standards which are likely to be the defining standards for their portion of the OSI model - e.g., TCP/IP and X.400. Lastly, before investing in specific IT products, organizations would do well to consult some of the data bases which list OSI-compliant products.

Business Reasons for OSI

Adoption of a set of non-proprietary organizational standards such as OSI permits the use of standardized specifications for procurements. This would not only place pressure on vendors to supply technology which is amenable to use with the products of other vendors, but it would cut the costs and red-tape associated with the procurement process. At the same time, it would avoid the purchase of costly interfaces which are necessary in the absence of such standards, if inter-connectivity or inter-operability is among the information management aims of an organization. It would also permit greater use of electronic forms and files and thus reduce costly office space requirements for paper storage. Finally, it offers an insurance policy against dependency on single vendor, and promotes better more competitive products.

WHAT CAN BE DONE IN THE SHORT TERM?

Create a Vision

Every organization needs to create its own vision of what it desires organizational performance and associated information management support to be like in the future. Here is one simple vision which the author has for what it should be like in a quality, knowledge-based organization by the end of the Twentieth Century. Well run organizations should have:

- An improved sense of organizational and managerial accountability, internally and to the public,
- Better return on information investments for core business aims,
- Easily visible trails to trace past actions and decisions,
- Improved operational continuity - minimum re-invention of wheels,
- Easy access to relevant information, including both current and non-current records, from the office, the home or while traveling,
- More responsible management of information in terms of information access, privacy and confidentiality.

Doing the right things now is possible without a master plan; but it is not possible to do with any likelihood of success in the absence of a vision of the future. That is a good place to start.

Take Some First Steps

Just as there is no single technical approach which will satisfy every technological environment, there is no single plan of action which will meet every organizational need. There are many, however, which do have broad applicability. Following are some steps which offer the prospect for getting organizations which are already in trouble on a path of recovery.

- Make a commitment to begin to tackle mid- and long-range issues

- Establish a cross-functional policy group for managing corporate information assets, specifically including electronic records

- Develop priorities for short- and mid-term action plans to address high risk applications

- Internalize policy issues and solutions

- Take short-term damage control steps

    - Assess mission-critical and financial, security, legal and regulatory applications to determine where the organization is presently at greatest risk
    - Copy records to institutional media (disk, tape)
    - Where not feasible, copy to paper or microform

- Devise strategies for making later retrofit easier and less costly

    - Establish appropriate electronic filing schemes now
    - Provide a bridge between electronic and paper files
    - Train staff: IT staff, Archivists, Record Managers, Users

- Involve multi-disciplinary team in design of new network systems

- Plan the transition to electronic media; develop transitional systems

- Take first steps to design disposition management into existing and planned systems

- Develop in-house specialists in text-based information technology

As well as providing a starting point for organizations already at risk, the above actions may also help organizations which are not yet victims, to position themselves to tackle electronic records issues before they become a serious problem. They also offer an approach for helping organizations in determining which of the two categories they are in.

Archivists have a unique perspective, opportunity and responsibility to join their information technology colleagues in making top management in their organizations aware of the issues surrounding the management of organizations with electronic records; to set a common organizational vision for the future; and to forge short-term and mid-term action programs which are geared to legal and regulatory requirements, core business processes, organizational culture and the technological environment of their organizations. Doing so will make it possible for archivists to become part of the solution to the mounting use of electronic information, and in 'getting it right' both within their organizations and externally in interacting with other organizations.

IN THE END...

"What is past is prologue."

- *The Tempest*
(engraved on the entrance of the U.S. National Archives)

**"If we do not honor our past,
We lose our future."**

**"If we destroy our roots,
We cannot grow."**

- Hundertwasser

NEW DEVELOPMENTS AND THE IMPLICATION ON INFORMATION HANDLING

By Charles M. Dollar

The paper I am presenting today is taken from a larger study of the impact of information technology on archival principles and methods, which was the subject of a Specialist Meeting in May 1991 at the University of Macerata.[1] The Università degli Studi di Macerata, Italy, and the Italian *Ufficio Centrale per i Beni Archivistici* co-sponsored this meeting in which specialists reviewed a draft of the study. Based upon the suggestions and comments of the specialists, the study was revised and will be published in English and Italian.

This study reaffirms the centrality of the principle of provenance for the intellectual control and preservation of electronic records and identifies critical areas where archival methods must be modified in order to accommodate new information technologies. The study is divided into five chapters, the first of which is a broad review of the most salient technological developments that already are or soon will be in the market place. This review provides the context for Chapter Two that focuses upon technological imperatives, which shape the way information is being used today and will be used in the future and ultimately the way work is performed. Thus, information technologies are mediated through these imperatives and constrain the context in which archival principles and methods are applied. Chapter Three addresses the impact of these technological imperatives on the concept of record and the principle of provenance. Chapter Four examines the concentration of selected records in a central archival repository and the methods used to carry out the functions of appraisal, arrangement and description, reference, and preservation. Chapter Five concludes the study with a discussion of why archivists must become participants in activities of the broader information handling community, and offers recommendations and guidelines on specific activities archivists can initiate that will ensure that emerging technologies take into account archival principles and methods. Five Annexes that supplement discussion in the text of certain topics round out the study.

The impact of emerging information technologies that this study characterizes as technology imperatives clearly will alter the environment in which archivists will work in the future. A review of this impact within a context of archival theory reaffirmed the centrality of the concept of record as recorded information conveyed in the course of business and the principle of provenance for emerging electronic records. Furthermore, a review of traditional archival methods in five areas - appraisal, concentration of archival material in central repositories, arrangement and description, reference, and preservation - within the context of emerging information technologies suggests the necessity of substantial modification of these methods.

[1] The actual paper itself is taken from Chapter Five of this larger study.

The combined effect of this two-fold review is the recognition of the necessity for archival intervention in standards development and information systems applications in order to ensure that archival concerns are addressed. An unambiguous implication of such intervention is the need for archivists to acquire new tools and skills, which usually are not taught in traditional archival education programs. Consequently, this morning I will discuss ten issue areas of importance to the archival community and suggest activities and actions that, if implemented, can help address many, if not most, archival concerns.

TECHNOLOGY OBSOLESCENCE ISSUE AREA

Probably the single most important issue posed by electronic records to archives and archivists is how to ensure access over time to records in electronic form when the information technologies themselves are subject to rapid and sometimes revolutionary change.

Rapid technological change is a basic condition of modern life as technological innovations fuel new innovations. Such technological innovations virtually guarantee that computer hardware and software will become obsolescent in less than a decade after their introduction into the market place. Two developments underway can help mitigate technology obsolescence. First, because many users have substantial investments in existing applications and data they are demanding that vendors provide cost-effective migration paths to new hardware and software. Although cost-effective migration paths may be limited to a single vendor product line, nonetheless they can be very useful in exchanging data over time. Second, the trend toward non-proprietary standardized open systems environments, which are designed to overcome incompatibility between computer systems and applications and are reflected in international standards, is another powerful tool that can be used to facilitate the transfer of electronic archival records across technology generations. Of course, migration paths are a one-time fix and must be updated to new hardware and software. Similarly, international open system standards will change as technology changes. Although both trends provide less than perfect solutions, nonetheless, they are the only practical alternative available.

Implications:

- Archivists should strive to stay in the technological main stream of information handling by monitoring developments in information technology innovation.

- Archivists should become actively involved in the development of information technology standards at both the national and international levels.

- Archivists should promote the adoption of open systems standards as a part of an organization's information policy.

- Archivists should identify migration paths as a major requirement for new information systems applications.

RECORD ISSUE AREA

What constitutes a record in an electronic information environment - particularly a complex one where there are virtual documents and database views - and how archivists ensure preservation of electronic records are crucial for the integrity of archives and the capability of program managers and organizational entities to document how policies and programs were conducted.

Electronic records consist of a series of digital signals and have few, if any, of the inherent physical characteristics of traditional records, which carry crucial contextual information. Nevertheless, the use of electronic information technologies has not altered the basic nature of recordmaking, whose purpose is to document the transaction that occurred, or the fundamental role of archivists to preserve evidence of such transactions. An electronic record is information communicated and maintained electronically in the course of a transaction between persons (natural or artificial). Automatic capture of electronic records could occur through software copying to an archives store the records associated with transactions meeting certain characteristics that are held in a buffer prior to transmission. Unfortunately, software tools currently available do not automatically capture all of the contextual information of electronic transactions that provide adequate evidence of such transactions.

Implications:

- Archivists should define electronic records as electronically communicated and maintained transactions.

- Archivists should develop tactics and encourage vendors to develop tools that permit automatic capture of electronic records.

- Archivists should identify and articulate to information systems designers and software developers the functional requirements for the capture of contextual information.

- Professional archival associations and national archives should establish a program that will facilitate and coordinate the development of these functional requirements.

PROVENANCE ISSUE AREA

Documenting the provenance of electronic records, particularly those for which there is no traditional paper equivalent or there is a shared information environment, is of central importance to archives. Although emerging information technologies pose difficult questions regarding provenance, archivists can develop tactics and tools that can ensure the maintenance of provenancial information.

Archivists in North America have tended to view organizational structure as the primary component of provenance while European archivists have tended to view the competence of an organization as the substantial meaning of provenance. In either case, identifying and maintaining the context of electronic records creates difficult challenges for archivists, because electronic records do not exist as discrete physical entities, and much of the contextual information about electronic records is either not visible to users or not routinely captured. Much of this provenance or context related information will be found in metadata (data about data) that describes information system applications. Increasingly, archivists will have to rely upon metadata in order to understand and capture the provenance of electronic records. Because information resource dictionaries (metadata systems) will play such a crucial role in understanding and using information system applications in the future, archivists must ensure that they contain all of the contextual information essential to a full understanding of electronic records. Accordingly, archivists must become involved in the development of the Information Resource Dictionary Standard (IRDS) in order to ensure that provenance related functionalities are incorporated into the system. Participation in such a development will require archivists to define explicitly the information requirements underlying these functionalities.

Implications:

- Archivists should develop strategies and tactics for intervention in the development of information system applications that ensure the capture and preservation of provenance related information.

- Archivists should identify and articulate to information systems designers and software developers archival requirements for the capture of essential contextual information.

- Professional archival associations and national archives should establish a program that will facilitate and coordinate the development of these archival requirements.

- National professional archival associations should sponsor pilot projects to evaluate the incorporation of archival requirements for the maintenance of provenancial information into existing and planned metadata systems.

- Archivists should work with national standards groups that are developing the Information Resource Dictionary Standard to ensure that the standard incorporates provenance functionalities.

CENTRAL ARCHIVES REPOSITORY ISSUE AREA

The notion of a central archives repository is rooted more in local political traditions than in a fundamental archival principle. Consequently, the information technologies that support low-cost distribution and duplication of electronic records and high-speed telecommunications raise fundamental questions about the necessity of maintaining traditional central archives.

In an emerging electronic information environment the factors that have influenced the creation of modern, centralized archives facilities for traditional records are not very compelling. Furthermore, the costs of migrating electronic records from old computer systems to newer ones in order to minimize hardware and software dependence are likely to be substantial, particularly for those applications that reside on special purpose computer systems. In all likelihood it will be cheaper for many organizations to maintain electronic archival records rather than to transfer them to a centralized archival facility. Electronic access to records maintained as part of an organization's record system is likely to cost no more than electronic access to records maintained in a centralized facility. Consequently, archivists must redefine the role and responsibilities of centralized archives with respect to electronic records. This redefinition includes helping to develop programs, tools, guidelines, and regulations that facilitate access across disparate databases and information systems. Under this redefinition, a centralized archives facility would take physical custody of electronic records only if an organization were no longer willing to continue their maintenance and migration across technologies.

Implications:

- Archivists should transform the role of archival institutions from a custodian to a regulatory and access facilitative role.
- Archivists should define a centralized archives as "an archives of last resort" and take physical custody of electronic records only when their maintenance and migration across technologies can not be assured.
- Archivists should facilitate access to electronic records over time by helping to develop, promote, and implement international standards that minimize hardware and software dependence.

APPRAISAL ISSUE AREA

The identification and selection of electronic records for continuing preservation is one of the most critical tasks that archivists perform. Although there is a substantial body of literature on appraisal of traditional records, the changes that emerging information technologies are making in the records creation/use/storage environment require archivists to formulate other appraisal criteria.

The appraisal methodologies and techniques that archivists have developed for machine-readable records created over the last thirty years or so have limited utility in dealing with electronic records for which there is not a paper analog or equivalent, particularly multimedia systems, geographic information systems, integrated relational databases, and complex databases that cross organizational boundaries. One useful approach involves focusing on appraisal at the information systems application level rather than the computer systems applications level. The practical effect of this would be to appraise the function or competence that produces records rather than to appraise the records themselves. A second useful approach is to incorporate appraisal and retention functionalities into the design of information systems applications. In both approaches, it is unlikely that appraisal criteria which emphasize historical research value of records will be attractive to information system designers. What will be attractive and useful to these designers is an emphasis on ensuring that electronic information of value to the creating organization is identified, retained, and made accessible for program accountability. Consequently, one of the more important contributions archivists can make is to incorporate the life cycle management of recorded information into information systems applications design in a way that could serve both organizational and archival concerns. This requires archivists to specify the life cycle functional requirements that should be mapped into the data elements in metadata systems.

Implications:

- Archivists should adopt an appraisal approach that emphasizes the competence that produces records rather than the records themselves.

- Archivists should identify the functional requirements for the life cycle management of recorded information.

- Archivists should intervene in the record creation process to select and retain records of continuing value through the incorporation of appraisal functionality in the design of information systems applications.

- Archivists should develop the appropriate skills and knowledge necessary to work effectively in designing information resource dictionary systems.

ARRANGEMENT AND DESCRIPTION ISSUE AREA

Traditional arrangement and descriptive methods that have focused upon physical order cannot deal adequately with the changing form of documents generated by emerging information technologies. Therefore, traditional archival arrangement and description must be transformed to accommodate these new forms of documents. However, this is uncharted area for archivists, and research/demonstration projects should be initiated before full implementation is begun.

Traditional archival arrangement and description serve the purpose of maintaining the context of records and facilitating access to them. Although archivists generally divide arrangement in physical and intellectual (i.e., maintenance of the logical connections and relations between discrete records and groups of records), the latter is far more important. Because the actual physical arrangement of electronic records is of little consequence for either maintaining context or retrieving the records, knowing the intellectual or logical arrangement of electronic records is absolutely essential. Although the development of standards for archival description that focus upon the intellectual or logical relations of records provides a solid foundation on which transformed archival arrangement and description for electronic records may flourish, there is a great deal of work that remains to be done in developing specific rules. These specific rules would support a type of arrangement and description of electronic records that could focus upon the information resource dictionary system incorporated in information systems application design. Such an information resource dictionary system would identify information elements, define their relations, explain their context of creation and use, and specify organizational responsibility for their maintenance. It would constitute a first draft of an information application system inventory and a finding aid to the products of the system to which a more comprehensive archival description would later add value.

Implications:

- Archivists should shift the emphasis of archival arrangement and description of electronic records to an understanding of the information system context that supports organizational-wide information sharing.

- Archivists should conduct research/demonstration arrangement and description projects that utilize information resource dictionary systems.

REFERENCE ISSUE AREA

The shift from print-based media to electronic media, which is already evident in scholarly research in the social sciences and humanities and in the library community, will effect a similar change in the users of archives. Archivists, therefore, will be under increasing pressure to transform the delivery of reference services to electronic records to accommodate researcher expectations.

The reference service that most archives offer is supply driven in that it requires researchers to come to a facility and search inventories and other finding aids, obtain boxes of records, browse through them until they find what they want or conclude the records do not contain the information they need. Supply driven reference forces researchers to adapt their search strategy to very broadly constructed search and retrieval tools. The enormous power of emerging information technologies, however, will increasingly encourage researchers to define access in terms of their specific requirements, especially when archives may not have physical custody of some electronic records. Furthermore, technology obsolescence will make it unlikely that the original software functionality associated with the creation and use of electronic records will be available as operational search and retrieval tools. These emerging research expectations and needs will require archives to develop a reference service strategy for electronic records that involves modifying established ways of dealing with researchers. This strategy would include transforming the primary role of archives from repositories where records are made accessible to intermediaries or facilitators of access to electronic records, especially those still in the custody of the creating organization; promoting the adoption and use of software tools and standards (e.g. IRDS) that facilitate access; providing access to information systems that support comparable functionalities of the original software environment; and developing a greater sensitivity to the protection of personal privacy and to forestalling the inappropriate use of archival information.

Implications:

- Archivists should develop a reference strategy that takes into account how emerging information technologies are changing the expectations and requirements of researchers.
- Archivists should acquire a detailed understanding of the information systems in which electronic records are created and the comparable software functionalities that current technology supports.
- Archivists should develop appropriate tools and techniques for facilitating access to electronic records not in archival custody.
- Archivists should promote the adoption and use of software tools and standards (e.g. IRDS) that may facilitate access across time.
- Archivists should foster the formulation of policies and procedures that protect personal privacy of individuals who are the creators or subjects of electronic records.

PRESERVATION ISSUE AREA

The emphasis of traditional records preservation on the physical carrier of information provides little useful guidance for dealing with such critical issues as technology obsolescence and access to electronic records. The high costs of minimizing the effects of technology obsolescence requires archivists to replace the concept of "permanent value" with that of "continuing value." In addition, the preservation of electronic records requires shifting the emphasis from preservation of the information carrier or physical storage media to preservation of access to information electronically captured and stored.

The inherent technological obsolescence of electronic media and the devices required to read them adds a substantial cost to the "permanent" preservation of electronic records, which few archives will be able to support indefinitely. However, the concept of "continuing value" of records, which implies that records may lose value over time, can free archivists from a rigid, absolutist position that is not economically feasible. The concept of "continuing value" is particularly useful when it is linked to a systematic assessment of the risks involved in concluding that the costs of retaining electronic records exceed the benefits of retention. The preservation of electronic records of "continuing value" requires a shift in emphasis from preservation of the information carrier or physical storage media to the preservation of the readability and intelligibility of records. Readability can be assured by periodic recopying of electronic records so that they can always be read by current technologies. Intelligibility is more difficult to achieve, particularly when proprietary storage and retrieval techniques are used and the hardware/software become obsolescent. Archivists may deal with hardware/software dependence in two ways: retaining a paper or Computer Output Microfilm copy of the records, particularly those records that have traditional equivalents or are self-referential; and adhering to information technology standards that support the transfer of electronic records across technologies.

Implications:

- Archivists should adopt a preservation policy that focuses upon the "continuing value" of electronic records rather than on their "permanent value".
- Archivists should develop strategies, techniques, and tools that can be used to apply the concept of "continuing value".
- Archivists should redefine "preservation" so that it encompasses facilitating access over time and across technologies.
- Archivists should promote access over time and across technologies to electronic records by developing programs and activities that assure their readability and intelligibility.
- Archivists should consider the use of COM as an alternative to electronic storage of records in traditional document form.
- Archivists should promote the use of Open Systems Interconnection and other related information technology standards in the electronic storage and transfer of electronic records across technology generations.

STANDARDS ISSUE AREA

Emerging international information technology standards can be indispensable and cost-effective tools for capturing the contextual information of electronic records and facilitating its exchange over time. However, this potential can be achieved only as archivists identify archival requirements and work to ensure their inclusion in existing standards or in the development of new ones.

The creation of an open systems environment to facilitate different computers, subsystems, and application and system software to operate together is well established and quite likely will continue to flourish. Interoperability in and of itself does not provide the functionalities necessary to support the capture of contextual information about records and the records themselves or their exchange over time. Several of the international standards designed to support an open systems environment, however, could be very useful to archives if they were modified to accommodate archival concerns. Among the international standards in place or under development that fall into this category are X.400, X. 500, SGML, ODA/ODIF, IRDS, and SQL. These standards can be modified only if archivists define their requirements and then work with standards developers to ensure that the appropriate functionalities are incorporated into the standards and implemented. Archivists can also help influence the development and use of such standards through supporting regulations that require computer procurements to conform to these standards.

Implications:

- Archivists should identify archival functional requirements for the capture of contextual information about records and the records themselves and their exchange over time.

- Archivists should participate in national and international standards programs to ensure that these functional requirements are incorporated into SGML, ODA/ODIF, IRDS, SQL, and other standards.

TRAINING ISSUE AREA

Traditional archival training courses do not provide archivists with all of the skills and tools necessary to deal effectively with emerging information technologies. The development of professional training that will provide archivists with the necessary tools and skills to deal with emerging information technologies is absolutely essential.

Emerging information technologies confront most archivists with problems and challenges for which traditional archival training or individual self-improvement are inadequate. Few archivists understand the concepts and procedures that information systems designers employ nor are they equipped to comprehend fully the archival implications of a new information system application. Moreover, many archivists do not have experience in rigorous analysis of archival functional requirements. Yet, in a number of University Information Science Departments courses are taught where students could acquire these skills and tools. A curriculum that includes course work in operations research and information systems design would address a number of issues relevant to archival concerns. Courses designed specifically for archivists and preferably taught by an information scientist would be of greatest benefit. Equally as important for established archivists would be the opportunity to take continuing education classes that address operations research and information systems design from an archival perspective.

Implications:

- Archivists involved in archival education programs should identify as their highest priority the modification of university curricula leading to a degree in archival science to include at least one course each in operations research and information systems design, which might be taught by a member of the information science department.

- Archivists involved in archival education programs should develop short-term, continuing archival education programs that expose students to the tools and techniques of operations research and information systems design.

- Archivists already working with electronic records should enroll in college or university education programs or short-term continuing education programs that will provide them with training in operations research and information systems design

THE EROSION OF TIME, GEOGRAPHY AND HIERARCHY: SHARING INFORMATION TROUGH AN ELECTRONIC ARCHIVE

By Tom Finholt

Various stages of this work were supported by the National Science Foundation Graduate Research Fellowship program, the Xerox Corporation, and Bellcore. Special thanks to the following (in alphamagic order): David Constant, Baruch Fischoff, Chuck Huff, Mark Kamlet, Sara Kiesler, Bob Kraut, Lee Sproull, Jimmy Treybig and Tandem Computers, and John Walsh.

ABSTRACT

This study examined the use of two electronic archives of help information by employees of Tandem, Inc. One archive consisted mostly of working expertise, or informal knowledge, while the other archive consisted mostly of canonical expertise, or formal knowledge. The location of sites, level of experience of employees at sites, and the size of sites within Tandem were predicted to influence both the selection of archives and the amount of use of archives by help-seekers. Remote, inexperienced, and small sites were expected to use both archives more heavily than near, experienced, and big sites -- and to use the archive with working expertise more than the archive with canonical expertise. Results showed that remote sites used the electronic archives more than non-remote sites. Further, sites with inexperienced employees used the electronic archives more than sites with experienced employees. Finally, these patterns were more pronounced for use of the archive consisting of working expertise than for the archive consisting of canonical expertise.

1. MEANS OF SHARING HELP WITHIN ORGANIZATIONS

1.1 Introduction

When overwhelmed by a problem, members of organizations turn to the larger organization for help. Many organizations, though, face difficulties in placing the fullest range of relevant information at the disposal of help-seekers. These difficulties are compounded by the nature of information within organizations which spans a continuum from canonical expertise, or information acquired through formal training, to working expertise, or information acquired through experience on the job. Organizational mechanisms for sharing information are not equally reliable or efficient across this information continuum. The most important mechanism for sharing information is proximity which works well for both canonical and working expertise. But when there are gaps in local expertise, people must turn to information stored by the organization in the form of files and archives. Canonical expertise is more amenable to retention in these "organizational memories" than working expertise. As a result, members of organizations with poor local access to working expertise, such as employees at sites that are distant from headquarters, small, or staffed by inexperienced workers, have few alternatives for obtaining working expertise. Electronic archives containing exchanges of expertise may improve the availability of canonical and working expertise for the "outsider" members of organizations. This hypothesis will be examined in the sections that follow. The first section describes some of the barriers to finding information in organizations and some of the direct and indirect methods that organizations introduce to overcome these barriers. The second section offers a set of specific hypotheses about how electronic archives might be used in an organization. The third section describes the study site: 151 networked sites within Tandem Computers, Inc. The fourth section offers an analysis of differences between the two study archives. And the final section offers an analysis of the main hypotheses and discussion of the results.

1.2 Mechanisms for making help available

When people in organizations need help with a problem, they often look first to others. Sometimes simply observing others reveals the answer. Sometimes people ask questions of their coworkers. Sometimes people look in archives or files for help. The difficulty in most organizations, especially of obtaining information from files, is matching the right information with the person who needs it. A solution discovered by an employee in Paris may not be available to an employee in Tokyo. The Tokyo employee who needs the information may not know the employee in Paris has it, and the Paris employee may not know the Tokyo employee needs it. Alternatively, either one of them may be reluctant to exchange information. These difficulties are compounded by the diversity of information in organizations, which falls on a continuum from "canonical expertise," or information acquired and credentialed through formal training, to "working expertise," or information gained and validated on the job. Mechanisms for exchanging information within organizations are not equally reliable and efficient across this information continuum. A comparison of the characteristics of canonical expertise with working expertise, and of the ways these kinds of information are exchanged, illustrates the nature of the difficulty.

Formal organizations have departments with specific jurisdictional domains (Weber, 1978). Within departments, job categories have required skills, or hiring standards (Pfeffer and Cohen, 1986). When an organization recruits job candidates, they are presumed to possess the knowledge mandated by the job definition (Simon, 1976, p. 155). Or, when an organization hires an employee they offer training to bring the employee up to the basic standards of the job. At a minimum then, when an organization hires an employee it absorbs the information the employee has acquired that satisfy hiring criteria. This constitutes canonical expertise. in the performance of a job over time employees of the organization become aware of: a) variations in routine procedures; b) variable and potentially alterable aspects of technology surrounding routine procedures; c) idiosyncrasies of clients or customers; and d) informal relationships among others in an organization (Kusterer, 1978, p. 138). This "know-how" constitutes working expertise.

Much of the difficulty in making expertise available to those who need it is eliminated by putting people who perform the same formal function at the same place (Allen, 1977). Proximity makes the most frequently needed canonical expertise readily available through unplanned, face-to-face conversations. Proximity also increases the probability that the most relevant working expertise will be available. In general, proximity reduces the effort required to contact other people (Ebbesen et al., 1976; Kenrick and Johnson, 1979; Riordan and Tedeschi, 1983). This leads to more frequent contact (Festinger et al., 1950); Allen. 1977; Kraut, 1990) and in turn produces "strong ties" (Granovetter, 1973) that allow people to know which nearby person has the necessary expertise, either working or canonical , to solve a problem.

When members of organizations cannot get help from people nearby, they turn to the organizational memory (Walsh et al. 1990; Levitt and March, 1988). The organizational memory is the physical accumulation of documents, memos, and reports that constitute its "files" (Weber, 1978). The unfortunate aspect of organizational memory, from the point-of-view of a problem solver, is that it makes available a much fuller range of canonical expertise than it does working expertise. Canonical expertise is better represented in organizational memory because formal offices, through standard operating procedures and other standing mechanisms, create regular opportunities for obtaining formal knowledge from individuals and then storing the results of these activities in organizational records. These records are addressable using the organizational chart. For instance, a phone directory or similar listing constitutes a rough map to guide seekers of particular kinds of canonical expertise retained within office archives. By contrast, working expertise is not part of the organizational memory because formal offices don't have a responsibility to obtain and process this kind of information. Further, because much working expertise is exchanged through face-to-face conversations (see O'Reilly et al. (1987) for a review of the literature on the preference of oral information sources over written sources) this information does not create a strong trace (e.g., in the form of memos or reports -- people might be in the practice of audio taping their casual conversations) that could be retained within the organizational memory. This means that retention of working expertise occurs outside of the organizational memory and within the heads of individual members of the organization. Working expertise that isn't nearby is largely identified and addressed through social or friendship networks that emerge within an organization. However, these networks and the information retained in these networks are not necessarily synonymous with the formal organization (Blau, 1955, pp. 99-115), which makes finding this non-proximate working expertise difficult.

1.3 Strategies for improving the availability of help

Organizations have formal strategies that make people temporarily proximate, and therefore make help more available. For example, conferences and workshops bring together people from different parts of an organization. During the duration of the conference or workshop, it becomes easy for people to establish links with those who would otherwise be very distant, and therefore unlikely sources of information. Yates (1989) documents an early effort at DuPont to reap the benefits of conferences for this type of interaction. Starting in 1904 the High Explosives Operating Department held plant superintendent meetings to bring together superintendents from a dozen plants to foster greater cooperation, broaden allegiance to the larger organization, and most important, expose superintendents to other managers' ideas and techniques (Yates, 1989, pp. 235-238). Unfortunately, conferences and workshops typically last only a few days or less, and are not a mechanism for sustaining high frequency contact.

Job rotation is another example of a strategy employed by large, dispersed, or diverse organizations that makes people temporarily proximate. Unlike conferences, which create proximity by locating everyone for a short time at a common site, job rotation creates proximity for longer periods by assigning one person to a new site or sub-unit within the organization. Individuals who are rotated carry with them the lessons and experiences from one area of an organization that may prove valuable in a new area (Kaufman, 1960). For example, in the biotechnology industry, the circulation of scientists through sponsored post-doctoral fellowships is seen as a standard practice for disseminating new knowledge and techniques (Cambrosio and Keating, 1988). However, at best job rotation affects a limited proportion on an organizations's membership. It's success also is subject to formal organizational policy. For example, in the NUMMI manufacturing joint venture between Toyota and General Motors, Toyota rotated many managers through the plant for short tours of duty while GM sent a small cadre of managers to work in the plant for a long period (Powell, 1989). Toyota's policy allowed experience gained in the joint venture to spread further than GM's policy.

Recent research on computer-mediated communication has identified a new strategy for getting help and retrieving expertise without knowing in advance where this information is located. One way that this is accomplished occurs through computer mailing lists, which are collections of addresses of people in an organization who are interested in a given topic. When a person has a specific question, the person's query is directed to the mailing list where it is distributed by the computer network to the dozens or hundreds of other people with similar interests who are also on the list. In this way a request for information can be shared among members of an organization, some known to the questioner and some unknown, some nearby and others faraway, with equal effort. Using features of computer mail, like mailing lists, it is no longer necessary to know where remote expertise resides to be able to access it. Recent studies have shown that members of organizations use computer mailing lists to retrieve information from remote members of organizations (Feldman, 1988; Finholt and Sproull, 1990; Hesse et al. 1990).

In a study of computer-mediated communication in a large office products organization, Finholt and Sproull (1990) found that: a) employees at every level of the organization used computer communication extensively, receiving an average of 26 messages per day; b) 78 % of these messages contained information that members of the organization reported they could not have obtained any other way; c) 71 % of the messages received by members of this organization were reported to come from people that were unknown to the recipients; and d) 81 % of the messages received by members of this organization were reported to come from people remote from the recipients (Finholt and Sproull, 1990, pp- 48-49). As an example, Finholt and Sproull offer an illustration of how computer-mediated communication was used to access working expertise. A manager who wanted input on the feasibility of building a spreadsheet package for one of the company's products queried a set of mailing lists for advice. Within two days, 25 people from several cities have responded to the manager's request. The manager did not have to direct queries explicitly to these people to receive replies from them. In fact, the response identified a group of people in the organization interested in spreadsheet applications who started their own mailing list just for talking about spreadsheets (Finholt, 1990, p. 55).

In another study of the same office product organization, Feldman (1988) showed that computer-mediated communication functioned to signal common interests among people who would otherwise be unaware of their common interests. By classifying messages according to characteristics of the people sending and receiving the messages, Feldman found that without computer mail: a) 82 % of the communication between people who reported that they did not know each other would not have occurred; (b) 72 % of the communication between people who were spatially distant would not have occurred; and c) 73 % of the communication between people who were organizationally distant would not have occurred. In a sample of "weak tie" messages that Feldman created, 35 % were work-related. Weak tie messages, after Granovetters's definition of weak tie (1973), were exchanges that: a) would not have occurred without computer-mediated communication; b) were between people who weren't acquainted; and c) were between people who were remote from each other. For example, sharing hints for using modems with personal computers, discussions of the timing of product development, and announcements about the status of software systems.

In studies of computer-mediated communication used within the physical oceanography community, Hesse et al. (1990) found that computer-mediated communication created benefits for remote scientists. Remote, in this case, was operationalized as "inland" on the assumption that non-coastal oceanographers were not as proximate to the center of activity, i.e. the ocean, in their discipline as coastal oceanographers. When scientific output, measured as refereed publications per year, was analyzed for coastal and inland scientists, a higher relationship between publishing and computer-mediated communication use was found for inland scientists, than for coastal scientists. Among heavy computer communicators inland scientists came to resemble coastal scientists in terms of paper production (inland = 3.5 papers, coastal = 3.6 papers). Among light computer communicators, inland scientists lagged behind their coastal colleagues (inland = 1.6 papers, coastal = 2.4 papers). Inland scientists also had a tendency to use computer-mediated communication more than coastal scientists. As one respondent noted:

> I use it several times a day, and have found it extremely valuable for communicating with colleagues across time zones. I have met new colleagues working in similar areas. I've answered some questions posed on bulletin boards, and made some contacts that wouldn't have occurred otherwise (Hesse, 1990, p. 22).

From these findings, Hesse et al. suggest that computer mediated communication may be a mechanism used by inland oceanographers to overcome the disadvantages of their non-coastal location by knowing more about activities at the center of their discipline.

Each of these studies indicates that computer-mediated communication, in the form of mailing lists, can improve the availability of information for individual help-seekers. However, subsequent help-seekers must repeat the same steps to retrieve this information. There may be costs associated with this redundant retrieval of information that diminish the usefulness of mailing lists. For example, if the time and attention of people who possess needed information are seen as a kind of "public good" (Schelling, 1971), then the ability of seekers of information to easily use this collective resource may lead to a "commons dilemma" (Hardin, 1968). A commons dilemma is a type of social dilemma where behavior that is beneficial at an individual level has negative consequences at a collective level (Messick and Brewer, 1983; Dawes, 1980). In the case of computer-mediated communication individuals querying mailing lists get answers to their questions. However, as the volume of questions increases, people providing these answers may feel exploited, or that they are poorly compensated for their effort. Much has been written about how motivations for sharing information under these conditions can influence the quality of available information (Thorn and Connolly, 1987; Connolly and Porter, 1990; Constant et al., 1991). Thorn and Connolly (1987) for instance, indicate that the lack of compensation for answers will lead people to withhold information in discretionary sharing situations, like mailing lists. Constant et al. (1991), however, found that economic considerations were not foremost in decisions to share information.

A solution to the information sharing dilemma has been proposed by information technology theorists (Huber, 1990; Ackerman and Malone, 1990). They argue that exchanges occurring via computer-mediated communication create a transcript of the exchange. These transcripts effectively represent a history of any given information retrieval that can be cataloged and stored in online archives or databases. In this fashion, rather than querying a mailing list as the first part of every information retrieval, seekers of information can first query these online archives, and therefore reduce demands on individuals or collections of individuals who possess particular kinds of expertise.

1.4 Why is access to working expertise important?

The preceding section suggests that members of organizations face difficulties in acquiring working expertise from others in the organization. Why does this matter? This question is addressable at two levels. From a practical perspective it is costly for organizations to have incomplete access to the array of working expertise held by their members. If, as recent reports indicate, the nature of work in organizations is becoming more cognitively complex this suggests that organizations will increasingly be composed of highly skilled employees (Cyert et al., 1990). In many cases members of organizations will possess a range of skills that go beyond those required to satisfy the hiring criteria for a particular position. These extra skills may consist of experience in other organizations, or with other products -- and hence be potentially valuable. But unless this knowledge is directly related to an individual's job, the organization faces problems in tapping this expertise. Consider, for example, the case of computer "gurus". In word processing pools individuals often emerge who, because of superior mastery of software and hardware, come to act as unofficial consultants on computer matters. Within the local setting, fellow employees know that the "guru" is much more than another pool typist, but in the organization beyond the word processing pool, the "guru" appears to be no different than any of the other typists. As a result, the guru's knowledge is not really available to others in the organization facing computer problems.

At a theoretical level, incomplete access to working expertise by members of an organization may impair the organization's ability to learn. For instance, recent work by Cohen and Levinthal (1990) asserts that for organizations to successfully capitalize on an innovation they must have enough "absorptive capacity" to recognize that a given innovation may be profitable. In their terms, "absorptive capacity" represents a store of experience or knowledge in the area of an innovation within an organization sufficient to allow the organization to recognize an important opportunity. This capacity can certainly consist of formal knowledge, in the form of corporate research and development labs, libraries, and marketing research. But it seems clear that the experience of individual employees, on the job, also makes some contribution to an organization's ability to identify important openings for new products or processes. For organizations in highly competitive environments the failure to incorporate this working expertise into the set of widely available information within the organization may critically diminish absorptive capacity.

1.5 Summary

Individual members of organizations rely on the larger organization for help when they are overwhelmed by problems. The difficulty for organizations is linking existing information within the organization with those who need the information. This linkage is particularly problematic for working expertise that is not proximate. Gaps in local canonical expertise can be covered by turning to the organizational memory -- the physical accumulation of documents and memos retained in files and archives -- for help. This is not the case for gaps in local working expertise because working expertise is poorly retained in the organizational memory. Instead, people must obtain non-local working expertise through informal networks which overlap with the formal organization in complicated ways that make retrieval of working expertise difficult. Computer-mediated communication provides a mechanism for identifying and obtaining non-local working expertise without negotiating elaborate informal connections. Electronic archives, or databases, of these computer-mediated exchanges hold the promise of creating an organizational memory of working expertise to complement stored canonical expertise.

2. EXAMINING THE USE OF ELECTRONIC ARCHIVES

2.1 Scenarios of archives use

The previous section suggested that databases of computer-mediated exchanges of help increase the availability of expertise within an organization, particularly working expertise. This section explores predictions about who will use this increased availability. Three scenarios are considered. The first scenario, termed the "poor get even", suggests that electronic archives of information will be most used by those members of organizations in settings with poor local availability of expertise. Under these conditions online information offsets the local lack of expertise and creates a situation more like settings rich in expertise. The second scenario, termed the "rich get richer", suggests that electronic archives of information will be most used by those members of organizations in settings with rich local availability of expertise. In these circumstances, online information supplements expertise already available and creates a situation that exaggerates differences between information rich and poor settings.

Finally, the third scenario, termed the "status quo", suggests that electronic archives of information do not particularly benefit either expertise rich settings or expertise poor settings.

Therefore, differences between setting, in terms of availability of expertise, are unchanged by the existence of electronic archives.

The richness or poorness of available expertise at a given site is assumed to be influenced by three factors: a) the remoteness of the site; b) the size of the site; and c) the age of the site. If remoteness is thought of as proximity to the center of a formal organization, such as the headquarters site, then being close increases the availability of expertise at a site and being distant reduces the availability of expertise at a site. For example, the constant traffic of branch and field employees through headquarters means that people at sites closer to headquarters have the opportunity to be temporarily proximate to a broad mixture of specialists within the organization's membership while people at sites farther away do not. Similarly, the constant traffic of branch and field members through headquarters refreshes the store of gossip and rumors that, in the absence of a direct contact to sources of expertise, provides access to many informal networks for people at sites near headquarters, but not for people at faraway sites. If size is thought of as the population of employees at a site, then being big increases the availability of expertise at a site, while being small decreases the availability of expertise at a site. For example, big sites are more likely to contain employees within different sub-units, and therefore places a wider variety of specialists nearby than would be the case with a small site. Finally, if age is thought of as the experience of employees at a site, then being older increases the availability of expertise, while being younger decreases the availability of expertise. For example, older sites are more likely to have employees who have accumulated stories and myths that embody certain kinds of expertise than would be the case at younger sites (Martin et al., 1983; Orr, 1989). Also, older sites are more likely than younger sites to have elaborated "information buffers," or collections of information in unofficial records (Kmetz, 1984).

2.2. Hypotheses about archive use

2.2.1 The "poor get even" hypothesis

Under the "poor get even" scenario, sites with poor availability of expertise will use online information to become more like sites rich in expertise, specifically in terms of the availability of expertise. From the description in the first section, poor availability of working expertise is predicted to be a more pressing concern since organizational memory allows compensation for poor availability of canonical expertise. The "poor get even" hypothesis states:

H: As a site is more emote, smaller, and younger, people will use online information more than people at less remote, larger, and older sites -- and this pattern will be more pronounced for use of online working expertise than for online canonical expertise.

Support for this hypothesis will strengthen the theoretical assumptions presented in the first section that online databases of expertise, particularly working expertise, help balance the disparity in availability of information between sites rich and poor in expertise.

2.2.2 "Rich get richer" hypothesis

Under the "rich get richer" scenario, sites with rich availability of expertise will use online information more than sites with poor availability of expertise. This may indicate that online information, rather than redressing differences between expertise-rich and expertise-poor sites, actually amplifies these differences. One possibility is that sites already rich in expertise, particularly working expertise, are in a better position to evaluate help from the electronic archives. For example, employees in expertise rich settings may be able to validate online information through comparison with locally available information. Alternatively, information stored in electronic archives may be largely generated by people at expertise rich sites, therefore use of online information is a way that people at these expertise rich sites identify themselves to each other in contrast to employees at expertise poor sites. The "rich get richer" hypothesis states:

H: As a site is less remote, larger, and older, people will use online information more than people at more remote, smaller, and younger sites -- and this pattern will be more pronounced for use of online working expertise than for online canonical expertise.

Support for this hypothesis will indicate that the richness or poorness of expertise availability does influence use of online information, but not in the anticipated direction.

2.2.3 "Status quo" hypothesis

Under the "status quo" scenario the expertise richness or poorness of a site will not predict use of online information. This scenario suggests that other factors effect use of electronic archives. For example the function of sub-units at a site, and not the remoteness, size, and age of the site, may determine availability of expertise. Or, use of electronic archives may be determined by individual characteristics of users -- such as their familiarity with computer networks and databases -- that are unrelated to site-level characteristics. The "status-quo" hypothesis states:

H: Remoteness, size, and age will be unrelated to use of online information.

Support for this hypothesis will strongly undermine the theoretical assumptions presented in the first section.

2.3 Summary

Electronic archives of computer-mediated exchanges of help information are assumed to make expertise more available within organizations, particularly working expertise. The question of who will use this increased availability can be addressed through three scenarios. In the "poor get even" scenario, members of organizations at sites poor in expertise will use online information more than members at sites rich in expertise. This will make sites poor in expertise similar to sites rich in expertise, in terms of the availability of expertise. In the "rich get richer" scenario, members of organizations at sites rich in expertise will use online information more than members at sites poor in expertise. This will exaggerate differences between expertise rich and expertise poor sites, in terms of the availability of expertise. And in the "status quo" scenario the richness or poorness of expertise availability at a site will be unrelated to use of online information. Richness and poorness of expertise availability rises from three factors: a) a site's remoteness, described as proximity to the organization headquarters; b) a site's size, described as the population of employees; and c) a site's age, described as the experience level of employees at the site. Under the "poor get even" hypothesis sites that are far away, small, and young will show greater use of online information. Under the "rich get richer" hypothesis sites that are close, big, and old will show greater use of online information. And under the "status quo" hypothesis remoteness, size, and age will be unrelated to use of online information.

3. SETTING FOR DATA COLLECTION

3.1 Electronic archives of two mailing lists

The data for this study were drawn from archived computer mediated communication from two computer mailing lists within Tandem Computers, a Fortune 500 computer manufacturing company. This firm, founded in 1977, has over ten thousand employees distributed across 307 locations on five continents. The leadership of Tandem is heavily committed to open communication and this, combined with the nature of the firm's business, results in technology, policies, and opportunities that encourage routine and extensive use of computer communication by employees at all levels and at all sites.

The basic procedure to access information using computer mail within Tandem was for a person ("asker") to send a message requesting information from someone else ("answerer"). This message could be sent to a computer mailing list or an individual. At Tandem, mail generated by a mailing list used to support Field technical staff was saved in an archive called Field. Mail generated by communication with a set of experts assigned to support Field technical staff was saved in an archive called Expert. The mailing list that created the contents of Field did not have designated answerers. Askers addressed questions to a corporation-wide audience of other Field technical staff. Anyone reading a question addressed to this list was free to answer. When a question and the answers it elicited were saved into a publicly-accessible online file, this file would be collected and incorporated into the Field database. See Figure 1 for an example of a communication stored into Field.

```
Field - Document #:   196 - Document length:    16 lines -
21 FEB 84
INFO TRAILS LTD. EQUIPMENT

QUESTION:
DOES ANYONE KNOW OF AN APPLICATION ON A SOLO THAT TALKED TO
ITL
(INFO TRAILS LTD.) EQUIPMENT?
REPLIES ARE IN \PHILA.$DATA.GOO.ITL
XZZZ,
***********************************************************
*************
MTS COMMENTS:                                      (DATE)
(INITIALS)
                        NOT YET VIEWED
***********************************************************
*************

MSG 03540  FROM:     \CINCY.COL.FOO           21 FEB 1984,
17:09

I think Info Trails is owned by NCR. You might check with
them locally. Sorry I can't be of more help.
Frank Olson
```

Figure 1

Mail that created the contents of Expert came from designated individual answerers. Askers addressed questions to specific computer mailboxes, publicized within the organization and corresponding to various Tandem products, that were read by company experts. These experts were required to answer questions sent to their mailbox. Unlike the mailing list above, which directed questions to an undifferentiated audience of Field employees, the destination for these individual queries was known in advance. Errors in addressing were sometimes corrected by the answerers. Questions, and the experts' replies, were collected and saved into Expert. See Figure 2 for an example of a communication stored into Expert.

```
Expert - Document #:     3 - Document length:    36 lines -
26 SEP 84
TRANSFER OF ACU UNITS TO THE WISDOM


QUESTION:

I have received a question wondering if asynchronous ACU
units which
now use 2 async patch panel ports can be transferred to the
Wisdom.
These are implemented with Ambassador on the async board,
and use a
special 'Y' cable.  Will the Wisdom support this?
Don HenField
 \world.support.don

XZZZ,
************************************************************
****

----- Following comments by \CASG.CASG.CCOOK on 27 SEP 1984,
16:21:05

THERE IS NOT, AT PRESENT, ANY SUPPORT FOR ACU's ON THE 2400
DSS.
HARDWARE ( A NEW LIM WITH THE RS-366 INTERFACE ) HAS BEEN
DESIGNED
AND BUILT BY ENGINEERING, BUT IT HAS NOT BEEN PUT INTO
PRODUCTION,
AND NO SOFTWARE HAS EVER BEEN WRITTEN TO MAKE USE OF IT, NOR
IS ANY
SCHEDULED.  AUTO-ANSWER IS SUPPORTED BY SOME TYPES OF LINES
ON THE
2400, E.G.  ATP2400, BUT NOT ALL.  ONE POSSIBILITY FOR YOUR
AUTO-DIAL
CAPABILITY MIGHT BE TO USE A "SMART MODEM" WHICH GETS ITS
DIAL DIGITS
FROM THE DATA INTERFACE.  THIS WOULD REQUIRE SOME
PROGRAMMING EFFORT,
AND MIGHT BE LIMITED TO CP2400 AND POSSIBLY ATP2400.  TO MY
KNOWLEDGE
NO ONE HAS DONE THIS TO DATE, THEREFORE I CANNOT GUARANTEE
SUCCESS.

CC
```

Figure 2

3.2. Using databases

The basic procedure to access Field or Expert was for a person to login to the Tandem remote database service. Here, a user was presented with a choice of 29 different databases. After selecting a database, the user could specify several kinds of searches. The simplest form of search asked the database service to return all stored communication in the selected database containing a particular keyword. More complex searches involved use of keywords and logical operators. The most complex searches involved use of particular Fields, such as the date a communication was entered into the database, as selection parameters. The results of a search could be printed, saved into a personal file, or read online.

The Field and Expert electronic archives were oriented to the same population of organizational users, were accessed through the same database system, were equally available to all employees, and served comparable functions. The most significant difference between them was that Field contained questions with multiple answers, generated voluntarily with a mailing list, while Expert contained questions with single answers, generated by communication with individual experts who answered as partial fulfillment of job requirements.

3.3. Description of the data

Records of logins to the Field and Expert databases during the period February to September 1988 were the source for data on database use. These records were automated system accounts of the data, user identifier, site identifier, search commands, and search result associated with each database login. These data are summarized in the first section of Table 1.

Full text of a sample of stored communications from Field and Expert over the entire history of each database were the source for data on the content of communications stored into the two databases. The sample consisted of a random selection of ten percent of the communications stored into Field and Expert per month from 1983 to 1988. These data are summarized in the second section of Table 1.

The Tandem corporate personnel data system was the source of data on employee characteristics.

Table 1

Data for database study

	Field	Expert
Section 1: User behavior--Febr. 1988 to Sept. 1988		
Users accessing databases	1831	718
Sites where users are located	87	85
Total database accesses	9046	1751
Section 2: Stored communications -- Dec. 1983 to Sept. 1988		
Total stored in database	4582	651
Sample	465	78

3.4 Summary

The data for this study came from archives of two kinds of computer-mediated exchanges within Tandem Computers, Inc. Both kinds of exchanges were generated by Field support employees of Tandem trying to get solutions for problems. The contents of Field came from mail generated by questions and answers shared between askers and multiple answerers within a mailing list for Field technical staff. Anyone reading the list was free to answer. The contents of Expert came from mail generated by questions and answers shared between askers and individual designated Expert answerers. These experts were required to answer as a function of their jobs. Field and Expert, along with twenty-seven other databases, were accessed through the same interface within the Tandem computer network. Field contained 4582 stored exchanges dating back to 1983. Expert contained 651 stored exchanges dating back to 1984. Over the nine month period of study in 1988 Field was used 9046 times (an average of 1005 times per month) and Expert was used 1751 times (an average of 195 times per month).

4. SITE LEVEL MEASURES AND ANALYSES

4.1 Analyzing the use of electronic archives

In this section, the theoretical hypotheses suggested earlier are tested at the level of individual sites within Tandem. Data on each site describe the availability of expertise, which varies with a site's proximity to the organizational core, a site's size, and the experience level of employees at a site. These site-level factors are contrasted with measures of database use, moderated by database type, to understand: a) whether online information helps compensate expertise-poor sites, helps supplement expertise-rich sites, or preserves the status-quo; and b) whether sites compensate for missing expertise, or supplement existing expertise, with either working expertise or canonical expertise. The independent and dependent variables used to examine these relationships are described below followed by a description of specific analyses.

4.2 Sources of data -- independent variables

The descriptive statistics for each independent variable are shown in Table 2. The first line summarizes the remoteness of the firm's sites, operationalized as the distance from the corporate headquarters. The second line summarizes the size of each site, operationalized as the number of employees at a site. The third line summarizes the experience level of each site, operationalized as the mean organizational tenure of employees at a site. The remaining independent variables, archive type and sales orientation were coded as dummy variables. Archive type of 1 corresponded to the Field electronic archive. Sales orientation of 1 indicated that a site was a sales office.

4.3 Sources of data -- dependent variables

The descriptive statistics for each dependent variable are shown in Table 2. The fourth and fifth lines summarize level of use for Field and Expert, operationalized as the mean logins to each electronic archive at a site. The fifth and sixth lines summarize the breadth of use for Field and Expert, operationalized as the number of different archived documents accessed per employee at each site.

Table 2

Descriptive statistics, network sites, n= 151

Variables	Statistics			
	Mean	STD	Min	Max
Remoteness	2628.5	2336.9	0.0	9181.4
Size	60.0	87.2	1.0	553.0
Experience	3.7	1.5	0.0	7.7
Field logins per employee	1.7	2.4	0.0	30.0
Expert logins per employee	0.3	0.4	0.0	3.0
Field breadth per employee	1.4	3.0	0.0	29.0
Expert breadth per employee	0.2	0.4	0.0	3.0

4.4 Site level analysis

4.4.1 Judging equivalence

In light of the theoretical hypotheses, the goal of the site level analyses was to understand how features of a site's environment influenced use of online expertise. This was done by treating the two databases, Field and Expert, as a variable that moderated the relationship between the environment variables and the level of expertise use variables. The analyses of these relationships were conducted, then, with the intent of discovering whether the environment variables had an equivalent impact on use of Field (working expertise) and Expert (canonical expertise). That is, were the logins and number of different documents used from Field and Expert the same for a given site remoteness, size, and level of employee experience?

4.4.2 Interpretation of interaction effects

Three criteria were used for evaluating the moderating effect of database type on the relationships between environmental variables and database use at each site (Jaccard et al., 1990). First, the presence of an interaction effect was determined through comparison of hierarchical regression models. A General F-test for a main-effects-only regression against a main-effects-plus-interaction regression was used as the significance criterion. Second, the strength of the interaction effect was determined from the difference between the explained variance (Adj. R^2) of the main-effects model and the interaction model. Finally, the nature of the interaction effect was evaluated based on the magnitudes of the coefficient estimates in the interaction model, and their significance.

4.4.3 Comparison of two login models

The data in the following models included only those sites with a documented connection to the Tandem computer network. Evidence of a connection was determined by the presence of a given site on the master list of all network accessible sites found in the corporate online database. Of the 306 Tandem sites, 151 had network connections. As a validity check on this assignment the mean proportion of employees without computer mail access at networked sites (mean proportion without mail = 7 %, SD proportion without mail = 19 %) was compared with the mean proportion of employees without computer mail access at non-networked sites (mean proportion without mail = 60 %, SD proportion without mail = 48 %). Network sites had significantly fewer non-users ($t_{(.05,204)} = 12.7$).

The two models used for comparison were specified as follows. The main-effects model was:

$$L = b_0 + b_1R + b_2SZ + b_3E + b_4S + b_5D + e$$

Where: a) L was use of Field and Expert per employee at each site; b) R was a site's remoteness from the corporate headquarters site; c) SZ was the number of employees at a site; d) E was the availability of expertise in the immediate environment; e) S was an indicator of whether a site was engaged in sales activity; and f) D was a dummy variable indicating the type of information being accessed, where Field = 1 and Expert = 0. The interaction model was:

$$L = b_0 + b_1R + b_2SZ + b_3E + b_4S + b_5DB + b_6DR + b_7DSZ + b_8DE + b_9DS + e$$

Where each interaction term (*DR, DSZ, DE*, and *DS*) was formed as the product of the database dummy variable with the remoteness, size, experience, and sales variables.

Table 3

Regression of mean employee use per site on independent variables and interactions

Predictors	Null model n = 282	Alternative model n = 282
Intercept	.00	.00
Remoteness	.27	.16
Size	.12	.08
Experience	-.16	-.10
Sales	.23	.10
Database	.44	.06
Db x remoteness	--	.29
Db x size	--	.08
Db x experience	--	-.18
Db x sales	--	.30
Adj. R^2	.35	.38
F	31.06	19.88

The results of the two regressions are summarized in Table 3. In terms of the criteria mentioned above, the General F-test was significant at $F_{(.025,4,272)}$ = 3.31. Therefore, an interaction effect was judged to be present. The strength of the effect was two percent (Adj. $R^2{}_{ME}$

$_{+ \text{INTERACT}}$ - Adj. R^2 $_{\text{ME} + \text{INTERACT}}$ = .02). That is the addition of the interaction terms explained an additional two percent of the variance in login behavior. The nature of the interaction was as follows. When the database variable was set to zero (i.e., for logins to the Expert database) the following equation described login behavior.

$$L = .16R + .08SZ - .08E + .11S$$

When the database variable was set to one (i.e., for logins to the Field database) the following equation described login behavior:

$$L = .06 + .49R + .11SZ - .22E + .29S$$

From these two equations, the relationship between remoteness and use, experience and use, and sales orientation and use appeared to be much different between the two databases. The slope for remoteness was 3.1 times greater for logins to Field vs. Expert.

That is, all things equal, peripheral sites used the online databases more than core sites -- and used Field information more than Expert information. The slope for experience was 2.8 times greater for logins to Field vs. Expert. That is, all things equal, less experienced sites used the online databases more than experienced sites -- and used Field information more than Expert information. Finally, the slope for sales orientation was 2.6 times greater for logins to Field vs. Expert. That is, all things equal, sites in the sales division used the online databases more than non-sales sites -- and used Field information more than Expert.

4.4.4 Comparison of two breadth models

The two models used for comparison were specified as follows. The main-effects model was:

$$B = b_0 + b_1R + b_2SZ + b_3E + b_4S + b_5DB + e$$

Where: a) *B* was the number of different documents from Field and Expert per employee at each site; b) *R* was a site's remoteness from the corporate headquarters site; c) *SZ* was the number of employees at a site; d) *E* was the availability of expertise in the immediate environment; e) *S* was an indicator of whether a site was engaged in sales activity; and f) *D* was a dummy variable indicating the type of information being accessed, where Field = 1 and Expert = 0. The interaction model was:

$$B = b_0 + b_1R + b_2SZ + b_3E + b_4S + b_5D + b_6DR + b_7DSZ + b_8DE + b_9DS + e$$

Where each interaction term (*DR DSZ, DE,* and *DS*) was formed as the product of the database dummy variable with the remoteness, size, experience, and sales variables.

Table 4

Regression of mean breadth of documents on independent variables and interactions

Predictors	Null model n = 282	Alternative model n = 282
Intercept	.00	.00
Remoteness	.26	.16
Size	.08	.06
Experience	-.13	-.08
Sales	.13	.00
Database	.44	.05
Db x remoteness	--	.29
Db x size	--	.05
DB x experience	--	-.14
DB x sales	--	.30
Adj. R^2	.30	.33
F	25.16	16.46

The results of the two regressions are summarized in Table 4. In terms of the criteria mentioned above, the General F-test was significant at $F_{(.005,4,272)} = 4.15$. Therefore, an interaction effect was judged to be present. The strength of the effect was three percent (Adj. $R^2_{ME + INTERACT}$ - Adj. $R^2_{ME} = .03$). That is, the addition of the interaction terms explained an additional three percent of the variance in the number of different documents used per employee at each site. The nature of the interaction was as follows. When the database variable was set to zero (i.e., for documents from the Expert database) the following equation described breadth of documents used:

$$B = .16R + .06SZ - .08E + .00S$$

When the database variable was set to one (i.e., for documents from the Field database) the following equation described the breadth of documents used:

$$B = .05 + .45R + .11SZ - .22E + .30S$$

From these two equations, the relationship between remoteness and breadth of documents, experience and breadth of documents, and sales orientation and breadth of documents appeared to be much different between the two databases. The slope for remoteness was 2.8 times greater for the number of different documents used from Field vs. Expert. That is, all things equal, peripheral sites used more different documents from the online databases than core sites -- and used more different documents from Field than from Expert. The slope for experience was 2.8 times greater for the number of different documents used from Field vs. Expert. That is, all things equal, less experienced sites used more different documents from the online databases than experienced sites -- and used more different documents from Field than from Expert. Finally, the slope for sales orientation was infinitely greater for the number of different documents used from Field vs. Expert. That is, all things equal, sites in the sales division used more different documents from the online databases than non-sales sites -- and used more different documents from Field than from Expert.

4.5 Summary

The scenarios described in an earlier section suggested three hypotheses about use of online expertise: a) the "poor get even" hypothesis where sites with poor availability of expertise would use online information more than sites with rich availability of expertise, and therefore become more like sites rich in expertise; b) the "rich get richer" hypothesis where sites with rich availability of expertise would use online information more than sites with poor availability of expertise, and therefore increase differences between expertise rich and expertise poor sites; and c) the "status quo" hypothesis where richness and poorness of expertise availability would be unrelated to use of online information. The analysis in this section showed strongest support for the "poor get even" hypothesis. Using two measures of online information use, mean employee use per site and mean breadth of documents accessed per site, online information use was found to increase with increasing site remoteness, increase with decreasing site size, and increase with decreasing site experience. Further, in tests for a moderating effect by database type, Field VS Expert, use of Field did incise more than use of Expert as the availability of expertise at sites became poorer.

5. DISCUSSION

The results presented in the previous section suggest that electronic archives may compensate for poor access to working expertise among remote members of organizations and among members of organizations surrounded by less experienced colleagues. The argument to this point has suggested that this improved access to working expertise is a good thing. However, it is important to recognize that facilitating information sharing, particularly of working expertise, may produce some unintended consequences. One framework for thinking about these consequences is provided by Weick's conception of "loose coupling" (1976) in organizations.

That is, if information sharing between units of an organization is imperfect or difficult this engenders a certain amount of local resourcefulness. People are not as free to borrow from people in other areas of the organization, under conditions of loose coupling, and hence they develop solutions to problems that are uniquely adapted to local conditions. This has many advantages, particularly in terms of creating a variety of approaches within an organization that provide some insurance against changes in the organizational environment.

Now imagine the situation where people in an organization are free to borrow solutions or approaches from other, in other settings and situations -- without any specific quality control or certification. This is exactly the case with information sharing through archives of working expertise. People draw on the experience of others, and apply it in their own circumstances, with potentially dangerous ignorance of the context or conditions that gave birth to the solution that is being borrowed. In this fashion the creation of electronic archives of working expertise seem to create a new set of vulnerabilities for organizations at the same time that they create new benefits. An important goal of future research on the nature of computer-mediated communication technology within organizations should be examination of the nature and extent of these potentially damaging characteristics of information systems.

References

Ackermann, M. / T. W. Malone, *Answer Garden: A Tool for Growing Organizational Memory*, in: *Proceedings of the ACM Conference on Office Information Systems*, 1990, pp. 31-39.

Alker, H., *Measuring Sociopolitical Inequality*, in: Tanur, J. (ed.), *Statistics: A Guide to the Unkrown*, San Francisco: Holden-Day, 1979.

Allen, T., *Managing the Flow of Technology*, Cambridge/MA: MIT Press, 1977.

Blau, P., *The Dynamics of Bureaucracy, Chicago:* University of Chicago Press, 1955.

Cambrosio, A. / P. Keating, *"Going monoclonal": Art, Science, and Magic in the Day-to-day Use of Hybridoma Technology*, in: Social Problems 35 (1988), pp. 244-60

Cohen, Y. / J. Pfeffer, *Organizational hiring standards*, in: Administrative Science Quarterly 31 (1986), pp. 1-24.

Conolly, T. / A. Porter, *Discretionary Databases in Forecasting*, in: Journal of Forecasting 9 (1990), pp. 1-12.

Constant, D. / L. Sproull / S. Kiesler, *Discretionary Information Sharing in an Electronic Network*. Masters thesis, Department of Social and Decision Sciences, Carnegie Mellon University, Pittsburgh/PA, 1990.

Dawes, R., *Social Dilemmas*, in: Rozenzweig, M. / L. Porter (eds.), *Annual Review of Psychology*, Palo Alto/CA: Annual Reviews, 1980.

Ebbesen, E. / G. Kjos / V. Konecni, *Spatial Ecology: Its Effects on the Choice of Friends and Enemies, in:* Journal of Experimental Social Psychology 12 (1976), pp. 505-518.

Feldman, M., *Electronic Mail and Weak Ties in Organizations*, in: Office: Technology and People 3 (1988), pp. 83-101.

Festinger, L. / S. Schachter / K. Back, *Social Pressures in Informal Groups: A Study of Human Factors in Housing*. New York: Harper and Row, 1950.

Finholt, T. / L. Sproull, *Electronic Groups at Work*, in: Organization Science 1 (1990), pp. 41-64.

Granovetter, M., *The Strength of Weak Ties*, in: American Journal of Sociology 73 (1973), pp. 1361-1380.

Haring, G., *The Tragedy of the Commons*, in: Science 162 ((1969), pp. 1243-1248.

Hesse, B. / L. Sproull / S. Kiesler, *Oceanography Study*, Working paper, Department of Social and Decision Sciences, Carnegie Mellon University, Pittsburgh/PA.

Huber, G., *A Theory of the Effects of Advanced Information Technologies on Organization Design, Intelligence, and Decision Making*, in: Academy of Management Review 15 (1990), pp. 47-71.

Jaccard, J. / R. Turrisi / C. K. Wan, *Interaction Effects in Multiple Regression*, Newbury Park/CA: Sage, 1990.

Kaufman, H., *The Forest Ranger: A Study in Administrative Behavior*, Baltimore: Johns Hopkins University Press, 1960.

Kenrick, D. / G. Johnson, *Interpersonal Attraction in Aversive Environments: A problem for the classical conditioning paradigm?*, in: Journal of Personality and Social Psychology 37 (1979), pp. 572-579.

Kim, J. / G. D. Ferree, *Standardization in Causal Analysis*, in: Sociological Methods and Research 10 (1981), pp. 187-210.

Kmetz, J., *An Information-Processing Study of Complex Workflow in Aircraft Electronic Repair*, in: Administrative Science Quarterly 19 (1984), pp. 74-97.

Kraut, R. / J. Galegher / C. Egido, *Patterns of Contact and Communication in Scientific Research Collaboration*, in: Galegher, J. et al. (eds.), *Intellectual Teamwork: Social and Technological Foundations of Cooperative Work*, Englewood Cliffs/NJ: Lawrence Earlbaum and Associates, 1990.

Kusterer, K. C., *Know-how on the Job: The Important Working Knowledge of Unskilled Workers*, Boulder/CO: Westview Press, 1978.

Levitt, B. / J. G. March, *Organizational Learning*, in: Scott, R. (ed.), *Annual Review of Sociology*, Palo Alto/CA: Annual Review, 1988.

Martin, J. / M. Feldman / S. Sitkin, *The Uniqueness Paradox in Organizational Stories*, in: Administrative Science Quarterly 28 (1983), pp. 438-453.

Messick, D. / M. Brewer, *Solving Social Dilemmas: A Review*, in: Wheeler, L. / P. Shaver (eds.), *Review of Personality and Social Psychology*, Beverly Hills/CA: Sage, 1983.

O'Reilly, C.A. / J. A. Chatman / J. C. Anderson, *Message Flow and Decision Making*, in: Jablin, F. M. et al. (eds.), *Handbook of Organizational Communication*, Newbury Park/CA: Sage, 1987, pp. 600-623.

Orr, J. E., *Sharing Knowledge, Celebrating Identity: War Stories and Community Memory among Service Technicians*, in: Middleton, D.S. / D. Edwards (eds.), *Collective Remembering: Memory in Society*, Beverly Hills/CA: Sage, 1990.

Powell, W., *Learning in International Business Alliances*, in: *Conference on Organizational Learning*, Carnegie Mellon University, May 1989.

Riordan, C. / J. Tedeschi, *Attraction in Aversive Environments: Some Evidence for Classical Conditioning and Negative Reinforcement*, in: Journal of Personality of Social Psychology 44 (1983), pp. 683-691.

Rosenbach, J. / E. Whitman / D. Moshkovitz, *Plane and Spherical Trigonometry*, Boston: Ginn and Company, 1943.

Schelling, T., *The Ecology of Micromotives*, in: Public Interest 25 (1971), pp. 61-98.

Simon, H., *Administrative Behavior*, New York: Free Press, 3rd edition, 1976.

Thorn, B. / T. Conolly, *Discretionary Data Bases: A Theory and some Experimental Findings*, in: Communication Research 14 (1987), pp. 412-528.

Walsh, J. / S. Kiesler / L. Sproull / B. Hesse, *Spontaneous Self-selected Participation in an Electronic Survey*. Forthcoming.

Weber, M., *Economy and Society*, vol. 2, Berkeley/CA: University of California Press, 1978.

Weisberg, S., *Applied Linear Regression*, New York: John Wiley and Sons, 1985.

DATACOMMUNICATION INSTEAD OF PAPER: THE USE OF ELECTRONIC MAIL IN DUTCH CIVIL SERVICE

By Victor Bekkers

1. INTRODUCTION

In 1987 the Dutch Cabinet Council decided that the exchange of documents within the civil service should be modernized by using the possibilities of electronic mail. This could lead to improvements in efficacy and efficiency, if a technological infrastructure could be implemented. The so-called DIS-program (DIS is the acronym for Documentary Information Systems) was born. Datacommunication instead of paper was the device under wich the program started.

In this article I want to address the relevance of electronic documentary exchange systems for the functioning and organization of central government. In doing so, we have to confront ourselves with some questions of a more empirical nature. The first step is that I will try to establish insight in the amount, the character and directions of the exchange of documents between departments. How many documents are being exchanged? How does this exchange take place? There are of course a lot of possibilities, varying from courier services to telefax. What importance do civil servants attach to the exchange of documents? What problems do they discern? These questions are examples of themes which I will address in paragraph three.

The introduction of electronic mail has consequences for the internal organization of a department. Which procedures are taken into account when documents are being exchanged with other departments? What does this mean for the position of the internal postal agency? Paragraph four tries to formulate some answers. In paragraph five I will evaluate the effectiveness and the efficiency of the DIS-project. Paragraph six presents a summary and an outlook, in which the earlier findings will be problematized.

Before addressing these issues, it is necessary that a sketch is given of the aims and the background of the DIS-program.

2. AIMS AND BACKGROUND OF THE DIS-PROGRAM

The aim of the DIS-project is twofold. The main goal is to establish a general standardized infrastructure for the exchange of documents within Dutch civil service. This could lead to an improvement of the efficacy and efficiency of the exchange of documents as well as of the retrieval of documents.

An important problem in establishing standardization was the fact that the responsibilities of each department regarding their internal information policies and the use of IT should be respected. Although the Minister of Home Affairs is officially responsible for the informatization within the civil service, in practice the departments involved are autonomous. The role of the Ministry of Home Affairs is therefore more of a facilitating and supportive nature. For the realization of the DIS-programme, the responsibility of the Ministry of Home Affairs is restricted to the implementation of information systems between, and not within the departments.

The existence of this power equilibrium between the Ministry of Home Affairs and the other departments has led to an 'archipelago' of hard- and software applications within the civil service. Data communication between departments faces therefore some compatability problems.

In the DIS-project a solution for these problems was found in searching for an infrastructure that is able to work with these different soft- and hardware applications. Standards had to be found for the transmission of documents and for the document format, which have no trouble with the different applications on the receiving and mailing side.

With a view to the process of internationalization in an EC context, an additional condition was formulated. The standards to be chosen had to be international ones. When these standards were not available, producer-dependent standards were chosen as a temporary solution.

The exchange of documents is based on the international ISO standard for Message Handling X.400 and X.500. The document format is based on the ODA/ODIF standard, which is not yet available, so that the short term solution is based on the T61 standard.

The DIS-program was operationalized in three pilot-projects, which were started in 1989. The first project is the project 'Parliament'. A large part of the documents which are sent to the Parliament and the State's Publishing Firm by the ministries of Social Affairs, Justice and Education could be sent by electronic mail. The second project is the project 'departments', which focusses on the electronic exchange of documents between the Ministry of Foreign Affairs and the Ministries of Economic Affairs and Agricultural Affairs. The Foreign Office has about 120 diplomatic agencies abroad. These agencies collect information which is also of importance for other ministries. Electronic mail tries to facilitate a quicker dispatch of the information collected abroad. One of the connecting aims was that e-mail should replace the use of telex. The last project to be mentioned is the project 'database rules and regulations'. This project aims at the promotion and improvement of the access of regulation databases for the civil servants and citizens.

Meanwhile, these projects are implemented. Although the amount of documents which are exchanged by electronic mail lag behind the orginal goals, the projects are considered as being succesfull (I will come back to this isssue in paragraph five). One of the major contributions of the projects is that the parties involved have reached an agreement on the standards to be used.

In July 1990 the Cabinet Council decided to continue the DIS-program, but under a new flag, namely 'Electronic Mail Civil Service'. First, this project tries to consolidate and to extend the communication infrastructure as was established in the pilot-projects 'Parliament' and 'departments' to other ministries. Second, the matching management structure, like protocols and procedures, should be hold against the light. In paragraph four I will further go into this matter, but first it is advisible to pay some attention to some of the characteristics of the exchange of documents between ministries.

3. AMOUNT, DIRECTION AND NATURE OF THE EXCHANGE OF DOCUMENTS

Number and nature of the documents

Of course it is a noble ambition to improve the electronic exchange of documents within the Dutch civil service, but what do we in fact talk about. How many documents are being mailed and received? What kind of documents can be distinguished?

On the basis of an inventory research project we can give some indications about the amount, the direction and characteristics of the exchange of documents between departments. A random sample consisting of 326 organizational units at the level of the bureau of secretary-general, the bureau of director-general and the directorates were being addressed in a survey with questions about the incoming and outgoing flow of documents within central government. Let's examine some of the results.

The research shows that per year approximately 700.000 to 800.000 documents, varying from a memo to concept-legislation, are being sent as well as received. Who are now the most important mailing and receiving departments? The research indicates that the ministries of Finance (Fin) and Home Affairs (Biza) are very important actors in the exchange of documents. About 75% of the units say they send documents to the ministries of Finance and Home Affairs. They also say that they receive most of their documents from these two ministries.

Figure I gives an indication of the amount of documents of the outgoing flow by using mean scores.

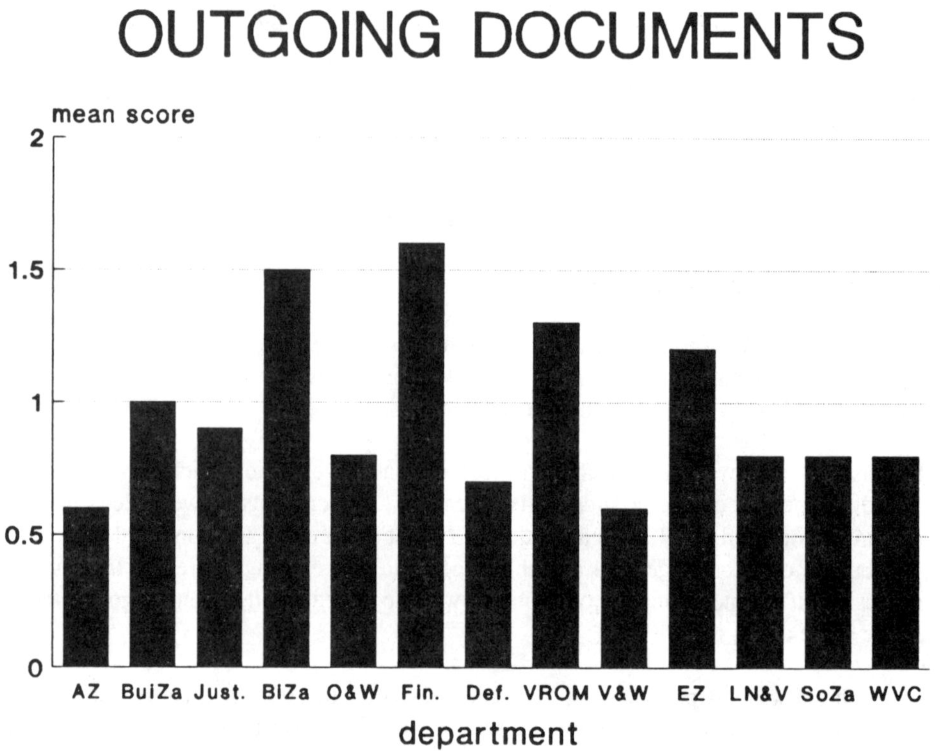

Figure I. **Amount of documents in the outgoing flow: mean scores**

What kind of documents are being sent and received? And, a more fundamental question is, what is a document. A document can be described as unstructured information in text form, but in the daily language of an average civil servant this is too abstract. In the research the idea of a document is being operationalized in several sorts of documents: letters (sec), notes/reports/minutes regarding policy formulation activities, sanctionized policy documents (which are no longer the subject of negotiation or dispute, e.g. legislation), documents which are sent to the Cabinet Council, memo's and financial reports.

Figure II visualises the different document types in the outgoing flow by using mean scores.

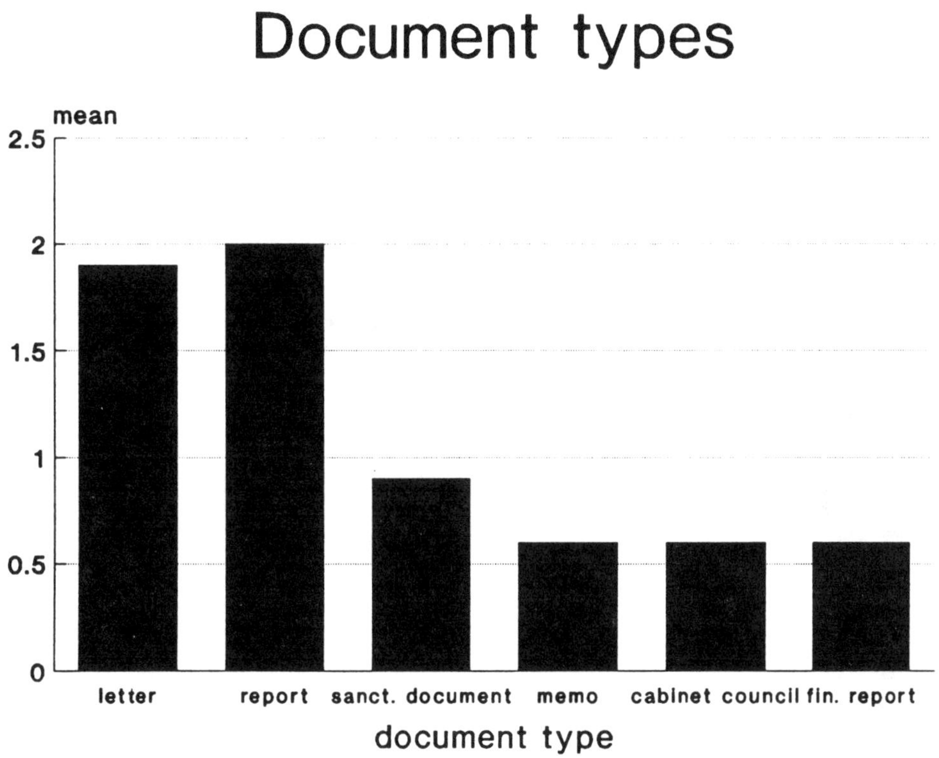

Figure II. **Document types: mean score in the outgoing flow**

A large majority of the documents exchanged between departments exists of letters and policy preparation documents. Very often other departments are being ask to give their comment or advice regarding the draft of a policy document. When units send sanctionized policy documents, documents for the Cabinet Council and financial reports, this happens occasional. The contribution of memo's in the exchange of documents is also limited c.q. not really visible.

The mailing of letters, reports etc. can be done voluntary, but they can also be the subject of legally determined, compulsory information procedures, like the procedures concerning the budgetting cycle. The research indicates that most of the mailed documents are not the result of obligatory procedures. Therefore a preliminary conclusion is that flows of documents are 'grey ones', corresponding with several stages in the policy formulation process. Most of documents involved are directly sent from one directorate to another, without mediation of a superordinated organizational level, like the director-general or secretary-general.

The way of exchanging

The way documents can be exchanged, differs. The following means of exchanging can be distinguished: through post, courier, telex, telefax, electronic mail, floppy-disk and the informal way of 'personal delivery'. The research indicates that post and courier services play the most important role in the more structural exchange of documents. Telefax is also very popular, but is mostly restricted to the exchange of documents of a more incidental nature.

Figure III gives an idea of the mean scores of the types of media used in the exchange of documents.

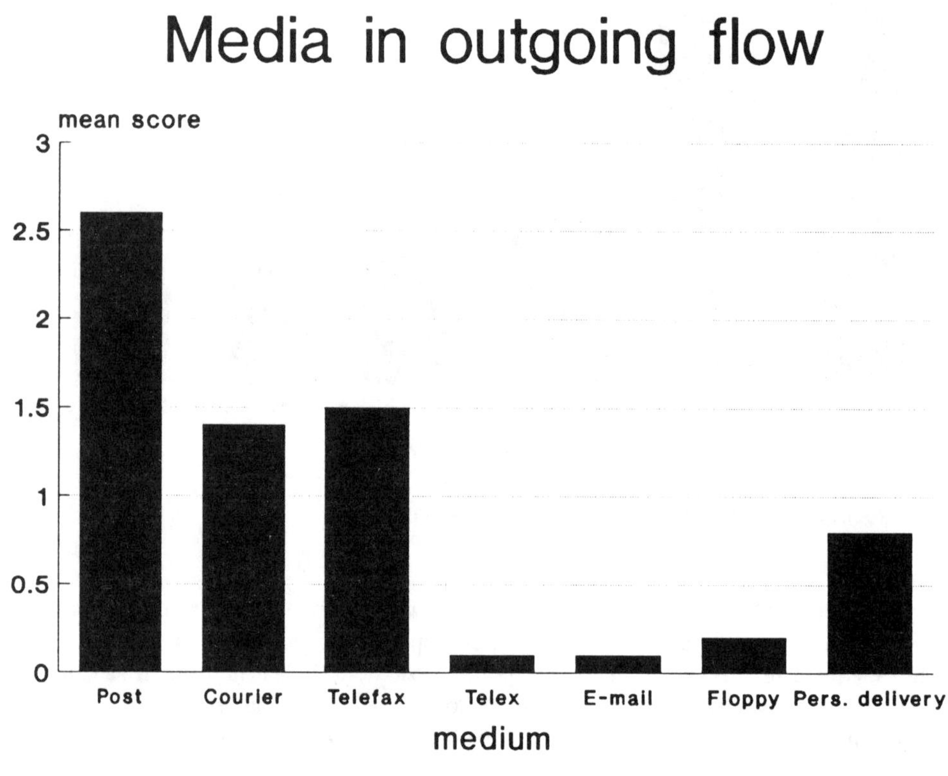

Figure III **Media used in the outgoing flow of documents: mean scores**

The importance of the exchange of documents

The selected units were asked, if and how much importance they give to the exchange of documents between the several departments, as well as what kind of problems occur. Almost everybody thinks that the exchange of documents is very essential for the policy formulation process. Therefore it may not be seen as a bureaucratic ritual. However, about half of the units approached think that a quarter of the documents exchanged can be omitted.

The large majority of the units questioned has the opinion that a speedy exchange of documents is necessary. This is not a surprise, if one considers the problems units face in exchanging documents. The slow dispatch procedures within the several departments is the problem which was mentioned mostly.

Almost 50% of the units questioned argue that one is using communication techniques which are out of date. Therefore, one wishes that advanced communication technology, like e-mail facilities, will be installed.

Figure IV gives the percentage of the answers of units questioned on the importance they attach to the exchange of documents.

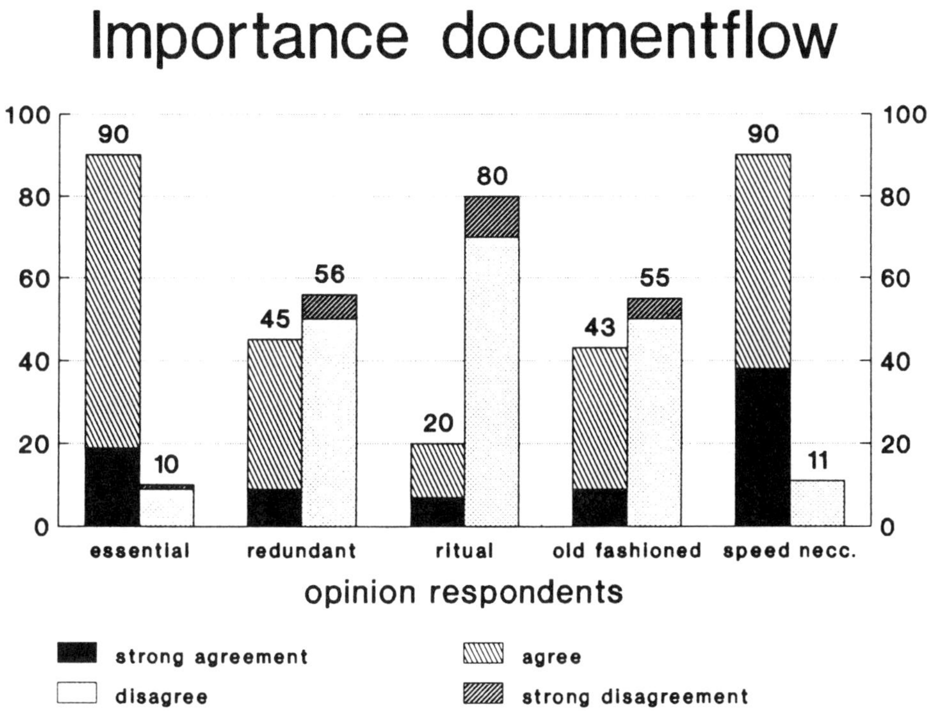

Figure IV. **Importance attached to the exchange of documents: percentages of the units questioned**

Relevance for the DIS-program

When we try to establish the meaning of these research results in relation with the aims and background of the DIS-program, some interesting obervations can be made.

First, e-mail facilities will never completely substitute other ways of communication. It is an additional medium for the exchange of documents, which is very often not profitable because of lacking utilization.

A selective and optimal use of these facilities depends on some characteristics of the document flow and the policy communication networks involved. Two charateristics of these networks are relevant for an optimal use of electronic documentary systems:

- the degree of formalization of the exchange of documents between departments. In what way is the exchange of documents the subject of legally determined compulsory procedures, like the budgetting cycle?

- the degree of stability and regularity of the exchange processes. A stable flow of relatively large quantities of documents will promote an optimal use.

Second, up to now most of the documents exchanged have been dispatched by using relatively expensive media like post, courier and telefax. Therefore it could be interesting to make a calculation of the costs of the distinguished ways of exchanging and costs of e-mail. What is the break-even-point for e-mail when we compare this with other break-even-points? And how can this break-even-point easier be realized when we relate it with some characteristics of the document flows and the policy communication networks involved?

4. EFFECTS ON THE INTERNAL ORGANIZATION

The use of advanced computer-assisted communication technology facilitates according to Huber (1990) the ability of the individual or organization (a) to communicate more easily and less expensively across time and geographic location; (b) to communicate more rapidly and with greater precision to target-groups; (c) to record and index more reliably and inexpensively the content and nature of communication events; and (d) to more selectively control access and participation in a communication event or network.

Let's try to examine if some of the effects mentioned by Huber can be seen, when we look at the consequences of the DIS-program on the internal organization and its procedures. Will we cross the traditional borders of time, place and hierarchy? However, a marginal note regarding this question is necessary. At this moment the effects on the internal organization are not quite clear, because of their ambivalent and contingent character.

Decentralization and the position of the internal postal agency

The first effect to be distinguished is the position of the internal postal office. In essence, the existence of an interorganizational network infrastructure, certainly when it is coupled with intradepartmental networks, facilitates a further decentralization of the exchange of documents. So, the traditional and centralized internal postal agency in the distribution of documents is diminishing. On a decentralized level several electronic post-office boxes are established. In the case of the Foreign Office each bureau has its own box with its own manager.

This means that the secretariat of each bureau sees its function enlarged and professionalized. The secretariat is responsible for the complete management of the document handling procedures.

This process of selective decentralization can be observed in the relationship between the Foreign Office in the Hague and the diplomatic agencies abroad. The introduction of e-mail implicated a break with the traditional way of exchanging documents. Messages of an administrative nature (the so-called A-messages) get the status of an internal memorandum, that no longer has to be addressed to the Minister of Foreign Affairs. It can be send to the specific bureau or office-holder in the Hague. A central address or distribution point within the Foreign Office is only needed for the so-called B-messages: messages which have the status of a policy document/report.

I said that the position of the internal postal agency lies under fire. But, is it defenceless? The position of the internal postal agency can be maintained, if the following pro-active strategy is chosen. The internal postal agency can try to profile itself as the 'communication center' of a department. It can try to support and facilitate e-mail activities on a more decentralized level. However, this could lead to domain conflicts with the central informatization and automation office.

Formalization and procedures

The decentralization of the exchange of documents could lead to some form of 'anarchy' in the handling of documents. Therefore procedures have to be developed for tackling this problem. There has to be agreement, amongst other issues, on the following questions: who is authorized to send a document; how do we organize the registration and keeping of the exchanged document? Another point of attention is the security problem: how do we safeguard documents against anonymous manipulation and unauthorized adding or deleting of information? The relationship between the exchange and manipulation of documents in the electronic way is much closer than in the traditional way. In the traditional way you can see alterations in the document, in the informatized way this is more difficult.

In the DIS-pilot project 'departments' the Foreign Office has developed interesting procedures. First, e-mail forced the Foreign Office to define and to formalize the status of several kinds of documents. There are P-, A- and B-messages. P-messages are of a personal nature. A-messages are, as I said before, of a administrative nature and B-messages are policy documents/reports.

A- and P-messages can immediately be send to the specific bureau or office-holder. B-messages have to be send to a central registration and distribution center. This center knows who gets a copy of what kind of B-message. With the help of distribution lists the B-messages will be send to the specific target groups.

The strict definition and formalization of the addressing procedure is another interesting point. When a traditional letter is sent, the delivery of the letter depends on the visual control of the written address. A letter which has an unclear address could wander through the organization. Using electronic mail has the advantage that it forces the sender to use a well-defined adress. Every address has to be unique. Daily messages will be earlier received by the persons addressed.

The mailing of the drafts of reports, notes etc. needs authorization. Someone has to be formally responsible for the content of a document. Validation of the authorization is therefore a necessity. In the traditional way of sending a report etc., authorization is done by the initials of an office and the signature of the office-holder. One of the problems is that it is often unclear if someone is the sender or one is pretenting that the document has not been send by him. Using electronic mail has the advantage that automatically the user name of the sender is inserted in the message. The usage of pass words in the authorization process is another advantage of e-mail.

One of the disadvantages of the electronic handling of documents is the adaption of the document. It is very difficult to see who has made certain adaptions (deleting or adding information) in the text. It is also difficult to comment on the text in the margins of the document. In the pilot-project 'departments' the following procedure has been established:

- making a draft with a computer (word processing);
- printing the document;
- circulation of and drawing up the printed document;
- the collected changes, comments etc. will be inserted in the document by the orginal drafter;
- the altered document will be sent.

The use of electronic mail has also advantages for the registration of the documents. Documents can automatically be given a registration number.

Information technology has the potential to facilitate control. When we look at the registration procedures within the Foreign Office we see that the controlling possibilities of e-mail are discerned. Offices have explicitely the possibility to control the progress of certain documents. The electronic registration of documents has also the advantage that a quicker retrieval of documents is being facilitated. In the traditional way a (voluminous) file is made which can be consulted. The electronic registration and management of documents has the advantage that the consulting of files can be done with certain headwords.

Electronic registration and managing of documents has also the advantage that the traditional space which is needed for the files diminishes. Documents can be stored digitally.

6. EFFICACY AND EFFICIENCY OF THE DIS-PROGRAM

In this section I will try to establish the efficacy and efficiency of two of the pilot-projects, namely the project 'Parliament' and the project 'departments'.

Efficacy

In 1990 the experimental project "Parliament" was finished and evaluated. When we look at the effectiveness of the project, we see that a re-definition of two goals has taken place. The first goal, at least 50% of the documents should be send by electronic mail, was altered in 'as much as possible'. The last goal, using producer-independent international standards, was amplified with the statement 'if they are available'. The absence of an international exchange format standard was therefore compensated by an interim-solution.

In the project 'departments' we see that the replacement of telex through electronic mail in the interdepartmental exchange of documents has been established for 50%. The original goal of the almost complete subsitution of telex by e-mail is therefore not realized.

In terms of efficacy I conclude that the major achievement of the project 'Parliament' was the agreement on and the establishment of a complete network architecture for electronic mail, which operates in accordance with international standards. This is important, because the choice of the network architecture had to have no consequences on the internal IT applications of the ministries involved. Each ministry should be able to read and work with the exchanged document on its own computer, in spite of the software applications which were originally used. Existing information technology created therefore considerable problems of functionality and compatibility, which were solved by using international standards. However, the problem was that these standards were not always available, so that ad hoc and short term solutions had to be developed, until these international standards were established.

The choice for a producer-independent network, as a result of the principle of departmental autonomy, can be evaluated in two ways. First, one could say that it created compatibility problems, which put the project under a lot of pressure: existing hard and software technology hindered the modernization of the exchange of documents. On the other hand, the mere existence of these problems was a necessary condition for achieving agreement on the standardization of the electronic mail network. So, existing hard and software stimulated modernization.

The major contribution of the pilot-project 'departments' is that it has led to a reflection on the procedures which traditionally guide the exchange of documents. These learning effects are very important, when electronic mail is implemented in the whole civil service. However, this does not implicate that these experiences will be given the status of a blue-print to be applied in the whole civil service. The recognition of the autonomy of the departments regarding their own internal organization of the IT-functions will hinder this. The ministries are free to organize their own procedures.

Efficiency

Another criterion for evaluating the success or failure of the DIS-pilot project 'Parliament' is the contribution of electronic mail to efficiency-improvement. In terms of efficiency, the conclusion can be formulated that the project 'Parliament' leads to considerable cost reductions, especially copying costs.

Another observation is that documents reach Parliament faster, so that they can be distributed among the Members of Parliament, their staff and the press more readily and more quickly.

For the State's Publishing Firm, electronic mail means that the possibilities of Desk Top Publishing can be used better and more efficiently.

Efficiency-improvements can also be discerned in the project 'departments'. The fact that the departments of Economic Affairs and Agricultural Affairs are coupled with the e-mail-network of the Foreign Office has shown interesting effects. For instance, the Export Office of the department of Economic Affairs has now speedier information at its disposal. This means that information about procurements abroad can quicker be given to Dutch firms. The mere replacement of telex through X.400 has lead to a reduction in duration of this process from 20 to 11 days. One is trying to reduce it further. This is a beautiful example of the effect that time and place are loosing their importance.

7. SUMMARY AND OUTLOOK

In this article I tried to evaluate the meaning of documentary information systems, especially the use of e-mail, for the functioning of the Dutch civil service. This was demonstrated by two pilot-projects, the projects 'Parliament' and 'departments'. In both projects one is trying to modernize the exchange of documents by using the possibilities of e-mail with a view to efficiency and efficacy-improvements.

These improvements can be realized when one is aware of the large amount of documents which is being exchanged within central government. Research indicates that 700.000 to 800.000 documents, varying from letters, drafts, Cabinet Council documents to memos etc., are being sent and received. E-mail can be an interesting (also financial) alternative for more traditional means of communicating, like post and courier services.

The introduction of e-mail in the civil service has also important consequences for the internal organization of and the procedurers within the departments involved. We saw that one effect is the further selective decentralization of mailing and receiving activities, which could threaten the centralized position of the internal postal agency. Another effect is that e-mail forces to re-think the traditional procedures which guide the exchange of documents. Procedures have to be strictly defined, formalization is being enhanced.

When we evaluated the achievements of the two DIS pilot-projects, we saw the main accomplishment is twofold. First, agreement has been achieved about standardization of the interdepartmental network structure, without being a threat to the departmental autonomy regarding their own IT policies and facilities. Second, a reflection on the procedures relating to e-mail activities has taken place.

But from a more theoretical and problematizing point of view, what does this all together mean for the organization of central government and its environment? Some statements can be formulated.

First, there is the co-ordinating role of the Ministry of Home Affairs in relation to the recognition of the departmental autonomy regarding their IT affairs. The co-ordination was a success, because it reconciled autonomy with interdependencies; it acknowledged the characteristics of the complex network, which government is. The acceptance was facilitated by a bottum-up co-ordination process. Top-down guidelines, instructions, regulations etc. fail in these kind of situations. The co-ordinating role of the Department of Home Affairs was that of a 'broker', a discussion facilitator, who is trying to point out the mutual benefits to the other actors in the network. This is very important because e-mail formalizes certain social communication networks inside and outside an organization. The success of such a network depends on the way it reconciles the interests of the actors involved.

The second statement concerns the way e-mail enhances bureaucratization. In this study bureaucratization is defined in a Weberian way. According to Weber and other students of formal organization (e.g. Pugh 1963) a bureaucracy or formal organization can be described in terms of the degree of standardization, specialization, formalization and centralization. The effects of e-mail in terms of more or less bureaucratization are ambigious. On the one hand we see that e-mail leads to a well-defined formalization of the documentary exchange process. Formalization which goes further than the traditional, more 'paper-orientated' procedures. On the other hand we noticed that selective decentralization of document handling was stimulated. Decentralized offices themselves are responsible for the management of the documents exchanged. This leads to an enlargement of the tasks of secretary staff.

Third, many authors (e.g. Beniger 1986) see technology and IT in particular as an instrument for control. The nature of IT is control and monitoring. The example of the Foreign Office underlines this statement. Although e-mail may be seen as a functional device, improving the efficiency of the exchange process, it is also possible to monitor the progress of certain documents as we have seen before.

Fourth, the establishment of interdepartmental electronic network puts the role of information and information relations in a new perspective. Information and informational technology are not neutral, they are no technical devices that enhance the rationality of the organization and its policy process, but they are powerful resources in a political game (e.g. Pfeffer 1981). Therefore we have to ask ourselves how and in what way information technology re-shapes the structure and culture of the political and administrative system. I will demonstrate the relevance of this statement by looking at the attitude of Dutch MP's regarding the use of e-mail in the relations between Parliament and the ministries.

We observe here a 'total' lack of interest in the possibilities which IT can offer for the fulfilment of their tasks and duties. Most MP's neglect and underestimate the political effects of this project, in terms of agenda-management and the execution of political control by MP's. Moreover, all the participants in the project 'Parliament' evaluate the project in terms of efficiency-improvement. Electronic mail is seen a functional and technical device, that replaces the traditional manual devices. Reflection on possible political effects in the near future is not taking place.

The fact that documents are received in a text pool means that everybody has these documents at his disposal at the same time. Also the transparency of the decision-making process can be improved. Lacks in information do not have to occur. This means that MP's can better execute their controlling duties. These controlling duties can be further optimalized when MP's could have access to ministerial data bases by using the electronic mail facilities: the transparent ministry.

However, MP's do not recognize these possibilities. They are not aware of the strategic possibilities that IT can offer. One of the reasons of this negligence is cultural. Most of the MP's are not used to work with IT: it is unknown, perceived as chilly and untangible and therefore it frightens people.

Not only do MP's not recognize the chances of IT, they also do not see the possible threats of IT for their own work. Because ministries have a knowledge advantage regarding IT, they could easier manipulate the information which is send to the department or, in a further phase, ministerial databases. An interesting question in this respect concerns the relationship between the ministerial duties to inform the Parliament and the use of IT. The optimal use that the advantages of IT for the exchange of information could implicate that ministries and their political apex have gained another power source to influence the agenda management of the Parliament and the political decision-making process.

References

Bekkers, V. J. J. M / W. A. J. Gooren / P. H. A. Frissen, *Inventarisatie documentaire informatiestromen. Een kwantificerend vooronderzoek in opdracht van het Ministerie van Binnenlandse Zaken*, Tilburg 1991.

Bekkers, V. J. J. M. / P. H. A. Frissen, *Informatization and Adminstrative Modernization in the Netherlands,* in: Frissen, P. H. A. / V. J. J. M. Bekkers et. al. (eds.), *Informatization in a European Context*, Amsterdam: Elseviers Science Publishers (to be published Autumn 1992).

Beniger, J. R., *The Control Revolution*, Cambridge/Mass. 1986.

Huber, G. P., *A Theory of the Effects of Advanced Information Technologies on Organizational Design, Intelligence and Decision-Making*, in: Fulk, J. / Ch. Steinfeld (eds.), *Organizations and Communication Technology*, Newbury Park/London/New Dehli: Sage, 1990.

Ministerie van Binnenlandse Zaken, *Eindrapportage project parlement*, Den Haag 1990.

Ministerie van Binnenlandse Zaken, *DIS-programma Project Departementen Eindrapport*, Den Haag 1990.

Ministerie van Binnenlandse Zaken, *DIS-programma Project Parlement: kamerstukken door de kabel*, Den Haag 1990.

Ministerie van Binnenlandse Zaken, *DIS-programma Project Departementen: electronisch berichtenverkeer van ambtenaar tot ambtenaar*, Den Haag 1990.

Ministerie van Buitenlandse Zaken, *Het berichtenverkeer bij BZ op nieuwe lees geschoeid*, Den Haag 1990.

Pfeffer, G., *Power in Organizations*, New York 1981.

Pugh, D. S. et. al., *A Conceptual Scheme for Organizational Analysis*, in: Adminstrative Science Quarterly 8 (1963), pp. 289-315;

Tweede Kamer, Meerjarenprogramma Documentaire Informatiesystemen, vergaderjaar 1987-1988, 20.471, nr. 2.

CHANGES IN ORGANIZATION AND PROCESS OF WORK IN ADMINISTRATIONS

By Heinrich Reinermann

1. "Interface" and "Gateway" have become important terms in informatics. They denote interchangeability between different systems.

In the following, I would like to concentrate on the interface between public administration and informatics:

- What is the potential of modern information technology to influence tasks and procedures of public administration?
- Is public administration utilizing this potential adequately? If not: Will it do so in the future?
- What influences of public administration on informatics are to be expected?
- How can special requirements of public authorities brought to bear on the suppliers of information technology?

Those two aspects, the influence of modern information technology on public administration and vice versa, are the subjects of "administrative informatics" as a discipline which is in itself a new interface between two older fields of scientific interest.

2. Looking at technical progress and its impact on the environment in general, one can observe at least three interesting features:

- First, the technical invention itself undergoes definite changes in response to the requirements of its environment. Take the automobile as an example, and it becomes very clear how the special needs of the various customer groups have contributed to the transition from the original motor-driven stage-coach to cars, trucks, golf-carts and the like of our days.
- Second, technical invention is not enough. In order to be able to utilize it, we need additional inventions in e.g. infrastructure. Without street systems, maintenance chains, traffic law or car insurance would not exist the "automobile society", as we know it today. High-tech, apparently, is not enough: We need "High-Org" and "High-Norm" as well.
- Third, after some time of rationalizing the given world with the help of a technical invention, we usually switch the perspective: We start to experiment with the new technology and try to change the world in a creative way. Once more the automobile can serve as an example: Obviously we didn't stop having made the horse-drawn carriage a little bit faster. Rather we created new ways of behaviour, as can be noticed

by looking at the arrangement of working and living areas in cities or at just-in-time production in manufacturing companies.

Before this background we should expect micro-electronics as a technical invention and public administration as the part of its environment we are looking into today, to interact in a similar way.

However, I would like to mention already here, that I regard information technology as a catalyst, comparable to a chemical substance which makes *other* substances interact whith each other. Information technology, like the catalyst, is not able to bring about administrative changes or administrative reforms by itself.

3. The technical invention, in order to be able to allow creative applications, must have reached a respective stage of development. In the case of EDP we can observe four broad development stages: The 60s were dominated by big and expensive computers; in the 70s, those mainframes were joined by smaller and cheaper minicomputers; in the 80s the personal computer wave spread virtually through all offices; an the 90s will see the expansion of local and wide area networks.

Now we have reached a state of information technology which is characterized by both - desk orientation and communication orientation. In addition, data of all types can be processed: written data, spoken data and images. Given this "state of the art", almost all phases of the typical work flow in public offices can be supported: the handling of incoming documents; the storage of documents; the communication process necessary to prepare a decision; the control of the work flow between cooperating units; the preparation of letters, decisions, or orders; and the dispatching of those. A product family, typical for this potential, is CSCW (Computer Supported Cooperative Work).

Therefore the result is obvious: information technology, as a catalyst, allows us to design our public administrations in ways different from those we have known in the past.

4. I would like to start my look into such administrative reforms with a hypothesis: Administrative behaviour is, among others, dependent on the available working techniques. The tasks we would like our public authorities to fullfill, the administrative procedures, and the working techniques available in offices - they are interdependent.

This phenomenon did not catch our eye as long as change in office methods was slow. However, confronted with today's leaping progress in information and communication technologies, such interdependencies become more and more apparent.

The reason behind this phenomenon is known as "means/ends-interrelation". Everybody knows at least one aspect of it by personal experience: The more money you have, the more wishes of yours can be fullfilled - and the other way round, as someone noticed who compared the defense efforts of various states and came to the conclusion: What is good for the USA is not necessarily good for Liechtenstein ...

There are several versions of means/ends-interrelation. I shall concentrate on just two: conflicting ends or goals and goal innovation.

The first decades of EDP in public administration were, at least in this country, characterized by discussions of negative side-effects which the new technology imposed on administrative work. Observers claimed that because of EDP, economy might have been improved, but that, on the other hand, division of labour went up, delivery periods between computer centers and public agencies became longer, client/administration-relations deteriorated and so on. The headline was "EDP is going to affect good administrative behaviour in a negative way".

Although it is still necessary to observe and control those conflicting goals, technical progress has given us the chance to shift the focus of our observations to goal innovation as another aspect of means/ends-interrelations. Let me start with an example.

It has become a general feature of public administration that it normally grants services on application only. This means that citizens

- must inform themselves about potential services
- must check the respective regulations for requirements
- must support their own files in order to prove that their personal situation complies with the regulations
- must find out which public agency is in charge
- must fill in application forms
- must file the application
- and the like.

When you consider the costs and benefits of the traditional "application principle" which has become an important part of our administrative culture, you might call it a benefit that citizens are not treated as wards of public administration, that they rather have the autonomy to decide and act, and you might call it a cost that quite a few persons entitled, don't make use of their rights because they don't master the necessary information work.

My point is, however, that one reason behind the principle of application is work technology. In order to follow the opposite strategy - public services granted ex officio, that means: without application - one would need "millions" of civil servants who would have to check the files in order to find out who could be entitled to what public service. And the big change brought about by modern information technology is that we in fact do have such "millions" of civil servants at our disposal - computers.

I hasten to report a practical example right away: A couple of years back, our Federal Government introduced a Child Education Grant (Bundeserziehungsgeld): For at least six months after a birth the mother gets a certain amount of money. When it came to administrating this new service by the *Länder*, one of our social ministers came up with a surprising idea. She said: Why should we wait for applications? We have all the necessary data in our computers anyway. Let's fill in application forms ex officio and let's waive the presentation of birth certificates and the like, because all this is in our machines from other sources already.

The important point is that it is office technique which makes the difference! Without modern information technology this change in perception of a public agency would not have been possible. Looking at costs and benefits again, you might call it a benefit that beneficiaries really get what they are entitled to, you might call it a cost, however, that government probably needs more money now for the same type of service. It is obvious also, that the change in work technique has led us into the middle of political and controversial considerations of the role and perception of public administration.

Now I can summarize my hypothesis as follows: Modern information technology allows new administrative procedures. But to change those, we need to shake up given means/ends-relations. Therefore, political decisions have to be taken with regard to the preferable model (Leitbild) of the respective agency. Only then can the new procedures be designed and implemented and safeguarded by rules and regulations.

This interdependence of work technique on the one hand and goals, norms, and procedures of public administration on the other should prevent from now on that people still claim "for me, modern information technology is just a working technique..."

5. One way of looking into the practical consequences of this phenomenon for public administration, is by distinguishing four layers of change induced by information technology as a catalyst: Change in data structures, in organizational structures, in personnel structures, and in task structures.

On the level of data structures we notice that data become ubiquitous. Whereas we are used to paper files which are unique unless we take special efforts to copy or mail them, electronic files are available anywhere on the globe, unless we take special efforts to protect their accessibility.

This is a prerequisite for change on the next level: organization. Not only can data be transfered via telecommunication lines, but so can jobs. A striking example is the citizen's office "BürgerBüro" in our *Land* of Lower Saxony. From here, the citizen in rural areas, supported by a civil servant, can communicate with remote federal, state and local agencies and, in addition, with private companies like banks or insurance firms as well. This way, those agencies and companies, having moved their physical locations into bigger cities, are at least "tele-present" in rural areas, and the citizens can do some of their business with them from a local office, the citizens office. Please note, that this is a definite change in organization or in the way tasks are assigned to agencies and positions. Such transfers of tasks via telecommunication lines to differrent positions can be noticed quite often. In general, this leads to holistic types of organization with less division of labor.

When you remember the civil servants in the citizen's office, one possible influence of information technology on personnel structures is quite apparent: The demand for qualification rises. Holistic patterns of organization require multiple qualifications and should have, in addition, an effect on status and payment of the employees. Another effect is higher motivation because of the higher influence and power which is given to civil servants in holistic forms of organization.

Finally, looking at the task structures we notice efforts to combine services in one hand which used to be separated and spread among specific agencies. Having ubiquitous data and software, it is, e.g., no longer necessary that a person who has moved adresses the citizen registration agency, the motor vehicles department, the school district, the post office, the telephone company, the tax agency, the utility company and so on; from the point of view of modern information technology all these services can be offered as one service package - and this package can be offered by *any* of the traditional agencies mentioned. Please notice that such an organizational pattern means competition between agencies which used to be sovereign and monopolistic. Similar changes are going on with respect to regional jurisdictions of agencies. A county, in charge of vehicle registration, converted its paper files to optical storage devices. Having made those files ubiquituos this way, it was possible to open up additional offices and to leave it to the car owners in which of the offices they wanted to register their vehicles. It is apparent that citizen/administration relations can be improved by such new arrangements of task structures. Also, citizen information systems and executive information systems can be mentioned as examples of change induced by information technology on this fourth level.

6. Comparing this potential of modern information technology to change the organization and the processes of work in public administration on the one hand and reality on the other, it is probably fair to say that we still are faced with a "damming up of innovation". Without doubt, one can detect quite innovative public agencies, but those still are pioneers. I think, the explanation is obvious: It lies in the very nature of such organizational changes. In the past computer support, more or less, required only to single out a certain area of administrative work, like payment, and to transfer it basically unchanged to the machine; now an integrative and holistic view is necessary. Reorganize before you automate, is the message. However, to redefine positions obviously can affect the interests of many employees and requires intensive leadership. However, given today's high demands for a raising productivity in public administration, for working environments which match the expectations of the public service, and for closer citizen/administration relations, public administration has no other choice than to utilize the potential of information technology for change.

7. As a last point I would like to reflect briefly on the consequences of this for public management. In my opinion, decisions about a working technique having as severe political implications as modern information technology has, must be the matter of regular public managers. A side-hierarchy for EDP as it can be found sometimes, is not able to handle adequately the intensive relations between goals, norms, and procedures of administrative activities. Rather each public manager must take responsibility, to answer three questions for her or his jurisdiction:

- Do we have, in my sphere of responsibility, adequate technical support?
- Do we utilize the available "data capital" sufficiently?
- Do we make use of the reform potential of information technology?

These topics should no longer be delegated but should be part of the regular duties of each public manager.

Of course, staff support in those three areas will normally be required. In one form or the other we need

- staff units to bring order into the technical infrastructure
- staff units to bring order into data resources, and
- staff units to bring order into administration in terms of tasks, organization, and personell.

But, as we have seen already, decisions in these fields are the matter of regular public managers. Given the difficulties to change organization and work processes in public administration they should apply Management by Vision and Management by Opportunities. Visions or models of preferable future states of an agency are useful as guideposts, and Management by opportunities is a strategy trying to approach those visions step by step and by gaining allies through convincing examples.

THE CHANGING FACE OF OFFICE DOCUMENTATION: ELECTRONIC/OPTICAL INFORMATION TECHNOLOGIES (IT)

An Analytical Framework for the Review of Trends in Office Automation and its Implications for Archives and Records Management

By Richard M. Kesner

ABSTRACT

Advances in information technology are transforming the way people work, communicate, and document their activities. At the same time, the global nature of the modern organization has dictated the development of convenient and economical methods of electronic data exchange. This series of events has in turn necessitated changes in the way archivists and records managers deal with their own responsibilities. The purpose of this essay is to characterize the operational, organizational, and technological developments that are transforming the work place; to discuss the advent of the "knowledge worker" and the "information utility"; and to consider how all of these factors provide new challenges for the archival and records management disciplines.[1]

Introduction:

The "Symposium on the Impact of Information Technologies on Information Handling in Offices and Archives" held in Gladenbach, Germany, on the 17th through the 19th of October 1991, brought together leading archivists from Europe, the United States, and Canada. Collectively they considered the growing use of electronic records by both public and private institutions and the issues that these developments raise for the archival profession. While the views of symposium participants ranged widely, the substance of what was discussed at Gladenbach falls into three broad categories:

(1) general statements concerning technology trends in the work place and their implications for electronic record keeping.[2]

---

1 This paper originated as a component of the Symposium on the Impact of Information Technologies on Information Handling in Offices and Archives, on October 17-19, 1991, sponsored by the Volkswagen Foundation and the Archivschule Marburg. The author wishes to extend his personal thanks to the many distinguished archivists and information managers who attended those sessions, the Volkswagen Foundation, and our host and "Symposium" organizer Dr. Angelika Menne-Haritz.

2 Rick Barry of the World Bank, Tom Finholt of the University of Michigan, and Richard M. Kesner of Babson College dealt with emerging trends in information technology.

(2) personal/institutional histories as to how particular organizations have addressed the issue of electronic records management in an archival setting.[3]

(3) a more contemplative focus as to what all of these technological trends and administrative practices imply for archival theory, training, and ongoing operations.[4]

This author fell into the first category of contributors. In his presentation and in the essay that is presently before the reader, he provides his audience with a view of the emerge office information technology (IT) environment. To do so, he has developed a series of definitions that will assist his audience in establishing a common basis of understanding and communication. He next characterizes the forces of change within the work place and how these are shaping information needs and uses. From this perspective, he then considers the implications of these changes for institutional IT services and hence the challenges faced by those charged with information resource management (IRM). To conclude, the author offers a number of observations and some modest strategies as to how information resource managers in general, and archivists and records managers in particular, might deal with these challenges.

A SELECT VOCABULARY:

To orient the reader for the discussion that follows, it is essential that we position his/her frame of reference away from the more traditional archival framework of concepts and responsibilities and towards a more comprehensive information resource management perspective. With this in mind, the author offers the following terms and definitions for the reader's consideration:

1. **end user** - Also referred to as "customer," "patron," or "constituent," the end user is the **knowledge worker** in the modern organization. IT systems, services and resources must be tailored to the requirements of the end user who in turn addresses through his/her efforts the primary mission of the greater organization.

2. **enterprise** - While "enterprise" may be used interchangeably with "organization" and "institution," it is the preferred term because it conveys action and the creation/delivery of value to the end user. Regardless of the strategic focus of the organization, enterprises must create "value" as perceived by their customers if they are to survive and prosper.

---

3 Victor Bekkers of the Katholieke Universiteit Brabant, H. Reinermann of the Hochschule für Verwatungswissenschaften, Peter Bohl of the Landesarchivdirektion Baden-Württemberg, Michael Cook of the University of Liverpool, and John McDonald of the National Archives of Canada all spoke of their first-hand experiences in the management of electronic records for archival purposes and in the use of automated systems for IRM.

4 Charles Dollar of the National Archives of the United States, Claes Gränström of the Riksarkivet of Sweden, Bruno Delmas of the Ecole des Chartes, and David Bearman of Archives and Museum Informatics raised broader theoretical and professional issues associated with archival electronic records management and the future of the machine-readable record.

3. **information resource management** - the economical and efficient management, servicing, and support of all information (in whatever format) that is of value to the organization. The value-added component of IRM is the information utility's ability to deliver accurate, specific information to the end user in a timely manner.

4. **IRM strategic planning** - IRM strategic planning is a necessary subset of the parent institution's process. It is necessarily shaped by the goals and objectives of the greater organization and must complement the more global directives established in the corporate plan.

5. **information services professional** - While the terms archivist, records manager, librarian, and systems analyst have relevance in today's information technology (IT) environment, the twenty-first century information utility requires the services of cross-trained, highly-integrated staffs of IT professionals to act as facilitators, catalysts for change, standards monitors, and resource managers for complex, user-driven and controlled, information delivery systems.

6. **information utility** - Within any organization, the information utility includes all of those resources, services, and facilities that comprise, process, and deliver information to the end user. More than computer hardware and software, an information utility is an approach to customer service that emphasizes availability, ease of access, economy, efficiency, and accountability to the community.

7. **knowledge** - We often think of "information" in terms of documents, records, files, etc., but these are merely formalized vehicles for the delivery of data to an end user. Historically, these information products were/are self-supporting and generally sufficient in terms of satisfy the needs of the end user. With recent developments in IT, "information" alone is not satisfactory - primarily because there is too much of it and the "products" in question are insufficiently focused and unadaptable. Instead, users seek "knowledge," that is: a higher level of information, at times in multi-media formats, that are tailored and processed to address a specific requirement. Correspondingly, **knowledge tools,** such as artificial intelligence systems, and hyper-text databases, facilitate the manipulation of information to meet end user needs.

8. **knowledge worker** - the end user who employs a wide range of information technologies to draw upon diverse information resources in a variety of formats to address his/her immediate needs through the sophisticated sifting, search, and reassembly of data into highly usable formats.

9. **meta-data** - The term "meta-data" refers to information about information, typically as this relates to electronic data. For example, an electronic spreadsheet's data may be a series of discrete numbers while its meta-data are the formula, formatting instructions, and programming commands that cause the data to appear in a specific manner. Similarly, the meta-data for a graphical representation of corporate financial performance includes information about the assumptions that went into the graph's

analytical model. While the archivist may be able to preserve the informational value (data) of such records, there are currently no easy ways to preserve their evidential (meta-data) value.

10. **strategic planning** - Strategic planning is that process of thought and action that directs the long-term growth of an organization. It focuses upon the clearly defined mission, goals, and objectives of the organization; assesses the available resources to bring these milestones to fruition; and establishes a method of performance measurement. The rigor of the process places considerable demands on management but is essential to corporate prosperity and hence to the interest of all stakeholders (i.e. organization members and those served by the organization).

11. **virtual documents** - Unlike paper or even machine- readable documents that have a tangible presence, virtual documents are information products created out of the confluence of information systems. They exist at a given time due to the instructions of a knowledge worker who has employed an array of information tools and resources to call them into existence. For example, a report on corporate performance may draw upon a number of information resources to produce images in graphical and video formats as well as text. The process, possibly driven by a artificial intelligence tool, creates the document and may recreate it at any given time through a further exercise of the logic or rules of the report generator. Latter iterations of the document may not report the same information because of the changes within the information resources that feed the document.

By way of orientation, examine **Exhibit I.**[5] This exhibit graphically represents the follow of raw data in various media and formats to intermediate data collection and distribution platforms (e.g. databases).[6] From there, it is manipulated by higher-level information processing ("knowledge") tools (i.e. applications) and then transmitted via an array of networks to the desk top of the end user, who in this illustration is either a living person or an automated process. The ultimate delivery of "knowledge" as defined above may then lead to specific, informed actions.

As described here, the entire set of transactions in **Exhibit I** constitutes modes of information resource management and use within the modern organization. The institutional context and corporate culture within which people work defines the unique character of these processes. Like the role of IRM itself, the modern organization is also transforming in light of

---

5 Exhibit I was prepared by Richard Wilson, Manager of Multi-Media Production, Information Technology and Services Division, Babson College at the request of Jerome Kanter, Director of the Center for Information Management Studies, Babson College.

6 For a consideration of current and emerging information media and formats, see James Martin, *Viewdata and the Information Society*, Englewood Cliffs/NJ: Prentice-Hall, 1982). See also Richard M. Kesner, *Automation for Archivists and Records Managers*, Chicago: American Library Association, 1984, pp. 12-31, and United Nations, Advisory Committee for Coordination of Information Systems, *Management of Electronic Records: Issues and Guidelines*, New York: United Nations, 1990.

Exhibit I

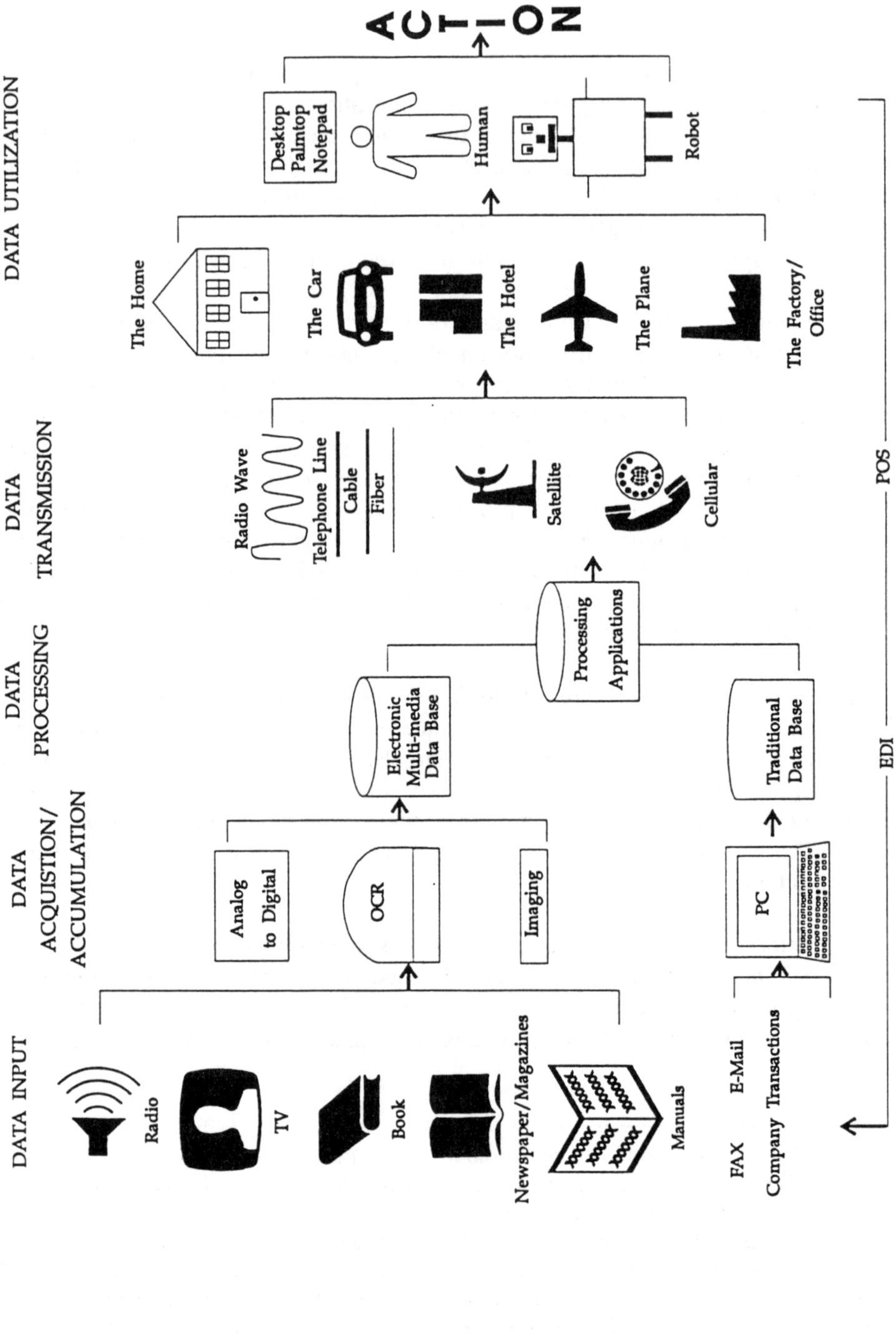
DATA INPUT
Radio
TV
Book
Newspaper/Magazines
Manuals
FAX
E-Mail
Company Transactions
DATA ACQUISTION/ ACCUMULATION
Analog to Digital
OCR
Imaging
PC
DATA PROCESSING
Electronic Multi-media Data Base
Traditional Data Base
Processing Applications
DATA TRANSMISSION
Radio Wave
Telephone Line
Cable
Fiber
Satellite
Cellular
DATA UTILIZATION
The Home
The Car
The Hotel
The Plane
The Factory/ Office
Desktop
Palmtop
Notepad
Human
Robot
ACTION
EDI
POS

technological innovation and adaptation. To better understand the forces at work and what they mean to the archivist and records manager, we will next explore the evolving corporate environment.

ORGANIZATIONAL ENVIRONMENTS AND IRM

As we proceed towards the twenty-first century, organizations will become less bureaucratic, more complex, and global in their orientation. Their management structures will flatten with senior executives playing a larger role in the direct management of people and processes. These players will map out the strategic programs for their organization, employing external alliances, resource sharing, outsourcing, and new information technologies to enhance their overall performance. Middle management will grow thin and serve primarily as a group of technical specialists developing policies, procedures, and applications for the rank and file. The vast majority of those remaining will directly contribute to value creation in terms of either products or services provided to the customers of the organization. In this more fluid, less hierarchical environment, most if not all employees will have both information resource management and production responsibilities.[7]

Information technologies have and will continue to play a central role in this restructuring of the enterprise. They facilitate streamlining and encourage a more entrepreneurial operating mode among managers now freed from dependence on others for vital information. They also tend to foster linkages with external global partners. Operationally, IT's allow senior management involvement in day-to-day business processes and communication with players throughout the organization. Furthermore, the ubiquitous and increasingly user-friendly nature of emerging information technologies has meant that line managers rather than technologists have taken charge of the resource, refocusing IRM requirements on core services and strategic business objectives.[8] The proliferation of IT and information resources throughout the organization is illustrated in **Exhibit II.** No functional area is without its IRM responsibilities.

As a result, information service providers within the modern organization are concerned less with the efficient and economical storage of data, and more with the proactive delivery of knowledge. Thus, the IRM shopping list includes such products as: intelligent, personal computer-based tools for end users; future-focused decision support systems; business simulation software; and expert systems.[9] Throughout, the objective of these IT scenarios is to empower

---

[7] See, for example, Charles R. Morris, *The Coming Global Boom*, New York: Bantam Books, 1990; John Naisbitt / Patricia Aburdene, *Megatrends 2000*, New York: William Morrow, 1990, and Tom Peters, *Thriving on Chaos*, New York: Knopf, 1987.

[8] Paul L. Tom, *Managing Information as a Corporate Resource*, 2nd ed., New York: Harper-Collins, 1991. See also James C. Emery, *The Strategic Imperative*, Oxford: Oxford University Press, 1987.

[9] For an excellent summary of what leading, international, chief information officers are looking for, see The Index Group, *Critical Issues of Information Systems Management for 1991*, Boston: The Index Group, 1991. See also The Index Group, *Europe in 1992, Winning Through Technology*, Indications (Fall 1988).

Exhibit II

The I/T Impact on Documentation

The Organizational Disbursement of I/T's

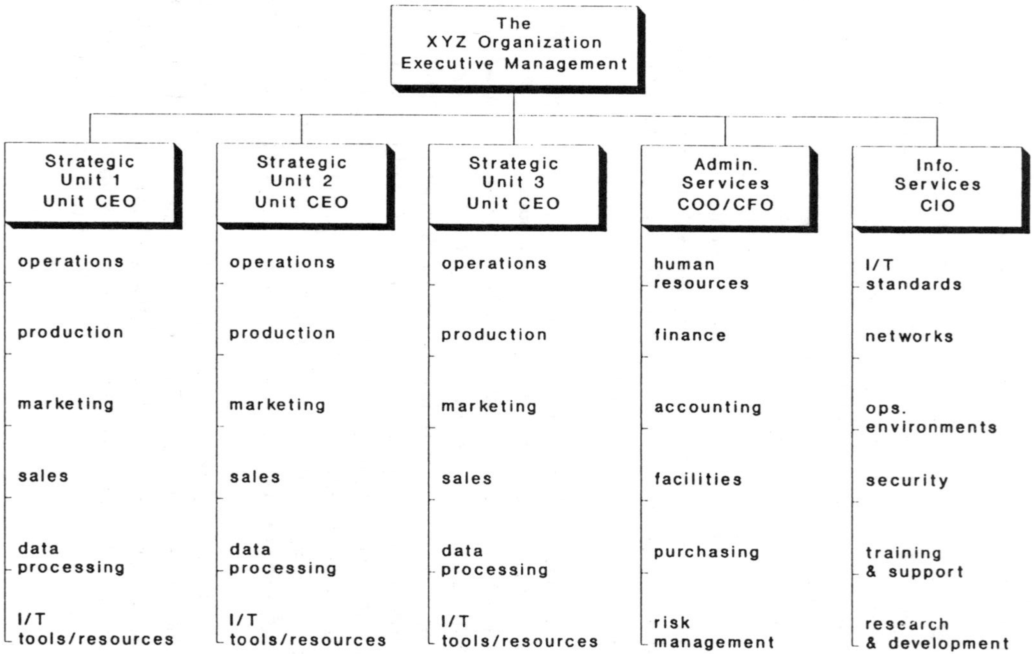

prepared by RMK Associates

the end user and to put this person in touch with the appropriate data to compete today and plan for tomorrow.

To manage the enterprise-wide use of information technologies and services, organizations are currently experimenting with a number of different reporting/management structures. The societal forces influencing these changes are easily discerned. In the first place, demographic shifts in both the work force and the customer base of many organizations have necessitated a reconsideration of IRM products and services. Today's economic climate with its accompanying resource scarcity is forcing overall corporate restructurings and a critical review of expensive operations, such as the IT functions. The technologies themselves are changing rapidly obliging those in charge to look for new opportunities and to rethink old strategies. Lastly, a new generation of skilled and knowledgeable IT users is exerting pressure on information services to perform and deliver as never before.

In response, many organizations are moving towards the development of an information utility (I/U) under the aegis of a chief information officer (CIO). Structurally, the I/U serves as an administrative umbrella for a mix of IT enterprises that may include: libraries, archives, records management programs, data centers, networks, technology training centers, media production and operations, and end user documentation. However, the heart of the I/U concept has less to do with departmental structure than it has to do with service. As its name suggests, the I/U exists to provide capabilities to its customers. Through computer hardware and software, communications networks, documentation, and training, the I/U seeks to empower its users to exploit all available information resources. Through direct participation in the strategic planning process, those who manage the I/U work with their customers to identify opportunities for the deployment of emerging technologies and the creation of new data resources.[10]

In focusing its IT capabilities in the I/U, the enterprise is making a statement as to the importance of IT within the organization. The CIO usually sits in the organization's senior decision making body and is instrumental in the development of internal and external linkages among information user communities. On the other hand, the I/U does not "own" corporate data and all of the associated systems and services. These tend to be the property of key I/U customers. By contrast, the CIO and his/her team facilitate, coordinate, and support the structures that deliver the data and enrich its value to the end user. I/U personnel are also responsible for the protection of the network and overall data integrity.

---

[10] The author has written extensively on this subject. See Richard M. Kesner, *Microcomputer Applications in Libraries*, Westport/CT: Greenwood Press, 1984, pp. 49-80; and *Information Systems: A Strategic Approach to Planning and Implementation*, Chicago: American Library Association, 1988, pp. 1-71; and Jerry Kanter / Richard M. Kesner, *The CIO/GIO as Catalyst and Facilitator: Building the Information Utility to Meet Global Challenges*, in: Shailendra Palvia et al. (eds.), *The Global Issues of Information Technology Management*, Harrisburg,/PA: Idea Group, 1991, pp. 465-483. See also F. Warren McFarlan / James L. McKenney, *Corporate Information Systems Management*, Homewood/IL: Irwin, 1983; Charles Wiseman, *Strategic Information Systems*, Homewood/IL: Irwin, 1988; and Anne Woodsworth, *Managing Information Technology on Campus*, Chicago: American Library Association, 1991.

Thus, the typical information utility must function in an environment that is both centralized and decentralized. On the one hand, it maintains and enhances the organization's core IT infrastructure, including: data centers, networks, data resources, and so forth. It also provides a wide range of user support functions, coordinates corporate-wide IRM activities, and polices system standards. On the other hand, it promotes user ownership and maintenance of data resources, client self-sufficiency in the exploitation of IT tools, and technology planning at the operating unit level.

The structure of the information utility and the role of the CIO may be illustrated by contrasting a more traditional organization with one employing the I/U model. For this example, let us consider the "XYZ Corporation" **(Exhibit III).** In this illustration the information service components of the organization are disbursed among various operating units. For example, "records management" is under "Administration" while "machine-readable records" are under I/S. Similarly, IRM functions are to be found everywhere. Clearly this more traditional structure does not afford opportunities arising from the combination of complementary IT services, such as the library, media, and computer services.[11]

Our second example assumes the structure of an I/U **(Exhibit IV - macro-level and Exhibit V - micro-level).** Here IT services are reorganized to take advantage of the synergies absent from the previous example. At the same time, it allows for the streamlining and downsizing of the IT team as well as the ability to focus the investment in people, hardware, and software where it will have the greatest impact. Furthermore, in this scenario the CIO is now a player of senior executive rank. He/she will therefore participate in the institution's strategic planning process and hence learn first hand how the development of the information utility can best address the organization's overall goals and objectives. Similarly, as the direction of the parent institution changes, the CIO has the advanced warning and flexibility to redirect I/U resources accordingly.

Unfortunately, the appointment of a CIO and the reorganization of IT will not in and of themselves lead to a successful implementation. Ultimately, the corporate culture of the I/U team must also change. Individually, players must become more flexible and proactive in their approach to their respective assignments. Collectively, they must commit themselves to a total quality, which in turn means an acceptance of the team's success over individual recognition.[12] They must also act entrepreneurially, seeking out opportunities to maximize the benefit of the I/U through the innovative use of new technologies and skillful change management.

This last characteristic is particularly important in an environment where team work will cut across organizational lines, where users "own" the data and may also control their own

---

[11] For two informative anthologies on this subject, see Brian L. Hawkins (ed.), *Organizing and Managing Information Resources on Campus*, McKinney/TX: Academic Computing Publications, 1989; and Caroline Arms (ed.), *Campus Networking Strategies*, Maynard/MA: Digital Press, 1988.

[12] John A. Buckland et al., *Total Quality Management in Information Services*, Boston: QED, 1991; David A. Garvin, *Competing on the Eight Dimensions of Quality*, in: Harvard Business Review, November/December 1987, pp: 101-109; and Peter Linkow, *Is Your Culture Ready for Total Quality?*, in: Quality Progress, November 1989, pp. 12-14.

Exhibit III: XYZ CORPORATION
TYPICAL ORGANIZATIONAL STRUCTURE
(INFORMATION SERVICE COMPONENTS)

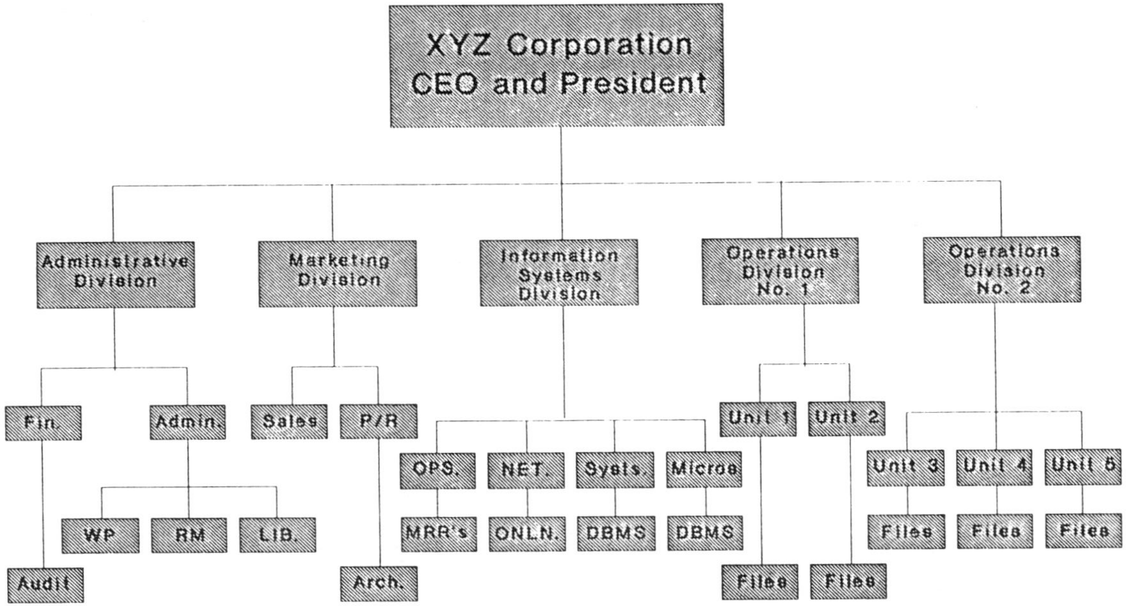

Exhibit IV: XYZ CORPORATION
INTERGRATED INFORMATION SYSTEMS & SERVICES DIVISION

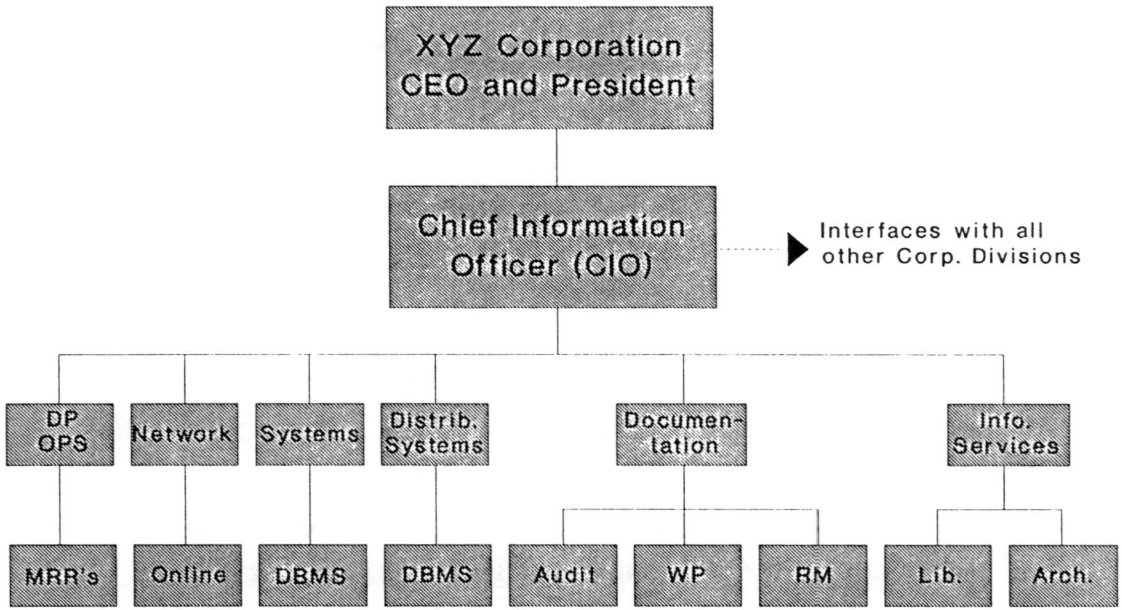

Exhibit V

The I/T Impact on Documentation

The Information Utility: Components

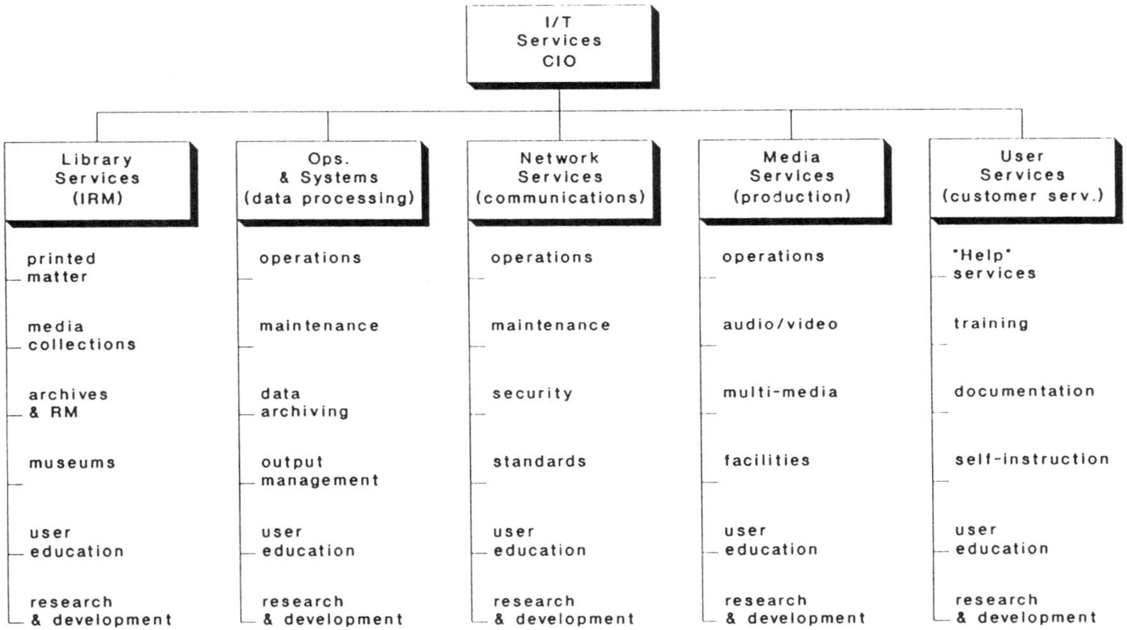

prepared by RMK Associates

hardware and software, and where those in the trenches not the technologists are the experts in specific applications. Under these conditions, process management will require the nurturing of alliances, where the common ground is defined by corporate strategic objectives and personal relationships rather than a rigorous reporting structure. Indeed, we are entering an era where organizational "authority" is being replaced by informal, complex, overlapping, reciprocal arrangements. In this setting, action steps will emerge from negotiation processes where all participants believe that they have a stake and will therefore benefit from a positive outcome. Similarly, the effective manager will be measured in terms of his/her success as a negotiator, facilitator, catalyst, and team builder.[13]

TO SERVE THE KNOWLEDGE WORKER:

Given this view of the modern organization and IRM operations, it is clear that the archivist must possess a different skill base than has hitherto been the case. Through formal training today, the typical archivist learns technical skills, such as collection accessioning and processing, preservation, description, and reference services. But, at least within the United States, he/she is never trained as a manager (even in the traditional sense of that term). Those who run successful programs have learned their management skills through practical experience and self-training or as the understudies to the rare management mentors of the profession.

The time has come to redefine the archival profession's educational goals and objectives. In our efforts to do so, we must define the training requirements and critical success factors for the archivist and records manager operating in the information age. Here is the author's short list of recommendations in this regard:

1. **Management Style and Leadership**
   Throughout this essay, the author has indicated the process management qualities vital to the success of an information services professional. These include: (a) a strategic focus, (b) flexibility in addressing tactical issues, (c) a people- as well as a task-oriented project management style, (d) the ability to delegate and manage through others, (e) ruling through consensus, and (f) a team approach to problem solving.

2. **Organization and Structure of the IT Function**
   The archivist will never be effective unless he/she and the IT group as a whole are appropriately positioned within the larger organization. First and foremost this means that the archives function within the context of the I/U model and play an integral role in the organization's IRM. Organizationally, the core IT group reporting to the CIO should include centralized MIS services (including archives, media, user support, et

[13] On the theme of influencing others within a complex organizational structure, nothing compares with Allan R. Cohen / David L. Bradford, *Influence Without Authority*, New York: John Wiley, 1990. See also *Managing for Excellence: The Guide to Developing High Performance in Contemporary Organizations*, New York: Wiley, 1984, by the same authors.

al.), network management, a standards committee, and a technology review team. IRM applications support could report to the CIO but will more likely report to the respective operational heads who employ these systems.[14]

3. **Skill Base: Individual and Team**
The archivist need not be a technologist but he/she must be conversant in computer and telecommunications technologies. More importantly, the archivist must have the vision to appreciate the potential uses of emerging IT and how they may benefit his/her own operation as well as the I/U enterprise as a whole. The archivist must also have a sufficient knowledge of the organization, its product lines/services, and its functional (IT) requirements.

4. **Total Quality Project Management**
The archivist must implement and enforce a total quality program with its focus on excellence in individual and team performance. To complement this effort, the entire culture of the archival organization must become team oriented usually implying an overall reduction in reporting levels, flexibility in project assignments, and rotating team leadership. This approach will foster a sense of ownership and commitment among participants that will lead to improved performance results.

5. **The Environment**
Rather than viewing the environment as an obstacle to success, the archivist should treat it as an ever expanding reservoir of opportunities. In this context, the archivist should turn to resources outside his/her own organization for guidance and support. For example, he/she should develop strategic alliances with institutions of higher education, research centers, and/or professional associations whose interests parallel those of the organization's IT programs. Instead of relying entirely upon home-grown solutions, the archivist might rely more heavily on outsourcing for specific expertise or on the cooperation of hardware and software vendors. Admittedly there risks associated with the development and nurturing of these and similar alliances. However, in the long run, such an approach will establish a reliable support network for the organization's IRM functions.

6. **Technology Transfer and Change Implementation**
In the area of technology transfer, the archivist needs to become more creative in his/her exploitation of procedures and systems developed in cognate disciplines. Finally, perhaps the most critical success factor of all, the archivist must become an agent/prophet of change within his/her organization. The archivist must assist in the evolution of a corporate culture that is receptive to change and a work force that is willing to forego old work habits in light of technological innovations. In this context, information will be viewed as the life blood of the organization and the archivist as part of a highly skilled and dedicated team devoted to its enrichment and support.

---

14 See footnote 9.

This additional set of skills will not be required of all immediately. However, as their institutions move towards a greater dependence on electronic and optical media for records creation, storage, and distribution, archivists and records managers will need these capabilities in balance with their more traditional expertise as they address the needs of end users.[15] Perhaps the most vexing of these challenges involves the servicing of the knowledge worker and his/her dependence on "virtual" documents for information sharing. The unique character of these records poses great difficulties for the archivist in particular because at present there is no way to preserve the context and in most instances the meta-data of these electronic documents. To clarify this point, let us examine the role of the knowledge worker and the nature of the virtual document in more detail.

THE KNOWLEDGE WORKER AND THE VIRTUAL DOCUMENT:

With reference again to **Exhibit I,** the work process of the typical electronic office may be summarized as follows: (1) raw data is created/collected - "input," (2) the data is enhanced through value-added services - "data processing applications," (3) the enhanced data - "information" - is distributed via electronic networks to the desk top, (4) the information is then received and manipulated by a worker or a work process, and (5) the resulting creation is a "knowledge product or process that exists for a specific purpose in time.

To achieve these ends, the knowledge worker needs access to a complex array of information resources, including: printed publications of all kinds, information systems documentation, bibliographic and other information utilities, proprietary and public databases, and the thoughts and voices of colleagues. But access alone is not enough. To be "empowered" and indeed to add value to the information at hand, the knowledge worker requires independent data processing capabilities, including: a personal computer work station with local and wide-area network connectivity, relational database tools, a multi-media receipt and transmission capacity, and even perhaps artificial intelligence-based IRM applications.

With these capabilities, each knowledge worker will develop his/her own personalized electronic information archives. However, unlike a more traditional paper or electronic record-based archives, the knowledge worker's holdings will not always include the data itself. Instead, these archives will possess "virtual" documents, that is: record shells that encompass the logic and rules to create documents out of the sundry information resources and tools at the worker's disposal. These "documents" do not exist in a tangible form (hence "virtual") but may be recalled and reconstructed at any time by executing the rules that called them into being. Since they are dependent upon other information resources that change over time, these virtual documents may have a slightly (or dramatically) different appearance each time they are summoned from the knowledge worker's archives.

---

15 See Richard M. Kesner, *Automated Information Management: Is There a Role for the Archivist in the Office of the Future*, in: Archivaria 19 (1984/85), pp. 162-172; *Whither Archivy? Some Personal Observations Addressed to Those Who Would Fiddle While Rome Burns*, in: Archivaria 20 (1985), pp. 142-148; and *Information Systems: A Strategic Approach to Planning and Implementation*, Chicago: American Library Association, 1988, pp. 1-13.

Harkening back to and paraphrasing the comments of one of the author's distinguished colleagues at the Gladenbach Symposium, "the real important information in contemporary electronic records is not the transactions themselves but rather the context and rules governing those transactions." In other words, each iteration of a virtual document is not anywhere as valuable from an archival standpoint as the record shell that causes that document to come into existence. The author apologizes for failing to do justice to the carefully developed analysis and arguments of his colleagues that arrive at this conclusion. None the less, the fact remains that from an archival perspective, the long-term value of most virtual documents will be evidentury rather than informational.

While established archival theory may be applied with considerable success to this new information environment, the practical implications of the virtual document to archivists and records managers are daunting. How are these information service professionals to cope? At this point, the author can only offer a series of strategic recommendations that must be field tested for their applicability.

1. Archivists and records managers must involve themselves in the initial processes of data structure design and collection. As part of this team, they must work to ensure that the evidential value (i.e. record shell logic and rules) are documented and preserved.

2. Through their national and international professional bodies, archivists and records managers must involve themselves in the standards boards that establish standards for all seven layers of the data communications typology model as applied to electronic information exchange.

3. These IRM professionals must also enlist the support of their colleagues in cognate disciplines through a process of systematic communication and education concerning archival issues pertaining to electronic records.

4. Last but not least, they must somehow educate knowledge workers themselves in archival principles so that these end users in turn will follow archival rules in the creation of information resources and the preservation of electronic documents of all types and descriptions.

The picture drawn in this essay of the information environment and knowledge worker is very real. The problems posed for the archivist and records manager are not widely recognized or perceived as pressing. It therefore comes as no surprise to the author that his readers may find his concluding recommendations impossible to contemplate. The fact remains that as a profession, archivists are just becoming aware of these problems and the significant barriers that obstruct progress. If the principles of archival administration are to be respected and applied to virtual documents, archivists must rethink the means of achieving their professional ends in a world of multi-media-based, network-distributed, information resources.

ARCHIVAL REQUIREMENTS FOR FUTURE DOCUMENTATION IN ADMINISTRATION

By Peter Bohl

INTRODUCTION

A short story to introduce the topic of the presentation:

Imagine that in the year 2020 a user will come to the archives to look for documents concerning the construction, operation, shut-down and demolition of a certain atomic power plant. The archivist responsible leads the user, who is equipped with a laptop, to an unoccupied work station with terminal and a keyboard. The archivist points out the sheet of instruction for gaining access to the archives and says that he will gladly help the user if he has problems using the machine or the software or if he needs any other assistance with his enquiries. He then gives the user his electronic mail address and says goodbye. After his application to use the facilities, which contains a brief description of his research subject, has been electronically processed and approved, a list of record groups containing information about the subject of his enquiries is provided on the screen in a new menu. For each individual record group, the reference number, the provenance, the recording media of information, the access date and the finding aids are given. He chooses a record group and is informed that some of the records are on paper, others on machine-readable recording media and that the inventory is stored in a data base. He calls the finding aid and looks for entries that interest him assisted by an information retrieval system. He marks them and copies them onto a file provided by the program for the user. Because the entries and the descriptions of what the data base contains are very detailed, he very quickly obtains an overall picture of the information content of the records. In some of them, especially those concerning measuring techniques, cartography and statistics, there is a note to the effect that they are on electronic recording media which are kept in a computer centre. Access to this information is achieved directly from the archives via a data network. As the user wants to look through his documents in the peace and quiet of his own home and also wants to prepare himself for a second visit to the archives, he copies the information in the inventory via an interface into the storage of his laptop. He thus finishes his day's work in the archives.

If a future user will take advantage of the facilities described above, a certain amount of preparation work has to be done first, both in the archives and in administration. In the following, I will go into the needs of the archives department for the use of modern information technology in administration. In administration, conditions must be created which make it possible for the information produced by administration to be made accessible to and usable by the archives when the information is no longer needed by the government agency and when it is of archival value.

As a starting point and a basis for my arguments for an administrative method of documentation which takes account of archive requirements, I refer to the automatic dataprocessing facilities in Baden-Württemberg which either already exist or are projected for the future. I can probably assume that not all the participants in the symposium know about the automatic data-processing facilities which are already in use or are planned in Baden-Württemberg. In the first part of my presentation, I will therefore briefly describe to what extent information technology has been planned and introduced in the public administration offices of Baden-Württemberg. The archival requirements for the use of electronic data-processing facilities in registries and documentation will be formulated with regard to the functions of the archives which are defined by law. These requirements are also based on the knowledge gained from working together with those responsible in administration and industry and from the analysis of the stated needs regarding the data-processing facilities and descriptions of programs.

1. THE DEVELOPMENT OF ELECTRONIC DATA PROCESSING IN PUBLIC ADMINISTRATION IN BADEN-WÜRTTEMBERG

The government of Baden-Württemberg recognised the significance of automatic data-processing for public administration at an early stage and supports the introduction and the use of modern information technology.[1] Since, however, there was no central coordinating office for the use of this technology in the early years, there was a wild proliferation of software and hardware. In 1971 a coordinating committee was set up whose agreement had to be obtained to any new acquisition of computer systems and to any employment of computer programs in state administration. It was also intended to serve as a medium for the exchange of experience among users. In spite of this committee, different hardware and software systems were purchased which were incompatible with each other. Problems in one area were therefore usually solved in isolation from other areas.

Computer systems were built up in order to perform those tasks required of them within each department. This was done according to the tasks of administration and the possibilities offered by technology. At the beginning, the processing of mass data was carried out in large computer centres.

At the end of 1983, a team of three management consultancies was commissioned by the government to prepare and present a report developping a total concept for the unified structure of information technology in public administration.

---

[1] VERWALTUNG 2000, Schriftenreihe der Stabsstelle Verwaltungsstruktur, Information und Kommunikation, Band 1, Gesamtkonzeption, die Ziele und ihre Umsetzung, Stuttgart 1990; Band 3, Bürokommunikation in der Landesverwaltung Baden-Württemberg, Stuttgart 1990; Band 5, Landesverwaltungsnetz Baden-Württemberg, Stuttgart 1991. Hermann Bannasch, Archiv und Registratur auf dem Weg in die Informationsgesellschaft. Die Reform des Registraturwesens und die Einführung elektronischer Bürokommunikation in der Landesverwaltung Baden-Württemberg, in: Der Archivar 39, 1986, Sp. 304-309; Hermann Bannasch, Archive im Netzwerk der Büroautomation. Das Beispiel "Landessystemkonzept Baden-Württemberg", in: Der Archivar 43, 1990, Sp. 96-101

The report given at the end of 1984 contained the basis, the principles and the conditions for the development of a state-system plan, in German *Landessystemkonzept* (LSK).[2] The concept encompasses all important details concerning the introduction and use of modern information technology. The word "system" refers to the structuring into different components; on the one hand the total scenario which discribes the organisational and technical guidelines and consequences, and, on the other hand, the individual scenarios which contain the concrete and practical realisation of the total scenario in administration.

The total scenario is of decisive importance for the realisation of the plan and the introduction of modern information technology. The aims are decided in the cabinet but putting them into reality is up to the individual departments. Newly set-up central institutions guarantee concepts and plans which are general and not limited to any individual department. The drawing-up of a total budget for information technology to finance state-system plan allows more flexible planning and investments. The organisation of information technology is the job of the departments.[3] The organisational guidelines provide a framework for the technical realisation of the plans. The technical guidelines are set down in order to make sure that the individual components of the system can communicate with each other. The standards required by the responsible institutions of the state, the basic pre-conditions for the integration of different systems, are orientated to the international OSI norms (Open Systems Interconnection Reference Model) of the International Organisation for Standardisation (ISO). Because some of the necessary standards are not yet available, manufacturer standards and industry standards have to be referred to. For the interchange of electronic data, the federal post service will be made use of. Starting from the existing information technology of the agencies, the future equipment will be unified in accordance with nationally valid guidelines.

At the same time as the total scenario was developped and laid down, ten individual scenarios were determined which should be regarded as examples of the application of information technology. These can be enhanced and extended if necessary. Fields of use for automatic data processing are as follows, some of which are planned, some of which already employ data processing methods:

- a network concept for state administration,
- (wide area network),
- budget management system,
- office automation in the offices of counties,
- administration (Regierungspräsidien),

---

2 Diebold-Dornier-IKOSS, Erstellung eines Landessystemkonzepts für einen rationellen und wirtschaftlichen Einsatz der Informations- und Kommunikationstechniken in der öffentlichen Verwaltung des Landes Baden-Württemberg, 1984

3 Gemeinsame Richtlinien der Ministerien zur Durchführung von Projekten auf dem Gebiet der Informations- und Kommunikationstechnik in der Landesverwaltung (luK-Projektrichtlinien) vom 25. September 1989, in: Gemeinsames Amtsblatt des Landes Baden-Württemberg 1989, S. 1162-1166; Richtlinien des Staatsministeriums Baden-Württemberg für die Planung, Budgetierung und Koordination des Einsatzes der Informations- und Kommunikationstechnik in der Landesverwaltung (luK-Planungsrichtlinien) in der geänderten Fassung vom 1. Juni 1987, in: Gemeinsames Amtsblatt des Landes Baden-Württemberg 1987, S. 346-349, 593-607.

- office automation in the offices of law courts,
- and public prosecutors (Staatsanwaltschaften),
- documentation and records management,
- pollution control information systems,
- (Umweltinformationssystem),
- personnel management systems,
- government management systems.

Not all the listed scenarios were realised by the middle of 1991. In spite of considerable investment, especially in the internal equipping of offices with modern office technology, some projects are still at the beginning stage. The number of screens at work stations varies a great deal from government agency to government agency. In some sectors the final stage of the projected goal in equipment has already been reached.

The employment of office automation systems is a major feature of the state-system plan. The tasks of public administration have become more complex and the carrying out of tasks concerning several subject-areas at once has become more important. Therefore the use of office automation systems is being extended even further. Tasks are carried out in a decentralised fashion with the help of technology at the work station from where access can be obtained via a terminal to internal and external data base systems and information systems. Not only data, but also text and graphics are procesed and later pictures, geometric data and language will also be processed. Some of the work stations are connected up to an information network which extends over the whole country so that the exchange of information takes place at a much faster rate. The exchange of information or documents between different office communication systems is ensured by prescribed standards such as SAN (System Network Architecture), DCA (Document Content Architecture) and DIA (Document Interchange Architecture). With regard to the employment of data base systems, a relational data base system and the data base language SQL (Structured Query Language), which normally belongs to it, are always to be used. Electronic document transfer to different public authorities takes place via the state administration network.

As well as the above-named projects of the state of Baden-Württemberg, there are further applications of information technology in public administration which are not dealt with by the organisational and technical guidelines of the state-system plan. These methods of processing have often been in use for several years and are employed for processing mass data, the production of statistics, the carrying-out and the monitoring of fiscal, business management and administrative measures. In addition, in agencies and at individual work stations, there are applications of information technology which have been developed by employees. These methods, employed in different departments and at all levels of administration, do not normally correspond to the above-mentioned norms and can only be used in conjunction with manufacturer-specific hardware and software. The number of such applications of information technology in state administration is not known exactly. In order to find out this number, the state archives administration of Baden-Württemberg has started a questionnaire survey.

2. CONSEQUENCES OF INTRODUCING INFORMATION TECHNOLOGY FOR ADMINISTRATION

With the introduction of modern technology in public administration not only the way in which tasks are carried out changes, i.e. quicker, more efficiently, more relevantly and more to the point, as it is described in the plans and descriptions for using information technology. The structure of information handling is also transformed and this transformation is in contradiction to traditional ideas. Information on which administrative activities are based, is no longer kept in case files, case papers and records, but is stored on recording media which cannot be read without the help of technical aids. Information no longer has to be kept in the office which uses it, but can be geographically far away in a computer centre which is connected to the producing government agency via a standing line.

The possibility of storing, processing and altering internal and external information, finding it again, and making it available for the people interested in, without loss of time, requires a different method of organization which is suited to electronic data processing. The working procedures and the processing and exchange of information have to be organized differently.

In this connection, there are basically three different applications of information processing systems:

1. Automation for extensive mass procedures such as in tax administration, calculation of salaries, and legal reminders, all of which are based on a fixed administration procedure with a relatively simple structure whereby large numbers of similar case papers are produced.

2. Office automation, office communication systems, records management and registry handling systems in which processing methods are applied which change the structural and procedural organization of a government agency, the way in which office products are created and handled, the general office methods and the registry system. These changes influence the future consistency of records.

3. Information systems, database systems which, because of their extensiveness, are also mass procedures. However, because they are complex and because it is necessary to integrate the most different kinds of information, such as geometric, graphic, numerical and alphanumerical data, they have a complicated, networked and multidimensional structure which is typical of expert systems. They wil usually replace methods of documentation, which are unclear and difficult to use, and also, to a certain extent, the case files in traditional registries and manual devices.

Each of these applications requires an independent and exactly-defined programming and organisational framework which is adapted to carrying out the relevant tasks. The structure of the stored data, their extent, the way in which they are handled, processed and altered are to be regulated by the responsible department. Data security and data integrity and the associated authenticity of records are essential preconditions for employing automatic data processing procedures to carry out tasks in public administration.

It is unrealistic to assume that government agencies will introduce processing methods which contradict legal requirements, the laws of administrative procedure, only to keep up with modern trends. The introduction of modern information technology in administration would already be more advanced if the computer programs developped for industry, especially in the field of office automation, could have taken over without any changes. As well as the development of programs by public offices with their own resource for special official applications, there is the possibility of cooperation with software suppliers who can help in the further development and adaptation of their products for use in public administration. It is to be seen that they are not determined by technical feasibility at the moment that determines which automatic data-processing programs are used, but by the fact that administration offices draw up concrete catalogues of requirements, orientated to the existing legal requirements and to the recognised necessities in administration practice.

3. CONSEQUENCES FOR THE WORK OF ARCHIVES

The introduction of modern information technology in administration necessitates that the archivists reorganise their work. For each of the three above-mentioned applications of automatic data processing (mass procedures, office automation and information systems), they have to develop their own appraisal criteria and transfer procedures. The life cycle, the meaningfulness, the usability in archives, and future accessibility of information are to be taken into account when appraising such information. As long as the long-term preservation of data on machine-readable recording media has not been ensured and the technical preconditions for the preservation and accessibility of such recording media are lacking, procedures of appraisal and transfer have to be applied which prevent gaps in the information from occurring.

1. With regard to **mass procedures**, a representative selection should be made which is put into the archives on analog recording media (paper, microfilm or microfiche). In Baden-Württemberg at the moment, with regard to the public utility files, a selective recording of the letters O and T is being carried out; for other records concerning people, the records of the letters D, O and T have been selected.

2. With regard to the processing procedures of **office automation** in the field of registry handling systems, the state-archives administration department was able to come to an agreement with the people responsible for the introduction of computer programs in administration and with the manufacturing companies. They agreed that archival requirements were to be taken into account during the development of programs. The retention periods of records will be supervised electronically. The disposal lists will be drawn up by the processing system when necessary. The data obtained during handling of records in registry will be transferred to the archives in machine-readable form in order to make it easier for the documents to be included and entered in the archives. To this end, the electronic registry finding-aids are given in a software-independent structured form. Since the transfer of digitalized records to the archives is a problem which has still not been solved, the administration has decided that all

documents must be available printed on paper before they are handed over. This guarantees that the archives can temporarily accept records on analog storage media.

3. The data stored in **data bases** and **information systems** are causing great problems for the archives at the moment. The complexity, the multiplicity of possible connections, and the continuous bringing-up-to-date of the information necessitate new criteria of appraisal and transferal procedures. As long as the technical preconditions for the long-term retention of data on recording media are not fulfilled and the financial, technical and personnel facilities for the archives are not provided, information cannot be received by the archives in machine-readable form. At the moment, it is only possible in the archives to record selected data on analog recording media at a date agreed with the person managing the data file.

In order to improve this presently unsatisfying state of affairs, certain steps have to be taken by the archives and also by the administration.

4. WHAT ARCHIVISTS REQUIRE OF THOSE RESPONSIBLE FOR THE DEVELOPMENT AND USE OF NEW TECHNOLOGY

Before the requirements of archives can be put to those responsible in administration and industry, it is necessary for the archivist to gain some basic knowledge of electronic data processing. The archivist who is concerned with automatic data processing must not be able to design and build a computer. Extensive programming skills are not necessary, too. What, however, he has to master are the most important basic concepts of automatic data processing. Only if the archivist, the government agency consultant for automatic data processing and the representative of the company are speaking the same language, the archivist is able to make his problems clear.

The first and most important thing the archivist requires from administration is that the archives are informed about the planning and any intended introduction of new information technology in administration. What they have to say must be listened to and they must take part in the development of any programs which concern archives. When doing this work together, organisational and hardware and software aspects must be taken into account as well.

For the archivist, not only contact with registrars and, possibly, organization managers is important. He must also get in touch with the responsible consultants, the automatic data processing specialists and the manufacturers before or at least during the introduction of modern information technology. This must be done to make sure that the concerns and requirements of archives are sufficiently stressed and satisfied. The committees set up for the introduction and use of modern information technology must be supported and advised by the archives in imposing the following guidelines:

1. **strategic guidelines** which provide a long-term safeguard for the use of information technology and the transfer of information from the government agencies to the archives:

   - consequential use of manufacturer-independent solutions, thus guaranteeing future security

   - keeping to international standards with regard to hardware and software

   - ensuring the compatibility, portability and interoperability of systems

   - use of open systems which prevent obstacles to the program, and allow data transfer and interchange within networks

   - standardisation of processing methods.

2. **organisational guidelines** which regulate the use of information technology, office automation systems and electronic registry in the agency and allow for suitable appraisal by the archives:

   - office procedure and conditions of access

   - the processing of records in the government agency

   - the documentation and registration of stages in the processing of information

   - data security, data integrity and the completeness of the data

   - the conversion of documents/information into files and records

   - files and records management in accordance with a standardized filing plan system

   - the uniformity of recording media (analog or digital)

   - the preservation of original documents, in spite of digitalization by scanning

   - the avoiding of redundant documents

3. guidelines which concretize the cooperation between administration and archives within the framework of the requirements of archive law:

   - The archives register the applications used in administration.

   - The archives are supported by the administration in the recording of machine-readable data by the automatic announcement of newly introduced applications.

- At an early stage, the archives appraise the machine-readable information produced during data processing, i.e. before the retention period of records has expired.

- The appraisal takes place in reference to the descriptions provided by the government agency of the application programs, the data contents the record structures and in reference to which tasks are carried out by electronic processing methods. If this information is not sufficient for a final appraisal, an autopsy is carried out on the spot.

- If the information on machine-readable media has **no** archival value, the archives issues an approval, which is valid indefinitely, to destroy it and this approval remains in force as long as no changes are made to the electronic process. The records on paper, microfilm or microfiche are subjected to a special appraisal.

- If the information is of permanent value, the archives department determines how and onto which recording media the records are transferred. Electronic recording media are then only to be transferred to the archives if long-term preservation and accessibility is guaranteed. If this is not the case, the records must be printed by the agency on long-life paper, microfilm or microfiche even if information is lost thereby.

- The registry data which is stored using office automation systems and electronic registry systems must be passed on to the archives on machine-readable recording media or via the wide area network. This must be done to facilitate appraisal, transfer, archival communication and description of the records to be dealt with. The data must be structured in such way that it can be further processed in the archives.

- By means of the strategies and organisational guidelines already described, it is ensured that transfer of electronic records to the archives and access to them is guaranteed.

- If the technical preconditions in the archives for the transfer, storage, processing and accessibility of machine-readable data do not exist, the recording media are kept in a state computer centre and are made available for access on demand.

- In order to allow access to machine-readable recording media, data base systems and information systems which are not kept in the archives, the archives must be connected up to the existing wide area network and information network. Via standard lines or switched lines, the archives and researchers have the possibility of access to different information networks in which information is stored which is relevant to the archives. The right of getting access must be specially decided upon.

5. SUMMARY

The story told at the beginning of the presentation is to show the services archives will have to offer future researchers. These services are necessary if the archives department is to maintain its position as a centre for the historical and social transmission of documents and information in an age when the procuring, availability and exchanges of information is of great importance for society. The securing and future access to the records produced today in administration which are of archival value can only be guaranteed if the archives take the necessary steps in time. The archives, together with administration, must work out guidelines which allow the transfer, the permanent preservation and the long-term accessibility of machine-readable data. The archives must insist on being connected up to existing communication networks in order to have access to external information systems and data bases.

The user who comes into the archives in 2020 must be sure that he can find and obtain the information which is kept in the archives or in a computer centre and which is available for use, it may have been recorded electronically or conventionally.

MANAGING INFORMATION IN AN OFFICE SYSTEMS ENVIRONMENT - The IMOSA Project[1] -

By John McDonald

The penetration of networked computer based information technologies into the Canadian workplace over the past ten years has been dramatic. From stand-alone micro-computers with limited processing power and memory, today's organizations are procuring sophisticated high performance multi-purpose workstations that permit users to create, use, transmit, and store a bewildering array of information types and forms. Text, graphics, data and voice are being used in increasingly sophisticated ways to record and communicate information. Although the products are often referred to as 'documents' their shape and even their existence can be in sharp contrast to the traditional paperbased concepts with which we are most familiar. Compound documents, dynamic documents, virtual documents and hypertext are no longer theoretical constructs - they are real things being created in today's business environment. On an increasing scale, and as the use of networked office systems grows in sophistication, electronic documents, regardless of their form, are being recognized as an important component of corporate memory[2].

Unfortunately, as much as electronic information in office systems is growing in importance as a valuable corporate resource, it is also a fragile resource. Archivists have known from years of hard experience that electronic information can be rendered inaccessible if:

- the magnetic and optical media upon which it is stored are not maintained;
- it is stored in environmental conditions that are subject to extremes in heat and humidity;
- it lacks sufficient documentation to permit ongoing intellectual understanding of its content and context;

---

1 The IMOSA project is managed by Susan Gillies of the Canadian Workplace Automation Research Centre of Communications Canada and supported by Christiane Desautels of the Government Records Management Branch of the National Archives. Many of the points raised in this paper resulted from their observations during this project.
The author is grateful to David Bearman, Margret Hedstrom, and Lisa Weber for helping to shape many of the ideas expressed in this paper.

2 For the purposes of this paper, corporate memory is the information required by organizations to support the delivery of their programs and to permit them to hold themselves accountable pursuant to law and policy.

- its access is dependent on software and hardware that can be expected to change over time; and

- accountability for ensuring that such information is identified and protected has not been assigned.

As a result of these factors there has been a growing concern that the corporate memory required by government agencies and by the Canadian government as a whole could be lost[3]. A closely related concern has been that the National Archives of Canada may not be able to carry out its role to preserve and make available that portion of the government's corporate memory that has long term archival value.

It was to address these corporate memory management issues that the Information Management and Office Systems Advancement (IMOSA) project was established in December 1989. IMOSA is a collaborative initiative between the Department of Communications and the National Archives of Canada in partnership with several other departments and private sector organizations. It is based on earlier work that was conducted as part of the federal government's Office Communications Systems (OCS) Field Trial Program. As part of that program, the National Archives (NA) was invited to participate in a field trial at the Department of Communications where a local area network linked 70 users in the Policy Sector. This provided a rich milieu for studying the impact of technology on the management of information from both the archival and corporate perspective[4].

Based on this experience, preliminary functional requirements were developed by the National Archives for managing electronic information generated on the office system used for the field trial. These requirements were further refined by the NA with the participation of the Department of Communications (DOC), Comterm Inc. and later Provenance Systems Inc. As a result of these activities, the National Archives produced **Managing Information in Office Automation Systems: Final Report on the FOREMOST Project** in 1990[5]. The FOREMOST (FOrmal REcords Management for Office Systems Technologies) report described the functional requirements for managing information in the office systems being planned for and installed in the National Archives and the Department of Communications.

---

3 Concern such as those described in this paper have been raised in a number of reports such as:
- National Academy of Public Administration, *The Effects of Electronic Recordkeeping On The Historical Record of the U.S. Government*, January 1989, Washington.
- Advisory Committee for the Coordination of Information Systems, *Management of Electronic Records: Issues and Guidelines*, prepared by David Bearman, United Nations, 1990.
- *Taking a Byte Out of History: The Archival Preservation of Federal Computer Records*, Committee on Government Operations, US House of Representatives, Washington, 1990.
- *Research Issues in Electronic Records*, published for the National Historical Publications and Records Commission, Washington, D.C. by the Minnesota Historical Society, St. Paul, Minnesota, 1991.

4 The report of the National Archives' experience in the DOC project is described in *Report of the PAC/DOC Information Management Working Group*, National Archives of Canada, 1985.

5 *Managing Information in Office Automation Systems, Final Report on the FOREMOST Project*, National Archives of Canada, Ottawa, 1990.

Although the FOREMOST report was initially prepared to respond to the needs of the two departments (NA and DOC), interest in and demand for the report from other organizations was substantial and copies were eventually distributed to over 1,000 organizations, both in Canada and abroad. As the requirements were attracting a high level of interest, it became increasingly evident that there was a need to test the validity of the FOREMOST requirements in an office setting, using a prototype application.

A meeting between representatives of the Government Records Branch (GRB) of National Archives, the Canadian Workplace Automation Research Centre (CWARC) of the Department of Communications and Provenance Systems Inc. resulted in an agreement to develop and test a prototype application based on the functional requirements. A joint venture agreement was established, and through CWARC's industry exchange program, IMOSA was launched in December 1989[6].

The prototype application was installed on the Novell local area network (LAN) in the Government Records Branch where users created and exchanged electronic documents using the software available on the LAN (WordPerfect, Harvard Graphics, electronic mail, etc.). The prototype application was available through a list of LAN menu options and provided end users with a tool to file, browse, search and retrieve electronic documents in a corporate database server. The database application was designed to protect the corporate holdings of the organization, while also providing functions allowing the records manager to control and manage both electronic and non-electronic holdings. Much of the departmental subject classification system (which was automated) was downloaded to the file server to ensure that consistency could be maintained between the hardcopy and electronic corporate holdings. The electronic holdings could comprise documents created using a variety of software that was available on the LAN (i.e. a document could be in the form of a spreadsheet, a graphic, or an electronic mail message as well as text generated by a word processing package).

The following describes the main functions and associated features of the prototype[7]:

1. **Filing: the "submit" function**

   Users could store their documents in two locations. The first was the user's own personal work space or directory and the second was corporate holdings (i.e the database application managed by the organization). For the purposes of the prototype assessment, the filing of documents into corporate holdings was at the discretion of the user. At the time of filing into the corporate holdings, a document profile was completed and appended to each document for indexing and retrieval purposes. The profile consisted of fields of information or attributes relating to the document being filed. At the point of submission, the document moved from the personal workspace to the corporate holdings. Once the document was submitted, the user could not delete

---

6 *The IMOSA Project: Information Management and Office Systems Advancement -Overview*, National Archives of Canada/Canadian Workplace Automation Research Centre, November, 1991.

7 *IMOSA Project: Functional Requirements - Corporate Information Management Application (CIMA)*, National Archives of Canada/Canadian Workplace Automation Research Centre, 1991.

it from the corporate holdings. Profiles of non-electronic documents could also be filed in order to provide a linked, integrated view of all documents contained in files regardless of the medium on which they were recorded.

As a new document was submitted to the corporate holdings, the DOS name (eight-character name plus three-character extension) was replaced by a number assigned by the application to uniquely identify the document. The document number also included a version number; through this numbering method several versions of the same document could be identified. Each time a document was retrieved from corporate holdings and edited, it could only be resubmitted under a new version number -- ensuring preservation of the previous version. The name of the user submitting a document was automatically recorded as part of the document profile for each version.

The document was also described by a "document subject" field (part of the document profile) which provided a 60-character field to be used by the user to abstract the content of the document. The "document subject" field and document number were displayed on the screen during the search and retrieval process, providing a much more useful description of the document than an 11-character DOS name (the use of a controlled vocabulary, however, would have enhanced further the effectiveness of the search and retrieval function).

2. Retrieving and searching: the "retrieve" and "search" functions

After a document was filed, it would be accessible to other network members. According to assigned security levels, users could browse, search, and retrieve from the database any documents submitted by their colleagues. Users could not delete or remove a document from corporate holdings; a copy of the retrieved document could, however, be added to the users' personal space.

Users could retrieve documents directly by the document number, or indirectly via the search function. While the "retrieve document" function required the user to know the document number (i.e. the unique number assigned by the system), that "search document" function offered three different ways of searching the corporate holdings.

- One method involved **searching by file number** of the departmental subject file classification system if the number of the file, or group of files, containing the required document(s) was known.

- The second method allowed users to **search on any one of the fields in the document profile** (i.e., attributes entered by the user or automatically at the time of filing; these included document name, title, file number, to, from, security level, document type such as graphic, spreadsheet, etc., and subject among others).
- The third method consisted of using a **full text search** of the document summary field (which forms part of the document profile). This latter search method was provided as an interim tool until it would be possible to integrate full text search

of entire documents. (This feature was slated for inclusion in a future version of the prototype software).

3. **Editing corporate documents: the "work on" function**

Once the document was retrieved from the corporate holdings into the user's personal workspace, the application provided an option to "work on" the document. The application retrieved the software program which was originally used to create the document, such as WordPerfect, allowing the user to edit the document (as long as the software was one of the packages - **and the appropriate version of the package** - available to the user on the LAN, such as WordPerfect or Harvard Graphics). The application then flagged the document which had been retrieved from the corporate holdings to inform any potential users that another user was working on the document at that time.

4. **Records management: the "verify" and other functions**

The application also provided the records management specialist with functions to manage and control the corporate holdings at both the file and document levels. For instance, when a new document was submitted to the corporate holdings, a "verify submissions" function permitted the records manager to verify the various fields of the documents profile which had been completed by the user to ensure that the information was accurate. Traditional functions performed by the records manager, such as "create a file", and "bring forward management", were also automated. Other functions were designed which allowed records managers to create new users and assign them security access levels which mimicked the paper file access scheme.

5. **Document classification: the "look-up" function**

The file classification index was fully automated. Using key words from the subject field or section titles, users could find the appropriate file number in the index -- allowing them to classify documents regardless of their knowledge of the classification system. Access to various files by users was limited by the security access level which was assigned by the records management specialist. The design of the application prototype was based on the block numeric file classification system and could be adapted to any one of the six variations of this system currently used by the federal government.

The prototype application was assessed by a small user group that comprised project officers and managers from the site as well as records management staff. The results served to highlight issues that were already known in an impressionistic sense but that were brought into greater focus through the experience gained in using the prototype and in contemplating its use on a broader scale by larger and more complex user groups and organizations[8].

---

8 *The IMOSA Project: Information Management and Office Systems Advancement -Phase I Report*, National Archives of Canada/Canadian Workplace Automation Research Centre, 1991.

Two general observations have emerged from the IMOSA experience. The first is that archival considerations can only be addressed successfully if they are considered in tandem with the information management considerations of creating organizations. Organizations will not tolerate the imposition of rules and procedures that are not in line with their own direction and/or implementation timetable. The successful archival program will be the one that incorporates its appraisal, acquisition and preservation requirements (identification, description, conservation, etc.) into the corporate memory management requirements of the organization. The second observation is that the efforts to address electronic records issues in the modern office have revealed the need to reexamine traditonal approaches to the corporate filing and retrieval of office generated information. As will become clear in the more detailed discussion to follow, existing approaches to the management of records may not be adequate in an office systems environment. This is particularly true in organizations concerned with 're-engineering' their functions and activities and using their information holdings to deliver more effectively their programs and to hold themselves accountable.

More detailed observations led to the conclusion that the incorporation of corporate memory management considerations in an office systems environment would be dependent upon six major factors. These include: 1) a policy to assign accountability; 2) rules of the road which, whithin the policy framework, guide users in managing information from a corporate perspective; 3) and understanding of how the office works in order to set the policy and rules of the road in context; 4) functional requirements to assist industry in building appropriate technical solutions; 5) the information technologies themselves, and; 6) the information technology standards that promote a consistent approach to implementation. These factors are described in greater detail below:

1. Policies that clearly assign accountability for the management of corporate memory.

   None of the issues raised in this paper can be addressed by organizations without someone being held accountable. In the Canadian federal government accountability at the highest level is normally assigned through Treasury Board policy. Prior to 1989, however, the information management policy framework was fragmented and the only policy that addressed the life cycle of records was the Records Management policy[9] which assigned accountability to the heads of government institution but only for non-electronic records under the control of only one information management jurisdiction (records management).

   Treasury Board's Management of Government Information Holdings (MGIH) policy, which was approved in 1989, provided the comprehensive framework that was missing under previous policies. It required institutions to manage their information holdings (regardless of their physical form) throughout their liefe cycle. While assigning responsibility for policy implementation to the head of the institution and even requiring a senior official to be named "for the purposes of the policy", it left the development of individual implementation strategies to each institution. As a result,

[9] *Records Management (Chapter 460 of the Treasury Board Administrative Policy Manual)*, Treasury Board Canada, 1983.

many institutions, faced with fragmented and uncoordinated approaches to information management, while welcoming the comprehensiveness of the policy, have been struggling with its implementation ever since its promulgation.

In the world of office systems, where control over the life cycle of information (particularly electronic) generally rests with the individual user, efforts to extend a policy such as MGIH to this world and related efforts to assign accountability to appropriate individuals is particularly challenging. As long as users consider the electronic records that they are generating as their own and as long as they have full discretion over their creation and disposal, then efforts to hold someone accountable at this level will be nearly impossible even if someone at a higher level has been assigned accountability pursuant to a government-wide or even department-wide policy.

From the IMOSA experience, it was determined that users generally will resist any outside interference with what they considered to be their own information 'turf'. As a result records managers likely will experience considerable problems in selling the idea of managing electronic records from a corporate perspective. Users will be resistant to change unless they can see some benefit and unless they can be convinced the managing information from a corporate perspective will not mean that they will lose control (i.e. their autonomy in carrying out the work of the organization will be respected even as the organizations interests in its corporate memory are met). As for the information systems specialist, the issues surrounding corporate information management are relatively foreign and until a user requirement is expressed that will cause them to pay more active attention then their involvement will be limited to the provision of technical support.

The issue of accountability may likely be resolved as organizations learn to migrate their office systems from utilities (i.e. using them to automate basic tasks such as creating a document or spreadsheet) to corporate support tools (i.e. using them to automate processes such as the executive correspondence application or the policy development application or, in an archives context, the processing of records disposition submissions, etc.). In this late environment, the assignment of accountability for the business application will dictate who is accountable for the associated information. As a result and in considering existing office systems environments where it is difficult to identify direct links between information holdings and specific business applications (i.e. creation, storage and transmission of information is ad hoc), it might be useful to turn to the accountability frameworks for existing and emerging business applications as a starting point for understanding how accountability might be assigned to other unstructured areas of a given office network (e.g. electronic mail messages forwarded in a seemingly ad hoc manner, or versions of electronic text transmitted to a seemingly arbitrary set of individuals for review purposes).
Ultimately the increasing reliance of individuals on the electronic version of documents, spreadsheets, etc. for decision making, the delivery of their programs or for holding themselves accountable for decisions made should lead to a greater interest in

the application of more disciplined approaches to the management of electronic information.

Such an evolution should foster a greater sense of accountability in much the same way as government officials currently feel a sense of accountability for financial and human resources. The end result (in an ideal world) is a user who feels a natural sense of accountability (linked directly to their program responsibilities) rather than a sense of obligation that has been imposed by some outside source.

2. Corporate 'rules of the road' that provide guidance to users in generating, using and storing information.

It is insufficient to provide users with a corporate information management software application (such as the prototype described in this paper) and then ask them to begin filing and retrieving 'corporate' records to and from the application without a set of rules and procedures. Users need guidance concerning why and how they should be interacting with such an applications. On a broader front, the planners and designers of office systems need to know what the application is supposed to support from a business perspective and then how the organization and its employees (regardless of their level) are supposed to interact with it.

As a result, and again, similar to the policy issue, corporate rules of the road need to be developed in accordance with the needs of the business, be it a social benefits delivery program or a policy office. When should the records of transactions associated with the business be captured? How much contextual information is needed to support the requirements of the business function or process? What security considerations need to be addressed? How long should captured records of transactions be kept? In what form and format should they be kept and why? The absence of clearly defined business functions and activities in the office system in which the IMOSA prototype software was assessed was a major roadblock to the development of responses to such questions and to the development of a comprehensive set of rules and procedures.

3. An understanding of how work is performed in the 'office' in order to identify business functions and activities to which both information management and information technology solutions can be applied.

One of the main objectives of the prototype application was to permit the management of both electronic and non-electronic records according to paperbased records management practices. The prototype succeeded in harmonizing the electronic system with the corporate paper-based records system. This was based on the concern that compatibility between the existing hardcopy records system and the emerging electronic system be maintained. In the task automation environment in which the prototype was being assessed this was a sensible approach. Users were concerned that they had a corporately defined repository application into which they could file and retrieve the electronic documents that they had generated through the use of the software (word processing, spreadsheet, graphics, etc.) supported on the local area network. The prototype supported this basic functionality and, moreover, ensured compatibility with the hardcopy system. Given the current level of office systems maturity (i.e. task transformation), this transitional approach to corporate information management in office systems will likely become a norm over the short and medium terms.

As previously indicated, however, office systems eventually will evolve beyond the automation of tasks to the transformation and automation of business processes. In progressive organizations, this evolution will occur in tandem with steps taken to analyze traditional processes and, through the innovative planned introduction of information technologies, to re-engineer these processes to the strategic advantage of the organizations[10].

Given that existing records management approaches were established before the days of the computer, office systems, and business re-engineering, it is highly likely that, as part of this evolution, these approaches may be transformed to more directly support the delivery of government programs and services. The growing need by users to use information within the context of business functions, activities, and processes (particularly in those organizations that are using office systems technologies as strategic business related resources) will have a profound impact on the shape of future 'filing' systems. As indicated in the descriptions of the other factors described in this paper, future filing systems will be molded around the transactions that comprise the busines processes of the organization. Although unstructured, seemingly ad hoc work flows will still exist (i.e. the transmission and storage of electronic documents according to user defined criteria), the shift to structured corporately defined applications (e.g. the development of policy, responses to executive correspondence, etc.) will become more pronounced. As a result, the criteria for defining when a records of a transaction needs to be captured, how it should be captured and for how long it should be captured will be easier to develop than if such applications were not in place. The reengineering of the records management function will likely be commonplace as organizations guide their office systems through the business process transformation stage. It is at this stage that the corporate rules of the road referred to in the previous section will become particularly relevant.

4. Functional requirements for the management of corporate information that would guide (and even leverage) the development of appropriate technology solutions.
   The functional requirements that emerged from the IMOSA project are intended to give expression to the needs of federal government institutions with respect to the management of their corporate memories. Based on the IMOSA experience, and as indicated in previous sections, it was learned that over the long term, functional requirements should be developed within the context of the needs of the business

---

[10] See: Hammer, M., Reengineering work: Don't Automate, Obliterate, *Harvard Business Review*, 68(4): 104-12, and Zuboff, Shoshana, *Age of the Smart Machine: the Future of Work and Power*, Basic Books, NY, 1988.

requirements of the organization. As most organizations are still at the task transformation stage, it may be sometime before organizations have evolved to the point where the requirements reflect this direct connection between information holding and corporate business applications. In the meantime most organizations will likely try to ensure that their evolving corporate electronic filing systems are relatable to their hardcopy systems. As structured corporate applications are defined, however, adjustments to **both** the hardcopy and the electronic filing systems are expected. This will lead to systems that are more relevant to the needs of the business.

5. Information technoliges that enable institutions to respond to the challenges described above.

   The technical solutions that respond to the functional requirements developed as part of the IMOSA project are emerging from existing computer assisted records management systems (CARMS). This follows from the natural inclination of organizations to apply easily understood and increasingly available 'records management' solutions to their information management in office systems problems. While such solutions are sufficient in helping organizations to take the initial steps required to bring their electronic information holdings under corporate control (i.e. based on the assumption that existing, albeit, traditional records management approaches should be adopted in order to maintain consistency and continuity beween hardcopy and electronic holding), over the long term these will evolve as the use of office systems moves from the automation of basic tasks to the automation of corporate processes.

   Consequently, as organizations manage the evolution of their office systems to the point where they are being used to transform and automate processes, they will be able to benefit from the emergence of automated techniques that incorporate object oriented approaches in which both process steps and associated information entities are seen as a single entity or object which, when combined with other objects (i.e. buidling blocks) can lead to the development of corporate applications.

   The future vision will be a fully automated set of corporate applications where corporate procedure, tasks and processes will be combined with communicated transactions to form applications. The repository or 'filing system' will be more than a database containing documents organized according to a subject filing system but a repository containing objects that comprise information on tasks (described in context with business processes and functions) as well as communicated transactions (the corporate information that needs to be retained for business delivery and accountability purposes). As a result, individual tasks and their associated information entities will be bolted together and placed within the context of the business processes of the organization. Emerging technologies such as Computer Assisted Software Enginering

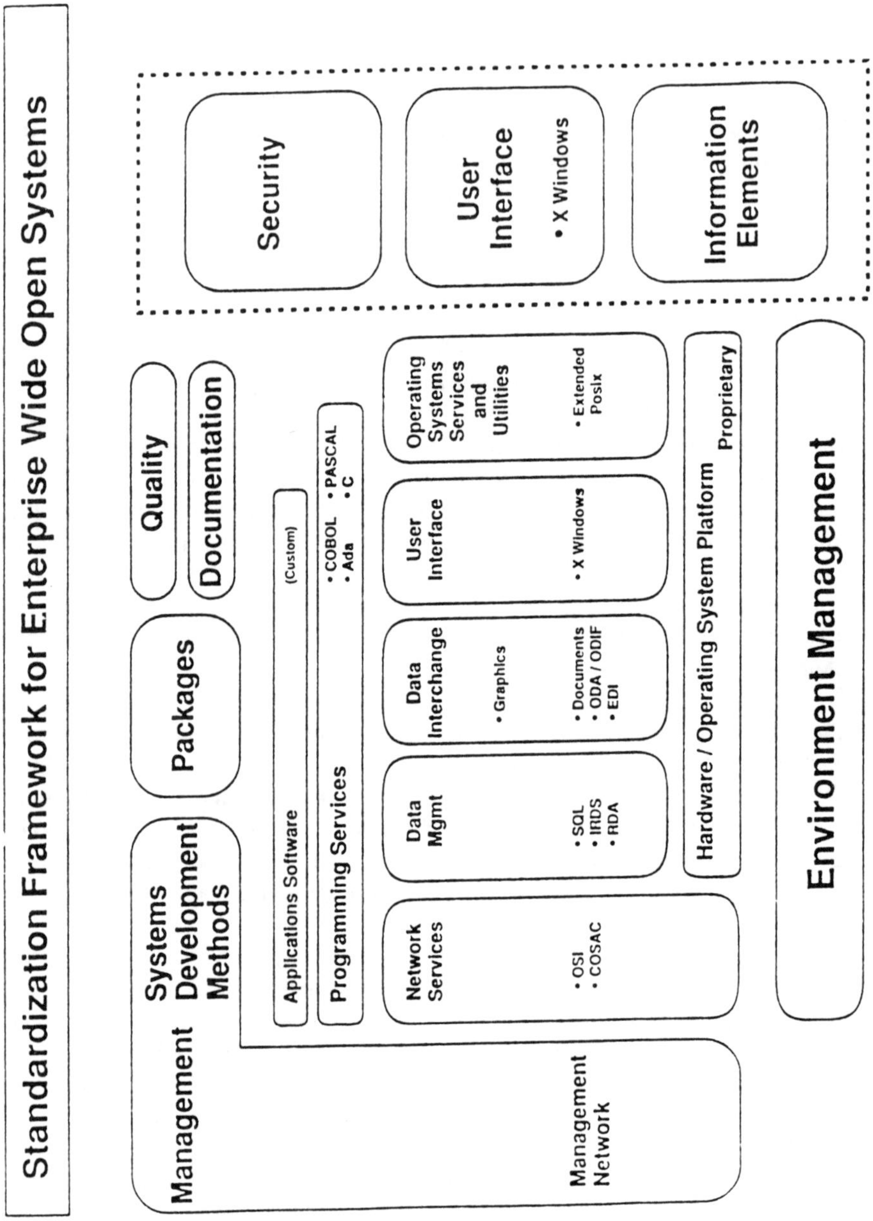

Standardization Framework for Enterprise Wide Open Systems
Management
Systems Development Methods
Packages
Quality
Documentation
Security
User Interface
• X Windows
Information Elements
Applications Software
(Custom)
Programming Services
• COBOL • PASCAL
• Ada • C
Network Services
• OSI
• COSAC
Data Mgmt
• SQL
• IRDS
• RDA
Data Interchange
• Graphics
• Documents
• ODA / ODIF
• EDI
User Interface
• X Windows
Operating Systems Services and Utilities
• Extended Posix
Hardware / Operating System Platform
Proprietary
Management Network
Environment Management

Figure 1

(CASE) tool sand, in particular, the integration of CASE and repository management tools (such as AD/CYCLE from IBM) will begin to provide organizations with such possibilities.

6. Information technology standard (including data standards) to ensure that technology solutions are in line with the government's direction towards enterprisewide open systems[11].

The first technology solutions to the requirements expressed as part of this phase of the IMOSA project will be proprietary or at the very least based on defacto standards. A portfolio of nationally or internationally approved standards for the corporate management of information in an office systems environment has yet to be developed. While the building blocks (e.g. Open Document Architecture/Open Document Interchange Foramt (ODA/ODIF), Standardised Generalised Markup Language (SGML), and the Information Resource Directory System (IRDS) are emerging, it will be several years before such a portfolio comes into clearer view. The growing significance of object oriented approaches to applications development may also have a strong influence on the nature of the standards that are developed to address corporate information menagement requirements, particularly over the long term. As a result, while existing standards for automated repositories such as the IRDS standard and the defacto repository standards that could emerge from the current efforts of IBM, DEC and others, will concentrate on the management of information about information (i.e. also known as metadata), future repository 'standards' will mange information about objects (i.e. processes and related data as single entities) as well as the business functions to which they relate. A number of CASE tools are pointing in theis direction.

For now, however, the development of standards compliant technical solutions to the issues raised in this paper, is only beginning to be considered. As a result, and although the prototype software developed as part of the IMOSA project was proprietary, future development efforts will be undertaken within the context of the enterprise-wide open systems model advocated by the Canadian federal government (figure1). This model places the seven layer Open Systems Interconnection (OSI) model within the context of standards that promote applications portability and, at a higher level, those standards that promote the interchange of both contextual information, the information itself, and the logical and physical processes that use this information to support the business of the organization. The element entitled "Information Elements" refers to the descriptive and data standards that need to be in place if such a comprehensive exchange of information is to occur. For archivists the enterprise-wide systems model offers an excellent view of a technology landscape to which all archives should subscribe - it not only promotes the exchange of informa-

[11] The chart provided in this paper was provided by Treasury Board Canada through the Treasury Board Information Technology Standards Program.

tion across space (i.e. spatial point to spatial point at a given point in time) but also across time (i.e. time point to time point withing a given space)[12].

The results of the first phase of the IMOSA project served as a catalyst to the establisment of subsequent projects that are currently underway. Some, such as the project to identify relevant software packages that meet the existing functional requirements, are intended to further the development of technical solutions that address the information management issues of today. Others, such as the project to study the redesign of work processes, are intended to pave the way for the development of technical and procedural solutions that will respond to the information management needs of the emerging office. The projects that comprise the current phase of IMOSA are as follows:

- the design and validation of requirements that address retention, disposition and archival considerations (neither the FOREMOST requirements nor the requirements that emerged from the prototype addressed these considerations);
- an assessment of the extent to which the requirements are reflected in existing and emerging software products;
- an assessment of the extent to which the requirements conform to the Treasure Board's Management of Government Information Holdings (MGIH) policy;
- a study on the redesign of work processes and their impact on the management of information;
- the development of core guidelines for the management of information in office systems (addresses the 'good rules-of-the road' that should be followed in integrating corporate memory management issues in office systems environments);
- the development of a quick reference guide to information technology standards that are relevant to corporate memory management in the office;
- the development of a guideline on the management of automated user directories (based on the premise that if a **consistent** approach to user directory management is established at the outset, then, as the office system evolves from one that is based on individual approaches to document management to a system that supports the sharing of information within and across corporate applications, user migration to an environment that is subject to corporate information management conventions will be easier);

---

[12] In fact the distintion between archival and corporte memory requirements is difficult if not impossible to identify (i.e. what is so different from the needs of an organization to maintain the integrity of its electronic records from the needs of an archives to maintain the integrity of its electronic archival holdings).

- an assessment of the retrieval capabilities of a nubmer of existing software applications (addresses emerging issues surrounding the use of full text, keyword, subject classification and other retrieval strategies and conventions);

- an assessment of the integration of image processing and multi-media systems with the kinds of corporate information management applications that emeged from the IMOSA experience; and

- a review of the relevant information management issues being addressed by various government working groups (to ensure that the direction set by IMOSA is constistent with these issues and the direction set by the groups).

These projects are being sponsored by a number of Canadian federal government and private sector organizations. The results will be reviewed by the Treasure Board Office Systems Standards Working Group before dissemination to a wider audience[13]. The involvement of other organizations as stakeholders is one of the major characteristics of the IMOSA project. Given the enormity of the issues and the extent to which the issues are commonly shared by most modern organizations internationally, it follows that, as much as possible, the solutions should be based on collaborative initiatives or partnerships. It is within this spirit that individuals and organizations are encouraged to contact the author to find out more about the IMOSA project and to share opinions and ideas.

[13] The Treasury Board Office Systms Standards Working Group comprises representatives from over 20 federal government institutions concerned about the impact of office systems on the management of information. In order to provide context for its work, the Group developed a report ("Issues and Directions: Treasury Board Canada, Ottawa, 1990") describing the issues that government was facing and the direction that the Group intended to take to address the issues. This was supported by a study, commissioned by Transport Canada, that described the characteristics of the modern office and the relationship between the use of technology and information resources in an office systems environment and the business functions of organizations.

E-MAIL SYSTEMS, OFFICE COMMUNICATION AND RECORDS MANAGEMENT

By Michael Cook

ABSTRACT

Examines records management practices in the context of the development of IT in administration. E-mail is considered in the light of information systems, internal to the organisation and external to it. Records management is essentially a structure of linked databases. The development of electronic communication in an organisation offers the possibility of building these into the common services provided by the system; details of these are given. Internal communications are matched by external ones, in the form of databases and systems for data exchange. Progress in adopting these methods has been slow, but has occurred everywhere. Citations are chosen from British sources on records management practice.

The electronic revolution offers many possibilities to records management. This simple statement is not controversial, but it has lost of its initial excitement. In most areas, electronic communications have developed in administration with unexpected slowness. Boasts of the coming 'paperless office', which were common 15 years ago, have proved laughably inaccurate. The communications revolution, first signalled in the early 1980s, looked set to go the same way.[1] Digital recording, and optical media also entered with a loud fanfare, only to suffer a mild debunking.[2] The IT consumer has grown cynical. Is there really any profit to be made by thinking technologically ?[3]

1. AWARENESS OF CONTEXT

The most successful records managers were always the ones who were most aware of what was going on around them in their organisation. Administrative instability, economic fluctuations and rapid technological innovation were three of the factors which made it especially necessary to be watchful. No aspect of management is likely to be successful in an enterprise, if it is planned in isolation from the whole environment in which it operates. This is true, whether the organisation is a government department or a commercial business.

---

1 *Office automation and records management: report of a working party.* (UK) Society of Archivists, Records Management Group, 1981.

2 *Computer-generated records.* Society of Archivists, Records Management Group. Approaches to problems in records management 2. 1986.

3 Conservative forecasts are set out in Peter Willett et al., *Information UK 2000: the technological imperative.* British Library Research and Development Report 6016. London, 1991.

Technological development has therefore to be planned in the full awareness of all the important environmental factors. Market pressures (which bear upon the organisation's objectives); legislation; social pressures and professional codes; user demands within the structure; and the pressure of technological change - these are all factors to be measured. An organised study of records systems within the organisation, and a survey of the records they produce, are more usually the starting point of records managers.[4]

The pressure of technological change is felt from several sources. Senior management is often keen to invest in new IT (not always from very appropriate motives); departmental heads and middle management are likely to be divided into opposing groups. Some wish to press ahead with new development, some are indifferent, and some actively shun it. Within departments, IT can often be seen as the immediate solution to specific problems, and waiting for overall plans or improved systems may seem frustrating. Hardware and software merchants bombard all management staff with discount, entertainment and training offers, and they constantly read and talk about new technology in the media and at home. The information providers (documentalists, librarians, consultants) all speak of the need for external technological information channels. The most routine of the administrative procedures are already automated, so that discussion of new technologies and their effect - such as electronic data interchange (EDI) and office imaging systems - seems to make sense.[5] IT seems constantly to be making new demands, but its rewards come slowly.

Records managers are no more able to resist these pressures than any other managers. The piecemeal advance of IT through the offices and departments presents them squarely with a first challenge: the need for the organisation to have an integrated plan for information management.[6] To put the thing at its lowest, there ought to be agreement on such broad questions as whether the PCs ought to be IBM-compatible; whether there should be a single family of software for word processing, local accounting and reporting. Records managers are among those most directly affected by this question, so it is natural that they should respond positively to the challenge. This plunges them at once into a sequence of planning activities with a highly political sensitivity.

"Planning of information systems is necessary because:

(a) the rapid changes in the technology require a clear view of what hardware/software will be most economical and compatible (the so-called 'migration path');

(b) planning data management successfully requires that the overall business objectives of the organisation be clearly stated;

(c) there has to be a methodology for monitoring the effectiveness of the plan (the so-called 'critical success factors');

---

4 These approaches to records management are elegantly summarised in S. C. Newton, *Strategic planning for records management and archives*. Society of Archivists, Records Management Group, 1984.

5 Tessa Atha, *Simpler Trade Procedures Board (SITPRO)*, in Records Management Bulletin 44 (June 1991), p. 5.

6 Barbara Reed, *Records management and information resources management*. Records management bulletin 44, June 1991, pp. 10-13.

While (a) does not affect the principles of records management, technological change is an important environmental factor and (b) and (c) are as fundamental to it as to any other function".[7]

2. RECORDS MANAGEMENT: AN INTEGRATED DATABASE SYSTEM.

Records management has always used sets of databases as part of its essential tools. In a context of IT it is possible to see these as essentially components of an integrated database system. In this respect also, records management resembles the complex of management and direction at the centre of any large organisation. In all of these, one or more large central databases are or can be linked, so that the whole system becomes relational. The various functions of the organisation - administrative, legal, financial, personal, manufacturing, etc. - draw their working data from some branch of the linked database system.[8] Up to the present, such integrated systems are usually partial and semidependent on manual inputs. When the linkages are nearing completion, then EDI becomes feasible, and the whole network takes on a higher level of activity.

An integrated database system in records management itself can be successfully operated at a much earlier point of development. The system would contain components like these:

Records survey findings:
- Register of series
- Retention schedule

Transfer lists: control of records disposition
- Issue and return of records
- Review and disposal of records

Departmental records:
- Costing use of central store;
- Costing records in office space;
- Staffing and resourcing costs

Appraisal record:
- Transfer to archives
- Access control
- Location control; repository management.

A model of this type shows quite a simple application of IT management which is easily within the capability of most sizable organisations in developed countries. In fact, it is probably within the capability of most moderately developed countries, and does not demand exceptional investment or input of expertise.

---

7 S. C. Newton, op. cit., p. 1.

8 This type of nexus is illustrated in M. Cook / M. Procter. *Manual of Archival Description*, 2nd ed. Gower, 1989, p. 246.

An interesting feature of this view of records management is that it is a readymade infrastructure for the arrival of E-mail.

3. OFFICE COMMUNICATION SYSTEMS: E-MAIL.

That computers are as much about communication as about data processing has been apparent for some years now. Outside organisations, very largescale communications networks are now in operation; and inside them, electronic mail is an established fact. For example, in Britain (not an exceptionally welldeveloped country in many ways), academic institutions are now accustomed to online consultation of each others' library catalogues, and have acquired the habit of corresponding with each other electronically. Their personnel consult electronic billboards to get uptodate information, and join forums to discuss technical and practical problems.

However, the e-mail revolution is making a curiously slow start. In the business world (except in merchant banking) e-mail is as yet not common. Where it is being introduced, it is often not used by senior managers, who tend to delegate it to their secretaries. To use e-mail effectively requires a total change of working custom, which has social and political consequences. Senior managers and professionals must work direct to the keyboard, for which they must acquire the skill, and they must have a terminal on their desks, constantly switched on. This means that the tasks delegated to clerical staff must necessarily be changed from the traditional ones. The way in which such staff are supervised, the manner used towards them, and the places in the building they occupy, are all novel. It is the completion of the social revolution which was first signalled by universal education and the employment of women in offices. No wonder the new technologies are resisted by older men who have reached moderate seniority by long service.

E-mail is therefore not yet well known, and its consequences not well digested. This is a favourable circumstance for records managers, who are well placed to join the planning teams.

When an organisation decides to embark upon e-mail as a method of office communication, it generally adopts a software package such as the IBM-designed PROFS. A package like this has three main aspects:

- it links PCs or terminals in different offices into a network, so that messages can be passed both in real time and from user storage space to user storage space;
- it provides a default filing system, so that messages received and sent by a particular station are preserved;
- it provides a set of common services.

Software salesmen are generally keen to sell their employers' products and therefore seek to include as many fancy features as they can. This is particularly obvious in the third category above. Common services usually include features such as:

- electronic diaries, with alarm bells, automatic booking of general meetings, public holidays, etc.;
- meeting room booking facilities;

- appointments and conference bookings, involving the comparison of several electronic diaries;
- sending round notices, automatic forwarding and dissemination of messages, etc.

Several of the components of the records management database system form a natural extension to this type of data and activity. For example, here is a list of records management information which could easily and usefully be provided as a common service in the communications system:

1. The retention schedule, with default display to the section dealing with the department accessing it.
2. Reports, including periodical statistical reports, could be automatically filed for access by all permitted offices.
3. Departments transferring records to intermediate storage could do so by entering data concerning them online, via a formatted screen; they could also order boxes, and arrange the transfer logistics.
4. Departments could order the retrieval of data from records or documents, again by a formatted screen. The records management staff could monitor the records issued in this way, and their return. An audit of issued records (or those overdue for return) would be possible, and an automatic count of records retrieved.
5. Records for review could come up automatically at the foreseen time. Departmental authorisation for disposal or transfer to archives could be made, using formatted screens.
6. Transfer to archives, and the archival finding aids might be added, though this is not so likely to appeal to current records managers.

Another feature of e-mail is that most often messages are filed by default in one of two chronological files, one for outgoing and one for incoming messages. This is a return to medieval filing practices, or it would be but for the useful fact that these files can normally be searched online. Most current operating systems or housekeeping software will allow basic search for textual strings. There is no reason why the default filing system need be so primitive, though it must be conceded that no complex filing system will ever be successful unless it is backed by both compulsion and a well-conceived training scheme; the system must also be constantly maintained and updated.

4. EXTERNAL COMMUNICATIONS

Records management and archival programmes operate on the materials generated within an organisation. The other branches of information management operate usually on materials bought in from outside. Traditionally, these were hardcopy materials, but now they increasingly take the form of access to online databases and the materials - such as CD-ROM - produced by information purveyors.[9]

Both these channels are of interest to archivists. They may produce data which can usefully be included in these general channels, and they may also buy in knowledge about relevant sources. The two approaches are closely linked. Archival data held in cooperative databases is useful to archivists as well as to researchers elsewhere. The more data that is held, the more useful are the databases. The experience of those databases which already exist shows this. Unfortunately experience also shows that the usefulness of such data depends to a great extent on the infrastructure of authorities and controls that are operated. Uncontrolled exchange of data is not efficient.

5. USER SERVICE AND EDUCATION

The response of the user is vital to the success of any of records management programmes. This is true of manual systems as well as of technologically based ones, but it is not so obvious. Many countries have a nonreference culture. To make it work, any records management system must have an extensive programme of user education. The records managers must also design their system with the user in mind. Systems like this will not operate if the records managers are intermediaries. Users must have direct access to data, and they must know how to do it.

This is probably the most serious problem in information management. There is also a technological answer to it, but it is one which has had little development as yet. This is to develop an expert system when designing the user interface. Progress towards this has not been rapid, but there are indications that it is going on. The adoption of the structured query language (SQL) conventions for controlling online search queries has greatly simplified this difficult aspect. The SQL standard has now been adopted in several popular database specifications. It is also used as the underlying structure for natural language searching, now under development. More fully developed user interfaces, involving expert systems in the proper sense, are in use in the most advanced centres.

CONCLUSION

E-mail, and the practice of electronic communication that goes with it, is probably the most important single development in automation in the 1980s. It is still very far from having achieved its full potential.

---

9 John Akeroyd, Vivienne Winterman & Catherine Royce. *CD-ROM networking*. British Library Research Paper 92. London, 1990.

E-mail is quite a simple development. It requires little more than telephone cables. The electronic standards that it uses for the most part exist anyway. This simplicity is the main reason why it is so important. Other developments are far more radical technologically and in their longterm implications, but they are not there, waiting at home to be used.

It is important that records managers and archivists should take an active interest in electronic communication as early as possible. In many cases, systems are already available, or may be made available easily. For example, archival and other data held on public databases is already accessible from relevant points in most countries, not all of them among the most developed. An example is the British Joint Academic Network (JANET). This carries a good deal of archival data, of international import, and is available to academic institutes (though not necessarily to government departments) in most parts of the world.[10]

E-mail is also usually available relatively cheaply within organisations, because it is essentially a simple extension of the facilities of standalone personal computers. Numbers of PCs grow daily. Their extension into local networks is a natural and unstoppable development. The databases generated and used by the use of PCs are the records manager's headache. Carrying these on the network is the records manager's solution.

10 Recent e-mail discussion on the 'Archives and Archivists List', carried by JANET, BITNET and INTERNET remarked on this feature. It was agreed by several correspondents, mostly American, that academic archivists seemed willing to participate in the electronic forum, but that government-employed archivists chose to avoid it.

WILL ARCHIVAL THEORY BE SUFFICIENT IN THE FUTURE ?

By Claes Gränström

This paper has been made with the help of Torbjörn Hörnfeldt. Hörnfeldt has taught computer science at the university of Uppsala and is now employed by the National Archives in Stockholm and is dealing especially with regulations concerning electronic media.

The title of this theme is formulated as a question. I will try to answer the question at the end. I will also mention very briefly how we work with records management and interprete archival theory in Sweden.

1. BACKGROUND

There are two factors/premises which govern records management. The first main factor is about archival theory. The archival theory dominant in Sweden is the principle of provenance, which is used in all three sectors, state, municipal and private. It was introduced in 1900 and 1903 by the ordinances issued by the Government, after proposals from the National Archives. From the beginning we, as it was said in the classical Dutch book by Muller, Feith and Fruin, stressed that this meant obedience to both *le respect des fonds* and *le respect de l'ordre intérieur*. This was to become of utmost importance.

The Government ordinances regulated amongst other things the obligation of all state agencies to catalogue all their records in a systematic inventory according to certain rules. All records as a rule were considered to belong to the archive regardless of age and media generally as soon as they were drawn up or received at the agencies. The inventory was the responsibility of the originating agency under the supervision of the archival authorities. The inventory must be kept up to date, which means that the process of cataloguing was an ever ongoing process. Also the records, which were going to be appraised, must be catalogued.

Thus the structure of the archival information was fixed in a certain structure in the inventory. When the archive or part of it was transferred to the archival authority, it was delivered in that structure together with the inventory. No rearrangement was necessary or permitted according to the archival theory. In this way the full value of the archival information, both regarding the direct informational value of each item and the evidential value, was shown by the surrounding and procedure in which the records were created.

The second main factor is the Freedom of Press Act legislation, introduced in 1766 mainly for political reasons, although the tradition of an open society can be traced to the medieval age, when all court proceedings should be public and attended by all free men. This Freedom of Information Act was considered more and more important as time passed and the public administration grew. It is now one of our three fundamental laws. Early the linkage between this legislation and archives management was recognized.

One important principle within this framework is the principle of equal possibilities of access. It means that the public including massmedia, researchers etc. shall have the same possibilities concerning access as the agency itself, not only to the individual record or file but to information composed of several records or files, that means to the total knowledge of the agency. To guarantee this over length of time is a formidable task. Here I would like to add that any move which threatens this, is considered to be appraisal, such as transfer from tape to paper or disc to tape, if the tape and disc with the relevant documentation is appraised.

If there could be difficulties for the agencies and archival institutions in coping with the paper records and for the agencies and for us to fulfil requirements of the Freedom of Press Act, this was nothing compared to the difficulties connected with electronic records of the new technologies.

You must understand that the vision that every record regardless of age and media should be accessible to all citizens and foreigners, whatever aim, has to be accepted. This was to be the guiding star in all the work.

One advantage is that the Parliament now has stated what aims govern the archival management and that the Parliament has stated what an archive and what a record is and the interpretation of the principle of provenance.

The aims are

- The right of access to official records
- The need for information for the administration of justice and public administration
- Research requirements

You have to consider the fact that archives are a part of our national cultural heritage.

COMPUTER RECORDS AND SWEDISH (ARCHIVAL) LEGISLATION

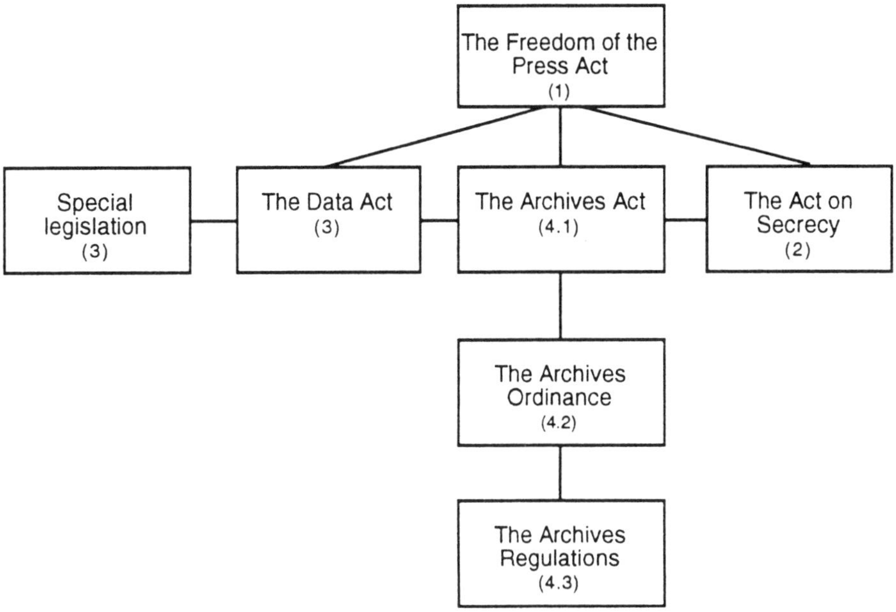

To further free interchange of opinions and enlightenment of the people the Freedom of Press Act, which is a so called fundamental law, guarantees every citizen free access to all official records. Furthermore the Act contains a definition of records and this definition is used in the Archives Act to define which records are part of a public authority's archive. It also specifies when computer records can be considered as public. The Archives Act is of decisive importance for the fulfilment of the aims expressed in the Freedom of Press Act. Main factors are amongst other things how the records are appraised, how the archives are structured and catalogued.

1.1 The Act on Secrecy (Privacy Act)

The Act on Secrecy regulates restrictions in the rights of access to public records according to the limitations given in the Freedom of Press Act. However, what is more interesting in this context is, that it also regulates the way all public records should be registered whether they are drawn up or received at the public authority in diaries/registers/finding aids.

It is vital to maintain the structure that is created at this stage, if one aims to follow the principle of provenance and also maintain *le respect de l'ordre intérieur* and also to be able to use finding aids stipulated above. The records are this way fixed in this structure in the agency.

The Act on Secrecy also stipulates that each agency should plan for and have a so-called "presentation terminal" available to the public in order to enhance accessibility. Besides that, it demands minimum documentation of public computer records that is required.

These demands are as follows:

- the name of the ADP system,
- the purpose of the ADP system,
- the type of information in the ADP system that is available to the public authority,
- at what other agencies the ADP system is accessible in readable form,
- the terminals or technical equipment at the public authority that are accessible to the public,
- the regulations relating to secrecy that normally apply, and
- the name of the contact person that can give further information concerning the ADP system and its use,
- the specification of appraisal regulations.

1.2 The Data Protection Act

The Data Protection Act is primarily aimed at guarding/preserving the integrity of the individual as his/her personal data is recorded and processed using ADP. The regulations apply to in what context personal data may be used in connection with computer records and special regulations concerning computer records containing sensitive data. Since there is a multitude of ways in which the term computer records may be defined, there is also a multitude of ways in which the protection from possible infringement into the personal integrity of the individual may come into conflict with the preservation of personal data. A new Government Committee is at present working with harmonizing the Swedish legislation with the international. It is also deliberating a new terminology, which will be of importance for the terminology used in the archival legislation.

The Data Protection Agency and the National Archives cooperate very closely, especially regarding questions about appraisal. The policy of the Agency is that preservation of personal data can be permitted if the individuals involved are informed and agree to take part in the investigation. The archival authorities are exempted from several requirements in the Data Protection Act regarding the Personal Data they have received from records creating agencies.

2. SPECIAL LEGISLATION ON CERTAIN AREAS

Certain areas in the society have been so important and sensitive that it is considered appropriate that the storage and use of automated data files is regulated in law by the Parliament. Such areas are for example taxation, social welfare, social security, census or residence registration etc. Also the question of appraisal is regulated in the laws in such ways that it can be stipulated in the law directly or given as a mandate to the Government and/or then to an agency to issue regulations about appraisal.

2.1 Archival legislation - the Archives Act

The Archives Act regulates that the archives of a public authority are assembled from the official records that relate to the authority's operations and from other records mentioned in the Freedom of the Press Act, i.e. those that become public due to the fact that they are made into archival records. The Act regulates which public authority shall keep computer records that are accessed and/or created by several public authorities. In the first instance this will be at the authority that is responsible for the major part of such records. The Act also regulates that the public authority shall

- pay attention to the importance of registration for longterm accessibility to the archives,
- choose suitable materials and methods for the creation of the records in order to guarantee that the information is understandable and can be kept as long as it is not appraised,
- organize the archives to facilitate the right of public access,
- draw up a description of the archives which provides an introduction to the archive and also a systematic, archival inventory,
- protect the archives from damage, theft and unauthorized access,
- clearly define the archives by deciding which documents belong there, and
- carry out appropriate appraisal (and subsequent disposal) of records.

2.2 Archival legislation - the Archives Ordinance

In the Archival Ordinance issued by the Government it is delegated to the National Archives to notify regulations concerning materials and methods of writing. The ordinance also regulates when records relating to a transaction shall be considered as an archival record, as well as definitions of when a record is to be considered being an archival record. This is an area where special regulations apply to computer records. They are considered "public" immediately when they come into existence, whether they contain data or not, and they immediately become "archival" as soon as the first data is entered into the records. What really constitutes a record has been much debated. There are also definitions on several levels in the legislation.

The Archives Ordinance gives the National Archives the authority amongst other things to determine where computer records that are accessible to and/or created by several public authorities, belong, which of those agencies is to be considered as the record-keeping responsible agency.

The National Archives can also issue regulations about

1. the use of writing material (all kinds of) and storage facilities (cartridges, boxes etc.),

2. the maintenance of archives such as

   - how the archives should be structured (organized so that the right of public access will be facilitated)

- description of the archives
- systematic archival inventory
- demarcation of the archives
- protection of the archives
- carrying out the appraisal,

3. the taking over of the whole archive or part of it to another agency or to an archival authority,

4. the returning of records.

The National Archives may also issue regulations about appraisal.

2.3 Archival legislation - the Archives Regulations

The new archives regulations presently issued by the National Archives are divided into four groups;

- general regulations,
- regulations concerning different mediums such as computer records, paper and micrographics,
- regulations concerning archival storage facilities, the selection of products and quality systems, and appraisal, and
- regulations concerning technical requirements on materials and methods (where we hope to use general standards).

The general regulations and rules concerning appraisal are mainly directed to those responsible for the archives and to archivists at the public authorities.

The regulations concerning different media are in part directed to archivists and in part to technicians. This also applies to the other regulations which apply to archival storage facilities and selection of products and quality systems.

The technical regulations are mainly directed to technicians, laboratories and the producers of paper, magnetic tape, film etc. intended for archival use. However, for legal reasons these regulations are directed towards the records producing public authorities.

The division of the archival regulations into these groups was a deliberate choice since it was felt that it will make it easier to update as well as amend them. However this division may also make it harder to understand how they interrelate and how they are to be applied in different circumstances. This difficulty is something we hope to circumvene by producing handbooks or guidelines which will include what the archivist generally needs to know, while targeting subject areas that frequently pose practical problems in specialised guidelines (directed at different interest groups).

These regulations are built in such a way that they can be regarded as the basis in a system to which you later on can add more regulations etc., as building units.

4. ARCHIVAL REGULATIONS CONCERNING COMPUTER RECORDS

The regulations relating to computer records may be related to three phases in the lifetime of the computer records. During each of these phases there are different requirements on the public authority. These are summarized in the following parts.

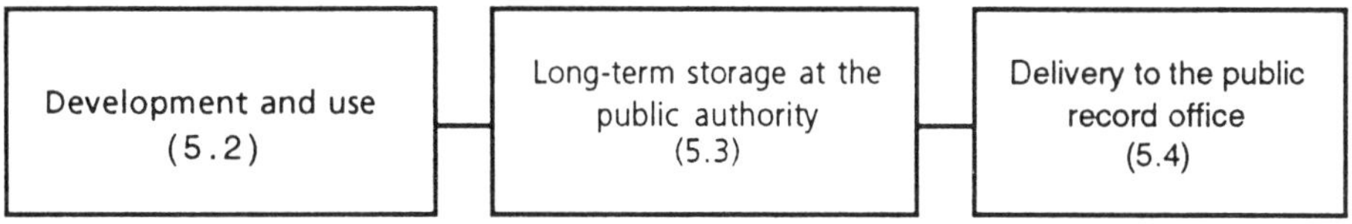

4.1 The ADP system in development and use

The first phase is when the ADP system is under development or in use, and no computer records have been moved from active use to longterm storage. During this time certain documentation should be assembled, or created if it does not already exist. The degree of detail required of the documentation is in some part determined by the complexity of the system. This means that the amount of effort needed to write the documentation hopefully does not exceed the effort of developing the system in the first place. However, this may not always be the case since the regulations are the same, whether or not the system is "large" or "small".

The documentation is divided into the following parts;

- the system/application (more or less in the form of a relatively short description),
- input and output data (forms, reports etc.),
- manual routines and how they relate to the system/application (i.e. access control systems and how these relate to the organization)
- regular/automatic routines (i.e. consistency checks, rules in expert systems),
- descriptions and definitions of data elements, records, relations etc. (preferably written in SQL),
- changes in functionality.

It is only required that applicable standards and technical norms as well as directions given by the manufacturer are followed. No specific standards and norms are listed at present, but the areas that they primarily apply to are data carrier, data representation, data organisation and methods of documentation.

4.2 Long-term storage at the public authority

The second phase is when computer records are moved to long-term storage at the public authority. At this stage there are additional requirements on which type of data carrier may be used, namely halfinch magnetic tape, magnetic tape cassette/cartridge or optical disk. At present there is ongoing research regarding technical characteristics and the first regulations concerning technical requirements will come into force within a year.

The most important regulation at this phase is that the agency is responsible for that it is possible to transfer the computer records to new data carriers as well as converting them to new formats etc. when this is needed, i.e. when acquiring new hard- and/or software.

There are also requirements regarding how the transfer of the computer records to data carriers used for long-term storage, handling etc. should be planned and documented.

4.3 Delivery to the public record office

The third phase is when computer records are delivered to the public record office. In principle all previously mentioned regulations still apply, but the public record office receiving the records may make additions and/or changes to previous choices of data carrier, data representation and data organisation. These additions and/or changes are made in the agreement on delivery and are not explicitly stated in the archives regulations. This makes it easy to adapt the requirements to a given situation and to make changes whenever new equipment or software is acquired.

The National Archives now receives on a regular basis deliveries with personal and other data stored on magnetic tapes, which now amount to about 20.000 tapes (10.000 in copy 1, 10.000 in copy 2). The work with preserving this information is very demanding.

5. RESEARCH AND DEVELOPMENT

Within the National Archives there is now a research programme, which to a large extent deals with problems linked to the ADP-technology. Examples of such projects are listed very briefly below:

- Record, what constitutes a record?
- Authenticity in relation to electronic signatures and scanning
- Principle of equal possibilities of access
- Levels of accessibility
- Linkage between information and integrity legislation and archival theory. Advantages and disadvantages with a close linkage
- Long term storage. How?

Together with this work we also work in order to make archives at archival institutions and later on at all archives-keeping institutions, agencies and organizations more well-known and available to all kind of researchers. The over all concept for this is known as NAD, a National Data Base. We try to use experiences and knowledge from all angles.

CONCLUSION

The answer to the question depends on how you define archival theory, what kind of information legislation you have and how it affects theory.

In our kind of society (the Swedish), with the now prevailing conditions, archival theory, developed and as we interprete it, will be sufficient and guide us as we have the political support expressed both in fundamental and normal level legislation.

I admit there are difficulties in carrying out these tasks and in implementing these visions. It is therefore imperative to define our tasks, roles and interests and those of all other parties who have interests in this matter.

ARCHIVAL SCIENCE AND INFORMATION TECHNOLOGIES

By Bruno Delmas

Many information technologies specialists consider that IT brings fundamental changes in the production, processing, use and storage of documents. Moreover, they think that not only the methods but the principles and even the concepts of archival science are outdated if not useless. In fact, IT influences the concepts and methods of archive administration and obliges it to adapt. With the existence of IT, archive administration is obliged to become more methodological, systematic and precise. But, in this paper I would like to demonstrate how archival science can help us to answer new questions that IT asks archive administration. So my point of view is academic, theoretical, but not practical.

As one knows, archival science is based on two complementary disciplines: diplomatics, the science of the archival document, and archive administration. Diplomatics study documents according to their form, origin and tradition. Archival administration studies principles and methodological means used to preserve archival materials in order to keep the rights, interests, know-how and memory of institutions or individuals. I shall illustrate my purpose with some examples from both diplomatics and archival administration.[1]

Examine the concept of an archive document, i.e. a diplomatic document: "document that has been naturally created or received by a human being or corporation, at a given time during their activities; document that this person, after having used it, preserves, by archiving it. Because it is hoped that the document can be useful later". This definition is valid not only for a document on paper but also for another medium such as a magnetic tape, a floppy, optical disk or even a card with a chip. The nature of an archival document is not linked to its form, medium, or date. Just as traditional documents, these electronic documents can be the medium for any purpose at a given time. But here I speak only about new information media.

Just as traditional archival documents, new media bring information of a special kind. They have a private or personal character linked with the activity of a person. So these documents are not normally accessible to everyone. They are confidential, or even secret, with limited access, because of the information they contain, they belong to their detainer's life (author or receiver). Because of this, just as traditional documents, they are rich and contain an infinite and inexhaustible variety of types of information.

Some aspects of these electronic documents have new types of difficulties from our point of view. I shall give four examples: the first one concerning authenticity, the second the form, the

[1] Ecole des Chartes, *Dictionnaire des archives, de l'archivage aux systèmes d'information* (sous la dir. de Bruno Delmas), Paris: Afnor, 1991.

third the periodically updated documents, and the last the archival documents with an oriented purpose.

Archives or records, even if they are not authentic strictly speaking, have a character of authenticity because they are created at the rate of a practical necessity, or legal or reglementary obligations (commercial correspondence, accounts etc.). So traditionally one considers that there is an authenticity presumptive of evidence that validates the information contained in paper documents, not found in a newspaper article for instance. But is this presumption of authenticity, transferable to electronic media? So it is necessary to first answer the question: are these documents real or virtual? Even if we cannot read a document directly, it doesn't mean that the document does not exist. Writing exists even if we do not see it.

The ease of modifying informations on the medium poses a real problem. However, we should not fall into the sterile quarrels that have opposed layers concerning the legal value of microforms during the 1970's.[2] Any technic or media for reproducing information can be falsified: paper as well as photographic or electronic records. Washing a check might not have any more of trace than modifying an electronic file.[3]

It seems that electronic documents must profit from the same presumed authenticity as other archival documents, as long as they are produced and kept in the offices with the same precautions and care as other office documents (for example: access to media, machines and filing limited to responsible persons having, for instance, a password or the software key, that even give more security). It is also clear that things are different for authentic documents, that even on a paper medium, are subject to precise rules of production. These restrictive conditions are true for a limited number of documents and should be able to be transposed when a new media is used.

Another point is the document form on electronic medium. We can create a draft with a computer and "throw this document away", just like a paper document. The electronic final draft created and recorded on a computer has by definition a different form according to the paper output. Is this a problem? A draft deed that is recorded in the notarial book is not the same document and the same text as the authenticated copy that is delivered to an individual. In both cases it is the same process: a final draft registered that serves to produce a copy according to needs ; giving two different forms of the same text.

This brings us to another diplomatic problem. There are documents that are updated every day: data bases for financial or staff management for instance. These data bases are archival documents and there is no difference between them and the book of accounts or the wage book or any other manual file that are also modified daily. In both cases there are documents where information or data continually change. The difference is that the last type retains the obsolete information, often cancelled; but the same information is removed from the electronic docu-

[2] G. WEILL, *La valeur probante des microformes: une étude Ramp*, Paris: Unesco, 1981 (PGI-81/WS/25).

[3] F. GALLOUEDEC-GENUYS, *Une société sans papier? Nouvelles technologies de l'information et droit de la preuve*, Paris: Documentation française, 1990, *Notes et études documentaires*.

ment (address changes in an electoral file, for instance). This point is not, however, a diplomatic problem but an archive administration problem. It is necessary to do periodical copies of the data bases to fix the historical informations at specific dates.

In the present information society, archived files contain more and more often not only archival documents but also what is called archival documents of oriented purpose. These are documents that are public and exist for every activity out of any file. The information they contain is used again and reworked by the manager for his use. So these documents are incorporated into the files and into the archives of the office that gathered them. Information technology developments (which increases every day and gives easy access to data bases) and the need for information and data will multiply archived documents and data of oriented purpose incorporated into electronic files. The importance of this phenomenon is new, but the phenomenon itself is not new. There is nothing in it that can disrupt our concepts or our ideas.

Archive documents are never isolated materially or functionally. A letter is linked logically and functionally to its answer, more than two articles side by side on a newspaper page. The different parts of a file (all documents put together to process a given purpose) are bound in a paper folder, a book, or recorded on a disk. The folder, the binding or the software must allow the user to access the complete and uptodate file when he wants to consult it. No matter how documents are stored and preserved, all have to be presented, in an organic and functional order, to the user when he needs them. So it does not matter if there is one copy in each file or just one copy broken into several files.

What we have just said about files can be said at a higher and more complex level of organization and integration of documents, represented by the archive funds. It does not matter how documents are stored, if we must be forced to go through the administrative structure, the organic set, bringing us to the document we are looking for and to the information. So, information is not taken by itself as self sufficient abstract data, but as an element of an action, in one context. This corresponds to its archival nature and gives us its complete sense.

These considerations help us understand what is an archival holding in the information technology context. It is a set of documents with whatever date, form, or material medium, automatically produced or received by someone because of his activities, and organically gathered and constituted because of the organization of this person concerned, and finally stored for a potential use.

The principle of provenance, the method of *respect des fonds*, does not mean that all documents must be stored together in the same location. It does mean that, when we search documents belonging to particular holdings, the set of documents, automatically gathered together, must be retrieved together. The *respect des fonds* is not a material obligation but a functional one and a necessity of information. The father of the principle, the French archivist, Natalis de Wailly, said in 1841: "*If instead of this method, which we can say is based on the natural things, it is proposed a theoretical order, all the advantages would be lost (...) the archives will fall in a chaos which will be difficult to correct.*"

I call "functional archival science", the science that defines, considers and studies documents, files, records groups and archival holdings as administrative tools according to their function. Information technologies, with the help of expert systems, can allow us to go beyond the intellectual and material problems of the confusion between arrangement and storage and perhaps also the problem of respecting the administrative structures and the functions.

To complete my paper after these theoretical remarks, I will now talk at an applied and practical level and show, with three examples, what diplomatic and archive science can bring to information technologies to contemporary documents and their archiving. The first example is related to studying the document tradition and the possibility to transpose this method for automatic document appraisal. The second example is about the diplomatic study of documents form and the structure of electronic documents. The third is related to transposing archiving models to electronic archiving.

One aspect of diplomatics is the study of text tradition. Tradition is the transmission through different means of acts, documents and informations. A text tradition study teaches us to distinguish between the different states of a text and informations: rough draft, final draft, engrossed copy, original, copies, certified copy, extract, etc. Methods have been established to evaluate and appraise successive versions of a text to prepare a critic edition. Through the original and copy notions, for instance, text tradition helps us to distinguish the document's value according to its place in the production process of text and legal validation. These rules and methods can help us to conceive the appraisal for selecting contemporary documents to conserve perpetually if the documents belong to a process.

Let us examine documents produced during the processing of statistical data for a population census and set up what we call the tradition schedule. The tradition schedule is the indication of all the documents and data status that has been created during this processing and that we know. It informs us about text or data processing and diffusion and enables a critique. For statistical data processing, the information follows a complex path and changes in form and in medium as the following table shows. It shows how information is processed and diffused (text or data) and allows us to evaluate it. We can: conserve basic information to process it again in the future; save it on an electronic medium if the working out has been sufficient; preserve the results published on paper or microform. If some documents are missing, we can easily see what substitution documents are to be preserved.

TRADITION SCHEDULE FOR CENSUS STATISTICS

	COLLECTING	**PROCESSING**	**DIFFUSION**
INFORMATION MEDIUM	ELEMENTARY	ELEMENTARY	SYNTHETIC
PAPER	- Working documents - enquiry - dataform - files		- general results table, listing, maps - report - study - official publication
ELECTRONIC	working files of samples (5% or 20%)	- basic file - working files - inverted file - table - software	- consult files
MICROFORM	disposal microfilm		- COM - microfiche published

(adapted from Michèle Conchon)

This table allows us to identify documents we have to save. It helps us to identify and search the essential informations to conserve according to the media that is best adapted to a future use. The electronic media is better adapted for reusing and changing documents. In the same way, we must keep results on paper or microfiche etc. But experience shows also that documents get lost, others are destroyed or changed, others reach archival services after much delay. The study of tradition allows organizing precautionary conservation in order to dynamically manage archiving.[4]

If, for instance, substitution microfilm of working documents, data base files, result tables, listings etc. exist, then we cannot save another category. But, if the data base file is missing, we have to keep the working files and results files. We can automatize these operations and set up software to simulate the appraisal. The document typology, as set up by the *Dictionnaire des archives* that I just published, with the participation of the Marburg School for the German-language part, is an element of this system with other components as dates, places, per-

[4] M. CONCHON, *L'archivage des fichiers magnétiques des administrations centrales, bilan et perspectives de "Constance"*, Paris: Archives nationales, 1987, in: *Les nouvelles archives - formation et collecte, Actes du XXVIIIe Congrès National des Archivistes Français*.

sons, etc. from the registered analysis. They are necessary elements but insufficient for this automatization. The system should also consider the primary and secondary value and the retention periods. At the same time, all new transfer in the archival service can modify the schedule. So for many serial and voluminous documents appraisal and selection would be done with the help of expert systems.

The study of the document's form is another topic of diplomatic. The form is the external (context) and internal (contents and structure) elements of a document. These elements give the document the aspect corresponding to its diplomatic and juridical nature, i.e. to its function, according to regulations and habits of the institution that establishes it. Internal characters are form elements of the text, for instance: protocol, preamble, content with pronouncement and final clauses, signature and so on. These are the elements of the text, the message structure. External characteristics are all the complementary information: marginalia, seal, visa, timber, registration mentions and so on. This is the service information that can be more or less assimilated to meta data and which are the text context.

The exchange of commercial documents such as invoices, orders, delivery notes etc. represent a large percentage of the expenses of many companies. If, for instance, we consider standards prepared to ensure the telematic exchange of these documents: Open Document Architecture (ODA), Electronic Data Interchange For Administration, Commerce and Trade (EDIFACT) or Standardised Generalised Markup Language (SGML), we see that computer specialists have rediscovered the study of the form of documents that diplomatic specialists have used for a long time.[5]

Computer specialists identify segments and sequences of data as basic elements of the data chain that constitutes a document that will be processed. Diplomatic specialists, however, knowing the function and importance of the content of each element of a document, give them a name, that allows identifying the information by its contents and not only by its logical segments. This knowledge can be useful for the information technologies specialists. In the same time, the normalisation and methodology of computer specialists can help the diplomatic specialists to perfect their intellectual or methodological tools to analyse the documents' contents. Both have a lot to gain from working together (fig. 1 and 2).

Now let us discuss one experience in archiving. Several years ago, the Club of the ADP staff of the main French companies (CIGREF) such as Saint-Gobain-Pont-à-Mousson (Glass), Société nationale des chemins de fer (Railways), Elf and Total (Petroleum), Banque nationale de Paris, Paribas and so on, created a mixed working group with archivists, to study the archiving problems of paperless office, internal network, and prewired buildings. They wanted to know the point of view of the archivists in this information technology context. They wished to conciliate the fact that on the one hand information is now an essential and strategic resource for the companies, of which the costs are important, so it requires rational and global management, and that, on the other hand, in fact, information is dispersed among autonomous workstations equipped with often incompatible hard- and software.

---

5 COMMISSION OF THE EUROPEAN COMMUNITIES, DGXIII-B, *OSI Model for Libraries Applications, A Tutorial* (by J. M. Cailloux et C. Casimir), Luxembourg: C.E.C., 1988.

The concepts and the principle of *respect des fonds* help to go beyond this contradiction. The computer experts did not know this. We identified three levels: the basic unit, the workstation or the desk; an intermediate local level, often defined by the structure of the enterprise, office, department; and a global level, often defined, in a paper system, by a material or geographic criterion. Archivists identified the four main functions to ensure: storage, preservation appraisal; communication; use and creation; description. The concept of archival holdings on which depends not only the method, but also the paper archiving systems, allows conciliating material autonomy and intellectual unity. Paper archiving process can offer models for electronic archiving.

By reference to a paper archiving system that is homogeneous and slow, information technologies allow to process information rapidly and even instantaneously. In the IT context we must not only keep the homogeneity of the four main functions and we have to integrate a paper subsystem.[6]

Other problems are: the evidential value, the permanency of the use of paper medium, the necessity of having also a new unmodifiable medium, the definition of the documentary units and information identification (document, files, series), the access to documents, the classification and the management of closed periods, the meta information created independently of the media.

An archiving system appears as two superimposed systems: hardware for storage and communication and software for managing and harmonizing means, process and retrieval systems.

When archivists work with information technologies or electronic archiving specialists, they have a lot to offer. They are the ones who have the conceptual key to the analysis and design of the new archiving systems.

[6] C.I.G.R.E.F., *Conception des systèmes d'archivage dans les grandes entreprises. Utilisation pertinente du disque optique numérique et du vidéodisque*, Paris: AFNOR, 1989, coll. *Les dossiers de la normalisation*.

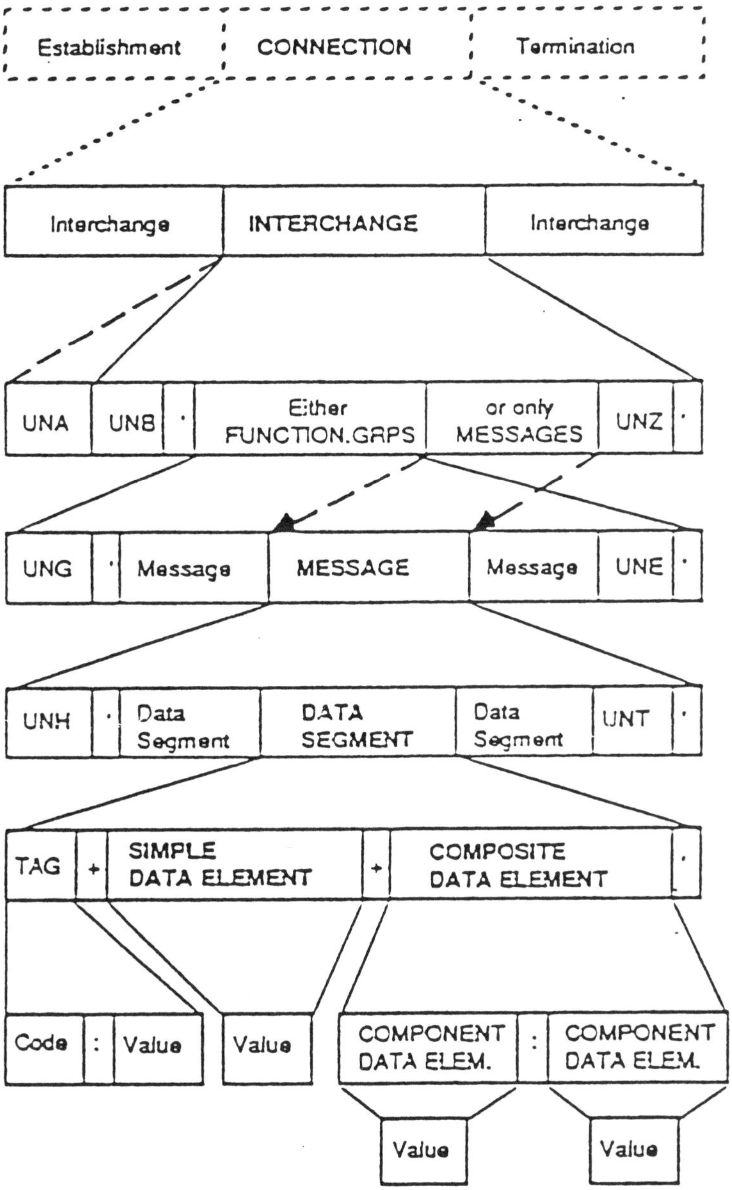

Figure 1: Hierarchical structure of an interchange
(Presentation of O.S.L. reference model and related services and protocols, p. 152)

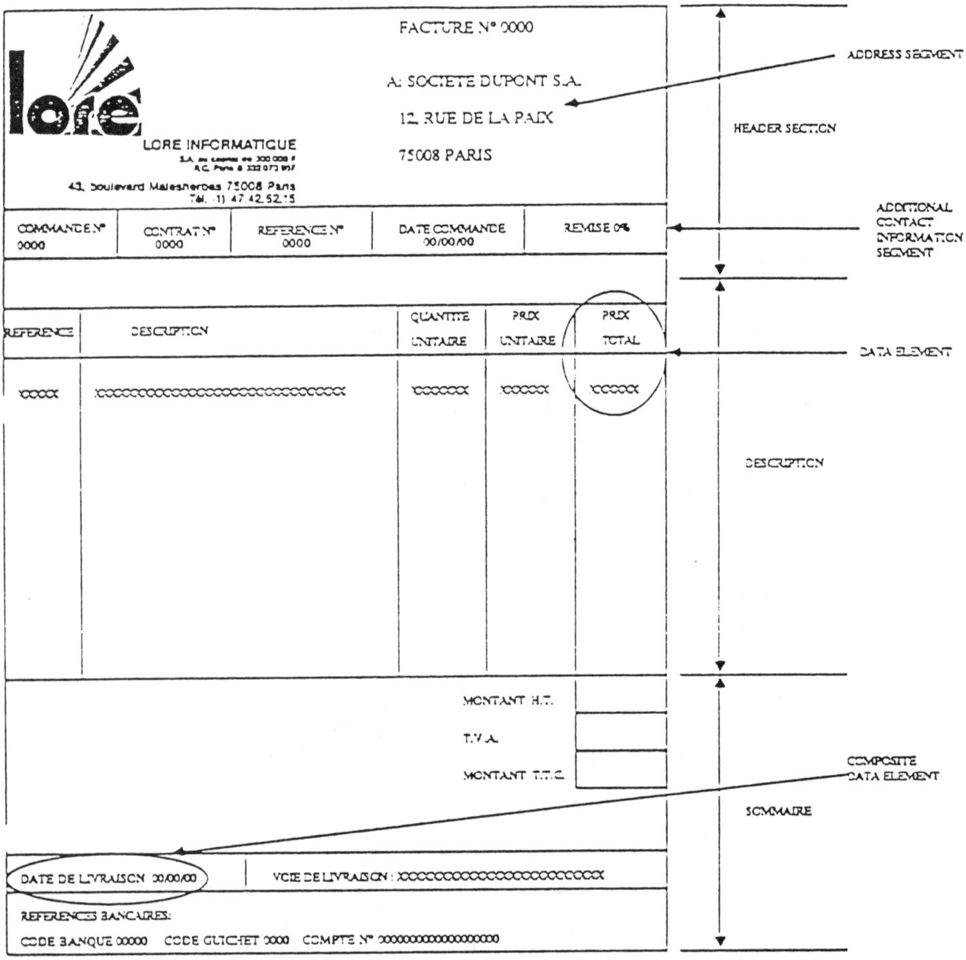

Figure 2: Example of message
(Presentation of O.S.I reference model and related services and protocols, p. 154)

ARCHIVAL PRINCIPLES AND THE ELECTRONIC OFFICE[1]

By David Bearman

I. ARCHIVES AS EVIDENCE

Responsible corporate management of electronic records, whether for ongoing operational purposes or for longterm retention of corporate memory,[2] depends upon an understanding of the fundamental archival principle of provenance. This principle is central to the concept of archives as evidence of activity and pertains with equal relevance to all forms of documentation. Two derivative archival methods, "respect des fonds" and "respect for original order" which are also often referred to as principles, are in fact only implementations of the principle of provenance which reflect the nature of record keeping in bureaucratic organizations during much of the era of paper records. Ironically, electronic records systems make it both possible to more fully capture provenance than paper records systems did and at the same time make it more likely that provenance will be lost and that archives, even if they are preserved, will therefore lack evidential value.[3] This paper explores the relationship between provenance and evidence and its implications for management of paper or electronic information systems.

Archives are recorded transactions created in the course of organizational activities of continuing evidential value. The criteria which distinguish archives from all of the information ever created or received in an organization are that:

1. archives are records of transactions
2. archives document activities or functions reflected in the mission of the organization, not just incidental to it, and
3. archives are retained for their continuing value as evidence.[4]

---

[1] An earlier version of this paper was presented at the National Archives of Canada, February 26, 1991. The author wishes to thank Terry Cook, Richard Cox, John McDonald and Lisa Weber for their thoughtful critiques which have contributed to improving the presentation.

[2] The term "corporate memory" is used extensively in the writings of John McDonald and the policies of the National Archives of Canada to refer to that evidence which it is important for an organization to retain for its ongoing operations and legitimacy. Cfr. *Strategic Framework for the Information Management Standards and Practices Division*, April 1991 (unpubl., National Archives of Canada)

[3] These concepts were originally developed in a discussion with Richard Cox, Margaret Hedstrom, John McDonald and Lisa Weber in January 1991 following the NHPRC sponsored working meeting on Research Issues in Electronic Records Management.

[4] Note that *archives* as used throughout this paper refers to a kind of records not to an institutional setting. The institutional setting called an *archives* may contain materials that do not fall within the scope of this definition of archives, such as personal papers, materials kept for their "informational" value, and information generated by archivists. The narrow sense of *archives* as evidence is explained further in David Bearman, *Management of Electronic Records: Issues and Guidelines*, New York: United Nations,

These three criteria contribute to an implementation guideline which has been central to records management and archival practice but is rarely made explicit: because the meaning of archives derives from the context in which they were created, and their evidential value is determined by the degree to which that context is still discernible, records management seeks to capture, and archives management to preserve, recorded transactions, their original form, and information about historical nexus of creation and use.

Archivists select records for their "evidential historicity". Evidential historicity is the sum of all information that can be determined about an accountable transaction, which is defined as the relationship between a record and an activity determined by archivists to require evidence. The information which contributes to evidential historicity is derived from analyzing the data, the structure, and the context of records, each of which testifies explicitly and implicitly.

- The data of the record are the words, numbers, images and sounds actually made by the creator of the record.

- The structure of the record is the relationships between these data as employed by the record creator to convey meaning. One kind of structure is the stylistic formalisms which we use to recognize the "address", "salutation", or "body" of written documents. Another kind of structure is the pointers between physically or logically distinct groupings of information as is the case with forms or databases where one aggregation of data elements is related to another aggregation in a separate record, but kept together in the same case file or in a "relation" in the database definition. Often structural information will be both indicated structurally and recorded explicitly in the data content of a record, as it is in the standard memorandum with the headings "To:", "From:" and "Re:".

- The context of the record is the testimony it provides about the nexus of activity out of which it arose and in which it was used and about how it appeared and behaved in that setting. Archivists recognize that a body of records that has lost its provenancial link has little or no value as evidence, but they have not analyzed the sources of information that reveal the relationship between the record and the activity out of which it arose. The most unimpeachable contextual information from which records derive their evidential value resides in the record system, not the individual records. Although this is the acknowledged reason why archivists retain record systems (which in paper based systems means "original order"), there is little analysis of how to read the evidence of records systems in the archival literature. As with structural information, it is also possible for contextual information to be carried as data in the record, as it commonly is in the case of dates on correspondence or reference codes in registry systems.

1990, pp. 17-70, and especially pp. 35-36. See also Sue McKemmish and Frank Upward, *The Archival Document, a submission to the Public Inquiry into Australia as an Information Society*, in: Archives and Manuscripts 19/1 (May 1991), pp. 17-31.

It is important to note that when information which purports to provide structure or context is carried as data it can be purposefully or accidentally misleading. The date on a document (data) may not be the date the communication was written or sent (context), and the distribution list may or may not be the same as the people who actually received a memorandum. Authors are free to invent data that purports to be context, and may even do so after the fact.

II. EVIDENCE AND BUSINESS APPLICATION REQUIREMENTS

Businesses maintain record systems to meet the requirements of on-going operations for evidence. Archivists retain those records required for on-going accountability. Archivists recognize the importance of contextual information to the quality of evidence in their appraisal practices where they consider the "evidential value" of the information in deciding about its disposition. Archivists reflect their belief that we can say significantly less about the meaning of records that are no longer in their "original order" than of those whose connection to the organization and activity which generated them, in their practices of arrangement and description. But archival theory has not articulated the link between the information conveyed by original order, which suggests how the records were used in the course of business, as a contextual information requirement of evidence even though courts have set such standards. For example, archivists and records managers know that only the systematic microfilming of records in the normal course of business, in which each record retains its contextual relationship to other records received and sent the same day, can assure the admissibility of a microfilm surrogate as evidence in a court.[5] Similar structural and contextual information requirements for evidential historicity are present also in all records systems. Here we argue that they can be made explicit, and that doing so is essential to defining the requirements for records management.

Different business applications will have differing requirements for evidence. The character, or degree, of requirements for creation and management of contextual information is directly related to the particular functions of each business. Once created to carry out a transaction, records are managed by organizations according to procedures dictated by ongoing needs of the application. In paper based records systems the primary need of an office can be implied from their filing sequence or "original order" of its records; secondary needs can be implied from the existence of indexes to those records. Thus contextual evidence tells us whether the critical organizing principles of daily work were time (if so we will find chronological files), responsibility (where we find project files), client (case files) or intellectual context (subject files). It is instructive to examine both the actual filing sequences required by given functions and the practices of record keeping surrounding some functions in which a greater degree of contextual information is kept in order to understand better the importance of

---

5 Digital Image Application and Optical Media Systems: Management Issues, Technical Trends, User Experience: Guidelines for State and Local Agencies, A Joint Report by the National Archives and Records Administration and the National Association of Government Archives and Records Administrators, July 1991; see also: Association for Information and Image Management, The Use of Optical Disks for Public Records, Technical Report #25, Washington/DC: AIIM, 1990, p. 33pp.

contextual data to evidence. This will also help us to appreciate why contextual data are of such great importance to electronic records management.

In an office conducting a single routine function, paper records are often filed according to a single salient feature such as the license number, plot identifier or date of application. "Line" offices, which are responsible for carrying out a single function of the organization, will have procedures that assure the capture and retention of necessary evidence of their activity. If the service they perform is based on priority for example, the date on which an application was submitted or a fee was paid will very likely also be explicitly maintained by the filing system. In such an office, incoming material will be subject to a transaction (receipt) which involves stamping the documents with the date of receipt in the office performing the application review function. Subsequent steps in the procedure will be subject to similar documentation, which could be recorded or stamped on the original document, or on the folder containing the case, or on an accompanying transaction slip. The consequences of transactions may be recorded be filing the documents in a distinctive file based on the outcome (approved, rejected, continuing under review, etc.) or such information may be reflected in data on the transaction slip and all records interfiled. In this hypothetical case, we can see the accumulation of data from a number of transactions (the original letter of application, each entry acquired along the way), along with structural information (the linking of an application to a license number), and contextual information (the form of the record revealing its provenance, the stamping on the record or file revealing the time of its receipt, and the folder in which the document is found suggesting, but not explicitly revealing, the activity locus and its relationship to other documents with which it is filed.

Since the late nineteenth century, client oriented functions have maintained case files for each client. These will typically contain both information about the client and information about the handling of the clients' case by the organization. Much of the latter, contextual, information about handling the case may take the form of dates and initials of various people who collected information, evaluated it and made recommendations, approved courses of action, and communicated actions to clients. It may also include notes indicating who has viewed the folder. These contextual data are not the text of documents in the folder, but may be marked on the folder itself or attached to documents in a variety of routing or transaction slips. They are reflections, in a "paper trail", of the procedures employed by the agency, and hence provide evidence of what procedures were followed.

For example, in the Office of the President of the United States, dossiers containing many briefing papers were routinely marked with their drafting history, the history of their review and approval and indications of their dissemination.[6] In such application environments, we must presume that the requirements of the function dictated that detailed contextual informa-

---

6 These paperwork practices in the office of the President were common in the Kennedy Administration as reflected in records at the Kennedy Presidential Library. Similar practices probably were not followed in the Reagan administration use of the IBM-PROFS electronic messaging system because the system provided some of these features as long as the records were active within it. We will know more as the suit by Scott Armstrong et.al. to prevent destruction of the Reagan administration White House PROFS files moves into the discovery process in late 1991 and early 1992.

tion about the use of data in the activities of the function. The fact that we don't keep every draft of paper documents or every copy of a document sent for information in most offices reflects the organizational and economic costs of implementing such a degree of contextual data capture exceeds the business requirement for it.

III. RECORDS SYSTEMS AND EVIDENTIAL HISTORICITY

Evidential historicity is captured in records systems which reflect the social and mechanical technology of the time and retained and retrieved by archivists whose selection of record shapes the archives. Explicit recording of contextual evidence is rare in paper-based environments because it is costly, inefficient and, given the amount of implicit evidence provided by paper-based systems, often unnecessary.

A cost/benefits plateau determines the degree of contextual evidence that will be retained. The contextual data capture plateau in paper-based environments typically excludes data on the intermediate transformations of documents; the bulk of paper that would be required to retain "version control" and the lack of means to link changes made within individual drafts to the individuals or offices making them, have generally prevented the long-term retention of drafts of all but the most important of documents. A different equation operates in electronic records environments where a multiplicity of versions will require incrementally more storage if the software environment stores only changes as it creates subsequent drafts.

In paper-based systems, evidence may be explicitly recorded for accountability as a matter of regular business practice, but still have very limited utility due to the limitations of retrieval. Such information is often retained only until an audit is performed. For example, in the licensing application discussed earlier, dates of application or final approval may be retrievable while intervening procedural states will probably not be, thus in this system, the question of who worked on a given case may be answered by the record system (retrieve by case, examine initials), but the question of what cases an individual member of staff worked on in a given week may not. As a result, archivists may decide to discard contextual data about transaction handling history which are recorded on the file folders when re-foldering the files themselves to better preserve their contents for archival retention.

Archival cost/benefits are not isolated, but rather reflect the cost/benefits of the implementation context. In the examples of version control and work analysis, an important consideration in guiding archival retention of evidence is the degree to which it was available, and used, in the course of the work of those who created the records. In the paper-based environment such data was also not used regularly in the course of decision making while in an electronic office it might well be.

But moving from paper-based to electronic systems is not a one way street towards greater ease in using and retaining contextual data. It is often not necessary to explicitly record much contextual evidence in paper-based record systems because they provide such a wealth of evidential historicity from implicit clues. Scholars working on pre-20th century records are frequently able to distinguish entries made by different hands and estimate the date by the ink used. In 20th century paper-based case files, the context of origin of records can often be inferred from the forms provided by different offices or functions. No one consciously designed the 19th century ledger to take advantage of the changes in handwriting and ink that serve the scholar in the construction of evidence, but these are nonetheless features of its design. The evidential historicity of these records derives from the immutability of the structural connection between entries on a page and the identifiability of handwriting and ink. Probably the handwriting and ink were used by the makers of the ledger, just as they are by the scholar, to retrieve records entered by a particular person. Although such evidential historicity could be captured in electronic systems where the invisibility of the evidence prevents us distinguishing the writer's hand or ink, and tools may be developed to allow authorship to be used as an attribute for retrieval, it is unlikely to happen unless we are conscious of the evidential historicity that will be lost without such design intervention.

Whether explicitly recorded or not evidential historicity may be subject to loss if the record system is disrupted. In the case of the 19th century ledger, a decision to microfilm these records might result in losing the identifiability of the ink. In the case files of license applications, refoldering will dispose of much of the contextual data now recorded on the folder itself, while almost any unsupervised use of the materials will disrupt the order of the documents which was originally filed according to a consistent filing procedure (such as "last to front"). In the case of electronic systems, the meaning of the pointer between a transaction record from 1980 and a client record updated in 1982 is obscured when both are written to a flat file for archival retention in 1985.

The costs of explicitly recording evidential historicity, the limitations in paper-based systems on retrieving information based on any recorded data, and the "eye-readability" of the residual evidence of activity in traditional office settings have collectively minimized the attention given to evidential documentation in the design of paper-based records systems. Because paper-based records systems lack methods to automatically capture, easily keep, or systematically analyze evidential information, business requirements have accepted a low plateau of evidential data capture, retention and access.

Electronic records systems do not have these limitations. They provide the opportunity to capture larger amounts of evidential historicity, and they create a need to do so. Greater amounts of contextual and structural information must be retained from electronic systems in order to assure that electronic records have evidence of equivalent value to that which was obtained from paper systems. In part, this reflects a greater degree of need for contextual information when records are not eye-readable. If we cannot see the documents then we need to have an external description of them. Not surprisingly, such descriptions, or indexes to records, were most often prepared in paper-based systems only when the records themselves could not be directly inspected for reasons of remote storage, security, etc.. But in the electronic systems that serve today's offices, we cannot inspect the records directly, so we must rely on information about them which is captured and retained by the system. As a consequence we must ask what evidential historicity should be captured by an appropriately designed system and how should it be retained?

An electronic system can track what function, activity, or transaction and what individual, contributed to or modified each item of information if only archivists articulated what evidential detail is required or desired regarding any given type of transaction. For example, in the electronic office we can easily track every modification made to a record during its drafting life, every recipient of an electronic message and when they read it, and even every time a document was consulted. However, the potential for automatically capturing large amounts of contextual information from electronic records systems is not simply a boon to archives. It is accompanied by a host of new problems, of which the most obvious is to determine what amount of evidential historicity is required and how to capture and retain it. Less obvious is the problem that much of the evidential historicity in electronic systems, just like the arrangement of records in a paper ledger or the use of different handwritings and inks, is hardware and software dependent, but the systems in which it is implemented are less easily preserved than paper-based systems were. Retaining evidential historicity also increases the complexity of the information system design and the amount of data that must be retained, and hence raises the cost of preservation both for storage and migration.[7]

To design records systems that meet organizational and archival needs for accountability requires that we understand not only that evidential historicity is found in data, structure and context, and that its character and degree reflect business application requirements, but also how records systems capture this information and the threats to its preservation. In the emerging electronic office environments that serve as the vehicles for creating and communicating the recorded knowledge of organizations today, the same relationship between raw data, structural information and contextual information can be identified. The raw data of the today's electronic office is the text of its documents. This text does not reliably tell us anything about the provenance of the information or the order in which it was kept or used. Like paper documents, electronic records may have data provided by their creators which is intended to tell us about context, such as the date of a letter, but which does not actually assure us that the letter was written on the date indicated or that it was sent. Indeed, in their ASCII form the data does not even tell us what the documents looked like to those who read them. This kind of structural information, corresponding to that provided by the form and filing of paper records in the past, comes from the documentation of the system in which the data reside. Contextual information about the actual use of data in the system and its communication to others (e.g. transactions) may or may not be kept by the software application based whether there is a technical requirement to do so in order for the software to function, and whether there was a business functional requirement dictated by the client(s).

IV. APPLICATION SOFTWARE AND INTERCHANGE STANDARDS

To provide concrete guidance on the capture and retention of evidential historicity in electronic records environments requires that we distinguish between the way in which evidential historicity resides in data, structure and context information in a variety of different applications. Specifically, we need to identify that evidential historicity which is a minimum technical

[7] Even though storage costs may prove to be insignificant in the future, it is evident that migration costs will not be trivial in the absence of complete interoperability standards.

requirement to support each application, and that which is the maximum observed evidential historicity implemented to support client functional requirements. This will enable us to develop strategies for capture and retention of evidential historicity, and to identify that evidential information which could be interchanged between software systems using existing standards and that which is not covered by existing interchange standards and must therefore be represented in proprietary ways. This in turn enables us to estimate the cost and effort involved in achieving certain plateaux of evidential historicity within a range of applications, thereby making it possible for archivists to return the decision about how much to capture and retain to the organization where the risks and requirements for accountability can best be addressed.

Electronic records present one management challenge less frequently encountered in paper-based systems: retaining records for whatever period of time they have continuing value necessarily means moving them from one software environment to another.[8] Because the data must be moved, and because their value as evidence depends upon their evidential historicity, the migration of records to future implementations including, but not limited, to archival implementations requires that structural and contextual information be moved as well. Interchange standards which accommodate necessary evidential historicity are essential to the survival of archives.

Interchange standards for data and for structural information are critical for organizations conducting their business electronically. Such standards have therefore received significant attention from information managers and the software industry. The case for migrating contextual information is most evident to those who need to keep information for a very long time, and who are concerned for its evidential value. Unfortunately, archivists have not yet articulated clearly the requirements for evidential historicity associated with particular types of information systems applications. As a consequence, such requirements have been inadequately addressed in the definition of data interchange standards. At the present time, as the requirement for evidential historicity increases, the standards governing the representation of the data become less adequate for migrating records and the degree of proprietary information structuring increases.[9] Archivists, records managers, other information managers and to a great extent program managers dependent on electronic information systems must become aware of the gap between the evidential information available to electronic application systems and the information that can be removed from the proprietary environment and maintained over time.

The degree of difficulty associated with contextual data capture and retention, and the types of information that could be captured in addition to "raw data" differ from one application

---

[8] The half-life of software products is less than 3 years, and less than 1 year between releases. In an environment ion which several layers of software will run between the operating system and the application, maintaining all these functional capabilities "as they were" would be technically impossible even if it were not the case that the software licenses do not transfer with the data if it comes to the archives, thus making it legally impossible to maintain commercially developed application software.

[9] As the users mental model departs from traditional paper models, the complexity increases. Hence, databases and GIS systems present require greater contextual data capture to represent transactions that word processing or electronic mail where the transaction is essentially like that conducted in the course of business in a paper based office.

software system to another. The way to begin to understand the implications is to analyze some generic characteristics of a variety of software application environments. Ultimately, specific software applications and implementations will need to be studied in order to derive the data required to define concrete cost/benefit plateaux.[10]

A. Word Processing

The most common office application of electronic information systems is word processing. The word processing file as created by the user (e.g. the data of the record) consists of ASCII text interspersed with display instructions such as punctuation, type size and font, tabs, and paragraph breaks. If users save the file, they must typically enter the document name into the appropriate component of the header. The display instructions indicate the logical structure of the file using typographical conventions which are familiar to readers of paper documents. The header consists of contextual information which is mostly supplied by the software system including, for example, the date and time of creation, the file size and location of the first physical data segment. In some software systems, especially in multi-user systems, the header might also include update history of the file, access rules, output format definitions and links to distribution lists.

An office system need not maintain a great deal of evidential historicity to manage word processing files if the word processing system is simply a means of making paper output products. But from an information management perspective, if the system serves as a repository of textual records created and maintained in the course of business, it is essential to retain evidence of the structure and context of the data, including information about the creation and use of the record.

Contextual information must be retained for operational as well as archival reasons. In electronic networked office environments that are now becoming the norm, there is a technical requirement to preserve evidence of what changed between versions of a document which is derived from the business requirement to be able to return to prior drafts, and from the audit requirement to identify who was responsible for all changes. The system may also have a technical requirement to identify the authors of each change in order to support security (permission) controls. Finally, the client may impose functional requirements on the software designers to create and retain information on the users and uses of documents. This kind of information is especially critical for records to serve as evidence in a shared filing system where many individuals have access to records and where "sending" the document in a transaction actually involves only making it accessible to another.

It is possible to design electronic office systems which record the evidential historicity associated with each transaction that creates, communicates, uses or modifies a document. For example, each transaction that is recorded and communicated beyond the boundaries of an individual workstation, a workgroup, an organizational unit or the organization (depending on what boundary the institutional policy decides is evidentially significant), could be captured in

---

[10] At present I know of no reliable studies of the costs of these migrations that can be used for archival cost-benefits analysis.

an audit trail, and written out as a data file. But in order for the system to use data of this sort, the information must be active with respect to the application software, as it is in a document header, rather than passively recorded as data of the document itself. Unfortunately, existing standards for office systems do not provide for interchangeability of header information regarding permissions, or file locations, of such documents. Existing standards don't even define methods of explicitly writing such header data to the file being kept as evidence.

Structural information must also be retained if we are to have adequate evidence, and conveying such structural information beyond the confines of the creating software is becoming more, rather than less, problematic. As the means of exchanging information created in electronic systems on media other than paper become widespread, we are witnessing a rapid evolution in "forms of material" which reflect new structural relations between data. Forms of material are socially or culturally constructed information containers with which we communicate.[11] It is as a result of these structural signals that literate people in our culture can immediately recognize the difference between a job application, a greeting card or a legal summons without reading the words which appear on each. We are currently witnessing a rate of change in forms of material that has not been seen since the advent of writing and the subsequent introduction of printing.[12] Because the appearance of electronic information is governed by software control of the application in which the information is made to appear, common conventions for rendering structural information are essential for the full meaning of records to be transferred.[13] Electronic technologies are now being used to generate an entirely new form of material called hypermedia or compound documents. These non-linear "documents" are composed of data objects in the form of text, image and sound that are linked by pathways defined by the author. The pathways are made manifest on being "played back" through software which is at this point still non-standard. Hypertexts and compound documents may, like the graphics generated from spreadsheets contained within word processing documents, point to dynamic data objects which take on characteristics of a changing environment, thus they may be different each time they are viewed. The implications for archivists are obvious: with these forms of material the transaction, and not the data of the document, is the archival record. Standards efforts for hypermedia have not yet succeeded in defining all the terms with which they must deal (the second NIST conference on hypermedia standards in the summer of 1990

[11] The definition I wrote for the NISTF data element dictionary has been used in the archives community but few have followed its implications. See David Bearman / Peter Sigmond, *Explorations of Form of Material by Dutch Archivists*, in: American Archivist 50/2 (Spring 1987), pp. 49-53 and Luciana Duranti, *Diplomatics: New Uses for an Old Science*; parts I-V, in: Archivaria 28-32 (1988-1992).

[12] Forms of electronic records are discussed in David M. Levy / Daniel C. Brotsky / Kenneth R. Olson, *Formalizing the Figural: Aspects of a Foundation for Document Manipulation (Systems Sciences Laboratory*, Xerox Palo Alto Research Center, 1988, p. 7p.

[13] The Text Encoding Initiative, an undertaking of numerous text oriented humanities disciplines, is developing methods of indicating the structural aspects of texts going back to the Middle Ages using Standard Generalized Markup Language (SGML). Twentieth century documentation practices are generally covered by a smaller set of declarations developed by the American Association of Publishers. More complex modern Document Type Definitions (DTD's) are being implemented for multi-media documentation for airplanes, battleships and like systems following the specifications developed by the Department of Defense Computer-aided Acquisitions and Logistical Support (CALS) initiative.

had to be canceled because of this), to say nothing of dealing with the contextual data questions raised by archivists.[14]

The challenge of retaining the evidential historicity of dynamic forms of material goes beyond what has been recognized by the standards efforts of today. These efforts have focussed on the interchangeability of the data content of documents and to a lesser extent on interoperability based on structural information without adequate regard for the need to capture and interchange contextual data about the particular transaction in which a user encounters a dynamic document. To do so, the standards efforts would need to address documents comprised of data objects that are brought together under user control though the functionality provided by one application, but which might themselves be created by other applications. In the moment of being brought together they have an evidential historicity which the systems designer could have designed to adhere to them. But the methods of representing the evidential historicity of the document would, by necessity, have to be non-standard because no such standards have yet been developed. Yet the new forms of material with which we are increasingly dealing require precisely such standards, operating above the application level, in order to survive with their evidential historicity intact.

B. Electronic Mail

Electronic mail is a deceptively non-traditional technology which can illustrate some of the problems and potentials of electronic environments. The speed with which electronic mail is delivered seems to reduce the length of individual messages within the communication. With electronic mail numerous messages will be exchanged as a dialogue in communications where the participants would previously have written a finished argument in a single exchange of letters. The velocity of electronic mail exchanges (the time between a message and the response) in many organizations is 2-3 times per day, thus the equivalent of a full complex exchange can take place incrementally over several days (in the length of time it would have taken to send a letter).[15] All the messages in the exchange can be sent to numerous individuals who respond asynchronously. It is necessary to know what messages have been received by whom, at what point in a discussion in order to fully understand the responses. In other words, the evidential historicity of the documents is essential to the reconstruction of the transaction.

In contemporary implementations of electronic mail, the "envelopes" of the messages are defined by the ANSI standards x.400/x.500 to carry the address to which they will be sent,

---

[14] The National Institute of Standards and Technology (NIST) called a conference on hypertext standards in the early spring of 1990. A follow-up meeting to have been held in the summer of 1990 was canceled because there was too little agreement about how to proceed to make progress possible. Currently two efforts are underway which emphasize different aspects of hypermedia interchange: HyTime, an extension of the SGML approach, declares the logical functions and links of objects being interchanged while MHEG defines the technical specifications for data representation in those objects.

[15] Tora Bikson / J. D. Eveland, *The Interplay of Work Group Structures and Computer Support*, in: Kraut / Galagher / Egido (eds.), *Intellectual Teamwork*, Hillsdale/NJ: Erlbaum, 1990. Observations on university campuses where electronic mail is widespread confirm that the medium is leading to the evolution of a truncated form of communication, sometimes resulting in exchanges analogous to the nod or grunt in face to face communications.

whether acknowledgement is required, and other information relating to the context of the exchange. Archivists require additional information about the communication context to be preserved for the record to retain its evidential historicity but they have yet to examine envelope headers to determine specifically what additional information would be required to establish the provenance, or originating context, of electronic messages. Systems designers have, to date, paid little attention to capturing the envelope data in their attempts to archive electronic mail. Thus we find ourselves in a world in which we have the technological capability to capture a level of context based information surrounding records that surpasses greatly any data we had in traditional archival provenance, but have settled for a plateau of data interchange that does not satisfy archival requirements. Higher plateaux can be easily envisioned, and the economic and technological costs (including the potential explosion of the size of information bases as they carry evidential historicity data concerning all their objects) can be calculated. Archivists need to participate in such efforts in order to articulate the functional requirements of archivally acceptable electronic mail environments.

C. Spreadsheets

If we look briefly at the spreadsheet, another common office application, we encounter these and other issues. The cells of electronic spreadsheets contain formulas relating to the nature of work in the organization. These formulas embody a great deal of knowledge about the organization, as anyone who has ever tried to use a spreadsheet developed for a specific office accounting function will recognize. However the nature of the data being cited and the history of the expression or formula are not documented in the application itself unless individuals make a concrete (and rare) effort to document it.

Transactions involving spreadsheets are even more complex. In addition to hiding their operative formulae, spreadsheets may draw their data from numerous active databases and they may be displayed to those making decisions as a series of graphs rather than as textual data points. Evidence of this transaction is not currently represented in application software except as the resulting graph, which is a print record surrogate, but which disguises the calculations as well as the raw data on which it was based. In short, the spreadsheet is rife with contextual data without which the "raw data" is hardly meaningful. In this and other many layered application software environments, standards for information interchange barely address the transfer of the data content and the structural information that assigns a calculation to the appropriate cell from one system to another, and none have addressed the contextual information interchange issues.

A spreadsheet, displayed as a graph, drawing data from a variety of contemporaneous database states may, furthermore, be displayed in a word processed document in which it resides as a pointer, rather than as a fixed manifestation. If such a document is used for decision-making, archivists will want to know what it said at the time the decision was taken, because if they save the document with its pointer, even if they could succeed at the task of keeping the associated information systems in tact, they would view a different image when the document is next displayed.

In the spreadsheet we are beginning to encounter a new kind of data - intelligent data - which could be major contributors to the productivity of the office in the next decade and which poses a serious threat to archives.[16] "Intelligent data" are aggregates of raw data created in a system which imbues them with contextual information that instructs them how to behave in that system; for example a text given the "intelligence" assigned to a memorandum, would "know" when to send itself and to whom to send itself. A word or two assigned the intelligence of a future date would "know" to remind the creator on or before that date. Creators need not assign this intelligence themselves, because in intelligent systems some of this work can be done automatically. Thus a program could determine the keywords under which to file a document, build a table of contents and an index, and screen readers for security requirements which it determined from reading the text. In the spreadsheet, each cell contains the formulae which it uses to analyze the raw data provided to it.

D. Database Management Systems

Database management systems are the next most common office applications. When we examine them from an archival perspective, some contextual information retention requirements present themselves immediately. The raw data in a database has some informational value, but it has little evidential meaning. The transactions in a database environment are input records, queries and output instructions. Without the documentation of the system, we do not know what data any given individual or office had included in their "view". Without update records, we cannot tell the state of a given piece of data at a given time. Without links to other systems that might have been provided to active users of the system, we cannot tell what use might have been made of the data. This kind of documentation of the "potentialities" of the data is recorded in meta-data systems called data dictionary/directory systems and Information Resource Directory Systems to which archivists need to pay greater attention. In addition, we could capture documentation of the actual uses, the actual updates, and the actual data participating in specific transactions. In principle a transactional audit trail could document changes so completely as to make possible a "time-travel" database, but the practical implications of maintaining a system so that it can back itself up in time are formidable. Therefore, archivists will need to work with systems designers to assure that database systems create certain transactional records (for particular types of transactions initiated by certain functions within the organization) that otherwise would not be created.

To get a complete picture of what the database does we need to document also whether it acts under human control at all times or if the database management system sometimes takes action (and creates records) on its own. For example, does it have a "tickler" report, or does it generate warning notices when someone tries to breech its security, or does it generate weekly, monthly and quarterly reports at the appropriate time without specific human request? Increasingly, software is being implemented in organizations so that the database serves each office differently, and that distinct facilities are provided for different functions. The trend in information processing is towards more and more "intelligent" systems. These include systems using "object oriented languages" and "artificial intelligence" but very traditional programming is also embedding growing amounts of intelligence in software. Unfortunately, the methods of representing this "intelligent" information surrounding the raw data, like those for

---

16 Timothy J. Heintz, *Object-oriented Databases and their Impact on Future Database Applications*, in: Information & Management 20/2 (1991), pp. 95-103.

representing contextual information, are non-standard. Nevertheless, the system rules are context to the transactions, and without them we can only poorly comprehend the evidential significance of a record.

E. Graphical Software

Beyond the office, a class of applications which include Geographic Information Systems (GIS), Business Graphics and Statistics and Computer-Aided Design (CAD) systems are growing in importance. These applications are characterized by a graphical presentation of data. They enable users to envision the relationships between large numbers of discrete data points by displaying them visually. As such they enable effective communication of complex information, and their outputs are records in such communicated transactions, but in order to employ these outputs as evidence the underlying data are required in addition to the visualization.

Geographic Information Systems (GIS), can serve to illustrate this. GIS environments are one of the most rapidly growing applications created by and used in government today because so much of the function of government involves delivery of services to the population of a geographic region and that population, and the infrastructures that serve it, must be envisioned by those delivering and receiving services.[17] Geographic Information Systems are databases whose records are data points in a spatial linking structure (e.g. a map). They are a powerful application environment precisely because data points derived from one source can be retrieved in conjunction with data points from other sources, thus building a comprehensive view of what is known about any space on the face of the earth (or under water). For government, the organization of databases by geographical locus is an important tool for management. However, the data points contributed to a geographic information system will have been established at different times, by different agencies and for different purposes (e.g. they will have a different provenance). Archivists need to decide both what data to retain about the context of creation and use of each discrete data point with respect to its original relation (which becomes simply another retrieval set within the operational GIS application) and what contextual data needs to be preserved as evidence of functions that subsequently use that data point in creating records (transactions) in other applications employing the GIS. Even if there were standards for the interchange of GIS data, or the interoperability of GIS systems, they would not address the retention of the evidential historicity of these new forms of material.

Another increasingly important, software dependent, data object is being created by Computer-Aided Design and Computer Assisted Manufacturing (CAD/CAM) systems. These systems employ vectorized information (formulae for lines) to generate displays of three-dimensional objects such as buildings or machine components. CAD/CAM files are used to make decisions about construction and maintenance of increasingly large portions of the capital assets of governments, but they are highly software dependent. Changes to drawing in CAD/CAM systems may or may not be documented and the contextual significance of the source of the data are not generally considered important by the architects, electricians, manu-

---

[17] Kentucky Information Systems Commission, *Current Issues in Government Information Policy Conference Proceedings*, Frankfort/KY: KISC, June 1991.

facturers, etc. who make and use the latest version of this data. Hence the implementation plateaux in these systems are set far below the levels regarded by archivists as important to record for evidential historicity. Meanwhile standards, such as IGES (Initial Graphics Exchange Environment), are focussed on interchange and interoperability below the application level.

V. ELECTRONIC RECORDS MANAGEMENT GUIDELINES

Electronic information systems, therefore, present at least two challenges to archivists. The first is that the designers of these systems may have chosen to document less contextual information than may be of interest to archivists when they designed the system. The second is that the data recorded in any given information system will, someday, need to be transferred to another system. As long as the information created in the course of work in an electronic environment remains in the software and hardware system in which it was created, it loses none of the contextual information which is critical to its meaning, but the transition, or "migration", of data to a new environment threatens to change the way the information looks, feels or operates, and hence what it means.

Archivists have always been dependent on the information systems implemented in working offices for the amount of contextual information that would be available as evidence. What has changed with electronic records is both that a greater degree of evidential granularity is possible, and that it may not be retained because program managers are less aware of its value, or of their ability to require its retention, than they were in paper-based office systems.[18] Archival retention of contextual data at appropriate levels of granularity is likely to depend, in the future, on program managers insisting on their requirements for this contextual data for information management within their functions. For this to happen, archivists need to articulate what contextual data are required as evidence, how it might be captured and at what cost.

Although archivists accession records at the level of the record series, we found very little contextual documentation at the series level in paper-based records environments. As a consequence, documentation of the paper-based records systems by procedures manuals rarely answers questions such as: - What functions and transactions within functions created records in the series? - What functions filed into the series and how did they exercise their judgement? - Which offices had access to information in the series and could they alter it?

---

[18] The practice of associating provenance with the governmental agency responsible for the creation of an entire body of records, which led to the establishment in the United States of the "Records Group" concept, has largely been superseded in the U.S. and Australia anyway, by the link between the record series and its functional provenance, or the activity of the agency that gave rise to it. The seeds for this move are found in the writings of Peter Scott in Australia in the 1960's and 70's and David Bearman, Max Evans, Rich Szary and others in the U.S. in the 1980's and in the practices surrounding the implementation of MARC, AMC and APPM. The increasing granularity of provenance may be a trend that will carry the assignment of provenance down to the contextual information in particular documents in electronic information systems.

Instead, in paper-based environments we find evidence of creation and use at the individual document or transactional entry, or at the level of file folders which detail who saw their contents, the time at which they received them, and what they did with them (forwarding, taking action, etc.). In electronic information systems, meta-data systems should explicitly document the activity context out of which records arise, and policy should be implemented to define forms of documents created in such contexts and the organizational retention requirements for each. Systems can then be implemented so that when a record is identified by its origin and date, appropriate retention policy can be automatically executed. Records which need to be retained for their continuing value can be protected from alteration or deletion.

The second threat is more insidious. It is expensive to transfer data from one system to another, especially as the information we are trying to capture in these transfers is the most system dependent and the least standard. Each system migration is accompanied by extensive planning, and often must include making modifications to both systems in order to preserve functionality associated with the old system and to retain contextual data, including that upon which systems functionality depends. In an operational environment, the decision is usually made to "migrate" as little data as possible into the new system and to preserve a minimum of contextual data. Archivists must realize however that data loss in migration, like data loss in copying is a one way street. As decisions are made to leave some contextual data behind, the evidence provided by the information that is transferred will be lost.

The current state of standards does not permit functional equivalency (by and large) to be communicated across systems. Only the "data" content of texts, images and sounds are accommodated by existing standards. New standards will eventually be developed (hopefully with archival input) to bring more and more contextual functionality across systems barriers, but new methods of data organization and new concepts in computing will also continue to emerge and will always lack standards when they are new so the problem will not go away. Archivists will have to continue to face the questions of how much functional equivalency they will try to transfer and how software dependent they will permit the data they manage to be. In other words, archivists will need to confront, on an application by application basis, the potential for capture of data with various degrees of evidential historicity.[19]

In each case, archivists will need to return to fundamental archival principles to determine just what they really wanted to save anyway. And they will need to look forward into the management of the current technologies to determine how practical it is, or will be, to save data of evidential value. It may be that archivists will be satisfied with the degree of evidential historicity they were able to achieve in paper based record systems, in which case there are very few barriers to implementing successful electronic based archival environments. Or archivists may decide that the fuller capability of tracking the actual participation of electronic

---

19 The identification of the business application as the locus of intervention by archivists is based on the realization that requirements for data retention derive from the combination of requirements by ongoing offices for information regarding their functions and the requirements of the organization for evidence of its activity over time. Both of these requirements are focussed at the program level and must be achieved through the implementation of software to support concrete functions of the organization. For more see: op. cit. #4, esp. pp. 19-27.

data objects in organizational activities needs to be documented by archivally satisfactory information systems, in which case they will need to define those levels of evidential historicity that must be attained, and specify the systems requirements for such environments.

At a meeting on electronic records management research issues sponsored by the National Historical Publications and Records Commission in January 1991, participants identified the concept of technological and economic plateaux in electronic data capture and archiving as an important arena for research. They proposed research efforts to identify such plateaux in existing applications and to define the technical challenges associated with the retention of greater degrees of evidential historicity within applications as well as the problems and prospects for longterm preservation of data representing different plateaux.[20] Their proposal would, for example, bring sociological evidence about transactions in organizations together with technical specifications of different degrees of evidential historicity of records, to generate preliminary estimates of the increases in data volume required to satisfy different levels of requirements imposed by the archival principle of provenance. Hopefully this research will produce information to help archivists make decisions regarding the amount of contextual information they can afford to capture and the requirements of systems designed to document context along with managing data content. In any case, the analysis to date has enriched the concept of provenance and reinforced its direct link to missions, functions and ultimately the activities or transactions of an organization rather than to organizational units, as was predicted by Richard Lytle and I in an earlier article.[21] I will not be surprised as we refine our concepts of evidential historicity to discover that the concept of provenance takes on even greater granularity, and is associated with the particular actions.

---

[20] The National Historical Publications and Records Commission, Research, Research Issues in Electronic Records, St.Paul:. Minn. Hist. Soc., 1991.

[21] David Bearman / Richard Lytle, *The Power of the Principle of Provenance*, in: Archivaria 21 (Winter 1985/86), pp. 14-272.

LIST OF CONTRIBUTORS

Barry, Richard E.

Mr. Barry is President of Barry Associates, 3808 N. Albemarle St., Arlington, VA, 22207, USA (telephone and fax: (703) 241-7968). He was formerly Chief of the Information Services Division of the World Bank, during which time he also served as Chairperson of the Technical Panel on Electronic Records Management (TP/REM), under the auspices of the UN Advisory Committee for the Co-ordination of Information Systems (ACCIS). The Panel consisted of a multi-disciplinary team of inter-agency specialists and consultants in information technology, archives and records management. ACCIS subsequently endorsed and published: *Management of Electronic Records: Issues and Guidelines,* 1990, which was produced by TP/REM.

Bearman, David

Mr. Bearman, founder of Archives & Museums Informatics, served as Deputy Director of the Office of Information Resource Management at the Smithsonian Institution in Washington for four years. He is a Fellow of the Society of American Archivists, President of the Board of Directors of the Museum Computer Networks, and the author of numerous published articles and reports.

Bekkers, Victor J.J.M.

Mr. Bekkers (1963) is Assistant Professor of Public Administration at the University of Tilburg, the Netherlands. He is a member of the Tilburg/Rotterdam Research Program on Informatization in Public Administration. His publications are in the field of steering and informatization, electronic mail and datacommunication networks, and the effects of EC-policies on federal and sub-central government.

Bohl, Peter

Mr. Bohl, b. 1955, holds a Ph. D. in German and History from the University of Konstanz. After his professional training in Stuttgart, Karlsruhe, Marburg (Archivschule) and Koblenz (Federal Archives), he works since 1990 in the Department for the Acquisition of Machine-Readable Archives of the Landesarchivdirektion Baden-Württemberg, Stuttgart.

Cook, Michael

Currently University Archivist and Director of the Archival Description Project at the University of Liverpool (since 1968); formerly Director of the Regional Training Centre for Archivists (English-speaking Africa) at the Department of Library and Archival Studies, University of Ghana, Legon (1975-1977) and Director of National Archives, Tanzania (1964-1966).

Consultant for UNESCO on archival training, Southeast Asia (1973), Caribbean (1980, 1983); British Council visiting lecturer in Turkey (1982, 1991); visiting professor at the University of Lisbon (1987-1989).

Chairman of International Council on Archives, Committee on Education and Training (1984-1988). Chairman of Information Technology Group of (UK) Society of Archivists. Member of ICA Ad Hoc Commission on archival description standards.

Author of *Archive administration* (Dawson Publishing, 1977); *The Management of Information from Archives* (Gower, 1986); *Archives and the Computer* (2nd ed., Butterworth, 1986); (with M. Procter) *The Manual of Archival Description* (2nd ed., Gower, 1989); and several technical reports on curriculum development for training, the impact of information technology on training, and the harmonisation of training between the information professions.

Delmas, Bruno

Bruno Delmas is a graduate of the Ecole Nationale des Chartes in History and Political Science. He began work at the French National Archives. He has carried out many planning and teaching missions for foreign governments, UNESCO and ICA. He has been elected as professor in the Ecole des Chartes in 1977 where he teaches Contemporary Archival Science and in 1988 as member of the ICA section for Education and Professional Training.

Mr. Delmas has extensively written in the fields of Administrative History and Archival Theory and Education. His main endeavor has been to assure the development of the contemporary Archival Science and Diplomatics. He organised in 1988 the First International Meeting of Archival Science Teachers and published the *Dictionnaire des archives, de l'archivage aux technologies de l'information* (French, English, German).

In the field of Information Sciences, he is since 1981 Director of the Institut National des Techniques de la Documentation.

Dollar, Charles M.

Charles M. Dollar has served as Assistant Director of the Archival Research and Evaluation Staff of the National Archives and Records Administration since 1983. In this capacity, he manages research projects relating largely to the use of information technologies in archives and records management. Prior to this, he was the Director of the Machine-Readable Archives Division of the National Archives. Mr. Dollar, who holds a Ph.D. in American History from the University of Kentucky, was a history faculty member of Oklahoma State University.

Mr. Dollar co-authored *The Historian's Guide to Statistics* (1972) and was general editor of *America: Changing Times* (1979, 1982). More recently, he co-authored *American Issues: A Documentary Reader* (1987). In the archives and records management fields he has written articles published in the *American Archivist* and *Prologue: The Journal of the National Archives*. In 1985 he wrote *Electronic Records Management and Archives in International Organizations: A RAMP Study with Guidelines*. More recently, he conducted UNESCO projects in Brasil and Mexico.

Mr. Dollar is a member of the Society of American Archivists, a Fellow of the Society of American Archivists, and the U.S. representative to the International Council on Archives Automation Committee. In addition, Mr. Dollar has served as a consultant in archives and records management to the Battelle Corporation, the United Nations, Guatemala, the Kingdom of Saudi Arabia, the Arab Fund for Social and Economic Development, and the Asian Development Bank.

Finholt, Tom

Tom Finholt is an Assistant Professor of Organizational Psychology at the University of Michigan, Ann Arbor. His research interests include the impact of computer communication technology on information processing in organizations, occupational diseases associated with computer use, and the design of collaborative computing environments. Mr. Finholt's recent work has focused on the use of electronic databases by peripheral members of organizations to overcome barriers of distance and time. He is currently involved in a five year project to design and assess electronic collaborative data collection and analysis in the international space science community, centered on the National Science Foundation and Danish Meteorological Institute's remote instrument array in Sondrestromfjord, Greenland.

Mr. Finholt has published scientific articles in the organizational literature, most recently in *Organization Science*, and in the psychological literature, most recently in the *American Psychologist*. He earned his B. A. with High Honors in History from Swarthmore College, and his Ph. D. in Social and Decision Science from Carnegie Mellon University.

Gränström, Claes

A graduate of the University of Lund, Mr. Gränström has worked at the National Archives of Sweden since 1969 and has been Deputy Director General since 1982. He has also served on a variety of national commissions and committees on electronic data and archival policy for the Swedish government.

Kesner, Richard M.

Richard M. Kesner currently serves as Chief Information Officer for Babson College, Wellesley, Massachusetts, where he is responsible for all aspects of the College's use of information technologies. He is also President and Senior Consultant for RMK Associates Inc., a management, strategic planning, and MIS consulting firm.

Prior to forming RMK Associates, Richard Kesner served as the V.P. of Development and Systems for the Parkman Companies, a diversified real estate development and management company. He also spent nearly four years as the V.P. of General Services and MIS for Multibank Financial Corporation, a $3 Billion bank headquartered in Dedham, Massachusetts.

Mr. Kesner holds a M. A. and Ph. D. from Stanford University, and an A. B. and M. B. from Oberlin College. He has also completed post-doctoral training in finance and strategic planning at the Wharton School, University of Pennsylvania. Dr. Kesner has spoken internationally before professional and business audiences, and has published seven books and numerous articles. He is currently at work on a book about information resource management within public sector institutions.

McDonald, John

While with the National Archives John McDonald has served a number of capacities related to the archival management of electronic records. During this time he also served on the Treasury Board Task Force responsible for the implementation of the Access to Information and Privacy legislation. Recently he assumed responsibility for a program that assists institutions in the management of their records, regardless of their physical form. A particular area of interest is the management of information in office systems. He received a B. A. in History and Geography and an M. A. in Geography from Carleton University, Ottawa.

Reinermann, Heinrich

Mr. Reinermann, b. 1937, is Professor of Public Administration Science at the Post-Graduate School of Administrative Science, Speyer (Germany), with a specialization in Data Processing and Computing in Public Administration, Information Management and Adaptation of Management Techniques to Public Administration.

1957-1958 commercial apprenticeship (Klöckner-Werke AG), 1959-1964 Studies of Business Administration at the Universities of Hamburg, Münster and Mannheim, 1964 Graduation (Diplom-Kaufmann), 1966 Ph. D. (Dr. rer. pol.), thesis won 1966's Academic Award of the University of Münster, 1967-1968 Visiting Scholar at Stanford University (Computer Science Department and Business School), 1973 Qualification as a University Professor at the University of Mannheim, 1981-1982 and 1987-1988 Visiting Policy Scientist at University of California, Irvine.

Publications: 22 Books (11 as author/co-author, 11 as editor) on efficiency, program budgeting, management by objectives, auditing, computing in public administration, some 163 articles in journals, handbooks etc.

ICA Handbooks Series

Hugh A. Taylor
The Arrangement and Description of Archival Materials
With a contribution: *Les Instruments de Recherches dans les Archives*
by Etienne Taillemite
1980. 181 pages. Softbound. DM 48.00
(For ICA Members DM 31.00)
ISBN 3-598-20272-5. (ICA Handbooks Series Volume 2)

Glossary of Basic Archival and Library Conservation Terms
English with Equivalents in Spanish, German, Italian, French and Russian
Edited by Carmen Crespo Noguiera
Compiled by the Committee on Conservation and Restoration,
International Council on Archives
1988. 151 pages. Hardbound. DM 68.00
(For ICA Members DM 46.00)
ISBN 3-598-20276-8. (ICA Handbooks Series Volume 4)

Manual of Archival Reprography
Edited by Lájos Körmendy
Compiled by James A. Keene, Lájos Körmendy, Ted T. Powell
and Georges Weill
1989. 223 pages, 77 illus. Hardbound. DM 78.00
(For ICA Members DM 52.00)
ISBN 3-598-20277-6
(ICA Handbooks Series Volume 5)